Managing Toxic Leaders and Dysfunctional Organizational Dynamics

Understanding experience at work, especially in organizations that have toxic leaders and dysfunctional organizational dynamics, is a multidimensional undertaking that must include in-depth perspectives informed by psychosocial theory. This may be best accomplished by relying on complementary theories to account for what is found and experienced in our organizations and in particular a better understanding of why this is happening. "Why did she do that?" "Why did he say that?" "Why did a group react the way they did?" "Why," is critical in terms of understanding organizational dynamics.

Our lives at work in large complex and multidimensional organizations are saturated with experience, some of which is fulfilling, and some are of a darker nature that arises from the presence of toxic leaders and dysfunctional organizational dynamics. Understanding these toxicities and dysfunctions and their effect on organization members is approached by first raising their awareness at the beginning of the book before providing psychosocially informed insights that form a basis for understanding and organizational change in the following sections.

This book explores these work-life dynamics by grounding them in concrete examples and then using complementary psychosocially informed perspectives to illuminate their underlying, often unconscious nature filling an important gap in management and organizational literature.

Managing Toxic Leaders and Dysfunctional Organizational Dynamics

The Psychosocial Nature of the Workplace

Seth Allcorn

Routledge
Taylor & Francis Group

A PRODUCTIVITY PRESS BOOK

First published 2024
by Routledge
605 Third Avenue, New York, NY 10158

and by Routledge
4 Park Square, Milton Park, Abingdon, Oxon, OX14 4RN

Routledge is an imprint of the Taylor & Francis Group, an informa business

ISBN: 978-1-032-73491-0 (hbk)
ISBN: 978-1-032-73490-3 (pbk)
ISBN: 978-1-003-46446-4 (ebk)

DOI: 10.4324/9781003464464

Typeset in Minion Pro
by KnowledgeWorks Global Ltd.

Contents

PART 3 Organizational Healing

Preface

If I were to ask myself why I wanted to author this book that answer would be telling a story that begins with my first management job where I managed a $25 million budget and 250 staff in a department of medicine in a School of Medicine. The often chaotic and marginally controlled experience of working within a large complex organization led me to wonder about *why* what I was encountering was often illogical. This began a quest on my part to understand *why*. I started with reading books on sociology and in particular books on bureaucracy. Many of these authors back in the 1970s and 1980s did an excellent job of describing the many pitfalls of bureaucratic structures and hierarchies and their spread around the world. These narratives matched with *what* I was seeing happening around me in my job. They, however, gave few explanations as to exactly *why* this was happening other than that these organizational dynamics were an outcome of human nature and personalities being expressed in our organizations. Nor did these books provide ideas on how to fix the many problems that had their root causes in the psychology of human nature.

Eventually, I began to look at areas like social psychology, psychology, industrial psychology, and abnormal psychology. Abnormal psychology offered some insights into human behavior that helped to explain to a limited extent what I was seeing, hearing, and feeling about my workplace. However, these disciplines still did not explain with sufficient depth *why* I was encountering what I did or even *why* many of those, especially in leadership roles, seemed to have "abnormal psychology." Eventually, I started to look at psychosocial theory which offered useful in-depth explanations of human behavior in large organizations. These theoretical perspectives allowed me to gain a better understanding of the *why* of the dysfunctional leaders and interpersonal, group, and organizational dynamics surrounding me.

Years of reading and study eventually led me to actionable insights into human behavior in large complexly structured organizations, especially when the behavior was irrational, antisocial, and toxic and led to group and organizational dysfunctions. This decades-long pursuit of understanding on my part informed by subsequent job changes that included responsibilities for up to one-half billion dollars in budget and thousands of employees is *why* I am still writing about it. This book represents my best effort to explain with sufficient depth *why* we find in large hierarchical bureaucratic organizations toxic leaders and dysfunctional organization dynamics that detract from achieving their missions. This hard-won understanding is shared in this book.

A FRAMEWORK FOR UNDERSTANDING TOXIC LEADERSHIP AND DYSFUNCTIONAL ORGANIZATIONAL DYNAMICS

Understanding leadership and organizational dynamics is challenging especially when there is a long-established dysfunctional organizational culture driven by toxic leaders. This insight building for understanding organizations begins with considering the dysfunctional dynamics that may be present within the management layers above and below one's position that have a long history and have become accepted as how we work here – our organizational culture. This makes responding to the leader's toxicity and organizational dysfunctions a challenging and time-consuming undertaking.

This book provides a much-needed psychosocially informed framework for understanding dysfunctional leaders and organizational dynamics that have become a part of an organizational culture and member identity that governs how we work and who we are as individuals, groups, and divisions with the organization. These cultural and identity dynamics can be helpful and reduce stress. However, they also often fall short of this admirable goal. Toxic leadership and dysfunctional organizational dynamics are common and stressful which makes them a common anxiety-ridden daily experience. These distressing experiences lead organization members to rely on psychosocially defensive individual, group, and organizational dynamics to cope with life at work. Ideally, these toxic and dysfunctional dynamics should be avoided but, should they occur, the defensive responses to them should be well managed and this requires an understandable framework to "unpack" what is going on. The three defensive directions of movement discussed in the book provide a straightforward way to recognize and understand organizational dynamics. They provide a framework, that when combined with the discussion of the psychosocial defensive perspectives, enables understanding *what* is happening and *why*. This understanding then informs *how* to meaningfully respond to toxic leadership and dysfunctional organizational dynamics. Answering the questions of what, why, and how to respond is the goal of this book.

ACCESSIBILITY

Throughout the book, every effort has been made to make the framework easily understood even though it is based on admittedly more complex and abstract theories of human nature and behavior. In my role as an executive, I found these insights could be adapted to my work of leading and managing. The accessibility of this book strives to inform understanding leader and organizational dynamics and more importantly locating ways to use the knowledge to improve organizational performance and work life. The keys to applying this knowledge are combining thoughtful observation, careful listening to others, reflectivity, and intentionality to build toward the cultural values advocated in this book: openness, inclusivity, transparency, and being collaborative, respectful, and trusting. These six words are often minimally present in organizations and sometimes entirely absent. They are a challenge to realize in our organizations and even harder to sustain.

AN ADVOCACY FOR UNDERSTANDING AND ACTION

This book advocates for an in-depth understanding of leadership and organizational dynamics that become dysfunctional. Oppressive, autocratic, and authoritarian leadership is all too common. These leaders are toxic to others and the organization. This stressful toxicity leads to reliance on individual and group psychosocially defensive responses that further increase the dysfunctional organizational dynamics and can become "normalized" as how we do work here, our organizational culture, and who we are, our organizational identity. Understanding these leader and organizational dynamics using the thought provided in this book "empowers" meaningful individual, groups, and organizational change even if it is localized as an organizational subculture within an unchanging larger toxic and dysfunctional organizational culture.

In sum, not trying to change toxic leadership and dysfunctional organizational dynamics is not a good option. The psychosocially informed framework in this book provides a foundation for meaningful change, a way forward for dealing with toxic leadership and organizational dynamics, and how to intentionally lead organizations.

Acknowledgments

This book is the product of decades of writing, consulting to, and managing large complex organizations. My progress along this pathway to learning has included the fellowship and support of many of my friends and colleagues who have also traveled this path. Michael A. Diamond and Howard F. Stein have coauthored and provided valuable comments for many books and papers as well as providing a rich and dynamic intellectual space and whiteboard to explore the possibilities of answering the question *why*. Thanks for the companionship on this journey of discovery. I have also been enriched by my colleagues Carrie M. Duncan, Nathan Gerard, Sara Elias, and Eda Ulus from the Center for Psychosocial Organization Studies (https://surfacingtheorganization.com). They and the center continue to create learning for understanding the *why* of toxic leadership and dysfunctional organizational dynamics. I also highly valued the rich and diverse intellectual community that the International Society for the Psychoanalytic Study of Organizations (https://ispso.org/) provided me at the start of my search for the answer to *why*. I have appreciated the experiential learning opportunities provided for me by the A.K. Rice Institute and from my early associations with senior members of the Tavistock Institute of Human Relations, London. There are also thought leaders who have contributed to this striving to understand toxic leadership and dysfunctional organizational dynamics. To list but a few, Manfred F.R. Kets de Vries, Yiannis Gabriel, Edgar Schein, Harry Levinson, Abraham Zaleznik, Howard Schwartz, Howell Baum, Melanie Klein, and Karen Horney. It is indeed the case that progress is always enabled by those who have provided thought that becomes the raw material for imagining the possibilities.

About the Author

Seth Allcorn authors his books from the perspective of a combination of decades of management experience in large complex academic health sciences centers, organizational consulting, and as a student of organizations trying to make sense of dysfunctional organizational dynamics by adapting psychoanalytic theory to their study. As a founding member of the International Society for the Psychoanalytic Study of Organizations, he is committed to understanding organizations, which he does so with an attention to making his learned psychosocially informed insights understandable to the reader. This is one of the strengths of his writing style that applies the theory in practice.

Leadership and management theory that is not informed by firsthand management experience offers the threat that what is actually going on in organizations is not fully understood. In particular, this is true of toxic executive and management styles and actions that are hard to understand without considering the experiential nature of our organizations. This appreciation is underscored throughout his work and his psychosocially informed study of organizations.

Seth Allcorn's management experience in academic medical centers includes managing large academic departments of medicine, having served as an assistant and associate dean of two medical schools including as the chief executive officer (CEO) of a three hundred million professional billing medical plan, and he has been responsible for the oversight of the health care system for over 30,000 offenders. He was most recently a Vice President of Finance and Administration of the University of New England that is developing an academic health sciences center focus. He also has over 30 years of organizational consulting experience working for public and private organizations focused on strategic direction, process improvement, and executive coaching. These decades of service at five universities when combined with the consulting experience permit him to ground the use of theory in practice and practice in theory. His ability to span theory and practice is his unique contribution to this book.

Seth Allcorn has a Ph.D. in higher education and an M.B.A. and B.S. in business administration. He has extensively published. He is the author or co-author of 16 books, half-a-dozen chapters, and over one hundred papers that have appeared in scholarly and practitioner journals.

1

An Introduction to Understanding the Psychosocial Nature of Organizational Life

The workplace, regardless of whether it is a small 50-employee retail store or a global enterprise employing many thousands of workers, is filled with a hard-to-know complexity that we most often try to overlook to function in our jobs. The vastness of the attributes of the psychosocial workplace can overwhelm efforts to enumerate them much less understand them as a dynamic whole with many interactions. This increases the challenge of knowing and understanding leadership and organizational dynamics. This appreciation amounts to a humbling proviso for this book and you the reader. There is no way all of this can be addressed for what it is. We are reduced to locating ways of thinking about this complexity that do not do an injustice to the true nature of our lived experience in our organizations. The cognitive maps that we do use to provide us with insights and understanding of the interactive nature of organizational life must include shedding light on how organizations influence us and how we influence them.

This chapter begins by overviewing the work of thought leaders who have contributed to developing psychosocially informed organizational insights. Many have made a wide variety of contributions. The few to be highlighted have formed much of the theoretical basis of this book. The chapters of the three parts of the book are then overviewed to provide an organizer to the book. These chapter summaries provide a framework for understanding how this book's content will provide insights into psychosocial organizational dynamics and how this knowledge can be applied in practice by executives, managers, supervisors, trainers, and consultants.

DOI: 10.4324/9781003464464-1

A GROWING UNDERSTANDING OF THE PSYCHOSOCIAL WORKPLACE

During recent decades organizational theorists have developed insightful ways to use psychosocially informed theory to better understand our organizations. Organization leaders and members are frequently observed to not always be logically pursuing profit-maximizing strategies or the goals for nonprofit organizations. The contributions of these thought leaders whose work began in the 1940s and 1950s are briefly overviewed. This 75-year history of trying to better understand individual, group, and leadership dynamics in our organizations is important to appreciate. Many important psychosocially informed perspectives have been created, and those on this short list were particularly informative for writing this book.

Wilfred Bion – Group Dynamics

Bion observed in the 1940s that in group therapy for soldiers suffering from war trauma, these groups included recurrent emotional themes he labeled as basic assumptions. These group dynamics contained tacit underlying assumptions that detracted from the group's healing work. The basic assumption groups he labeled as fight-flight, dependency, and pairing. These basic assumption group dynamics can also be observed to be periodically present in all types of organizations. Their potential presence makes it important to recognize them when they develop to avoid compromises to working on group and organizational goals. Avoiding retreats into these dysfunctional psychosocially defensive group dynamics is, however, challenging when organizations encounter highly stressful and anxiety-ridden circumstances such as losses of profitability.

These defensive group dynamics naturally emerge not only when group members experience stressful operating problems but also when the group's psychosocial dynamics contribute to the stress by detracting from the ability to work together effectively. Defending individually against stressful experiences is natural and can become shared by group members becoming a psychosocially defensive retreat to one of the basic assumption groups. Fight and flight group dynamics, for example, may develop when a distressing external threat is encountered at work. Fighting back against the threat may include identifying other organization members in specialized divisions as part of the problem that can generate hard-to-resolve organizational conflicts that engage everyone in a group dynamic that reduces voluntary coordination, cooperation, and operating performance. Similarly, flight from facing the problem at hand is often encountered. For example, a group that has met to solve a problem may prefer to speculate about its causes leading to imagining solutions for non-existent root causes. Doing the demanding work of data collection and analysis is avoided (defensive flight). These basic assumption fight and flight group dynamics and the dependency and pairing basic assumption group dynamics inform the development of the psychosocially defensive workplace framework in Chapter 2.

Harry Levinson – Organizational Diagnosis

Levinson, beginning in the 1950s, developed his approach to understanding our organizations by promoting an awareness of the importance of creating a context that supports the emotional well-being of organization members. He advocated for organizational consultants the value of conducting rigorous organizational diagnoses to inform the development of recommendations for organizational change in support of leaders and organization members. His diagnostic approach emphasized understanding the manifest and latent aspects of workplace cultures and practices (what it is like to work here) before trying to facilitate organizational change.

The focus of his work emphasized that the historical organizational concept of logically designed and engineered organizational operations based on rationality is an aspirational myth. He accepted that the daily reality of organizational life is often filled with out-of-awareness and usually the undiscussable leader and follower dynamics that lead to hard-to-resolve interpersonal and organizationally based structural conflicts and fragmentation. Conflict is generated in all organizations by various parts of the organization that have developed their own areas of expertise, goals, values, and methods. This appreciation led him to adapt psychosocial theory to better understand these not-so-logical or rational organizational dynamics. His work is an implicit basis of this book's efforts to embrace psychosocial perspectives so that they may be applied in practice by executives, managers, and consultants in our organizations.

Manfred Kets Devries – Organizational Psychosocial Dynamics

Kets Devries has focused his research and writing on leadership, the dynamics of organizational change, and exploring the interface between management theory and psychosocially informed perspectives. He advocates for an authentic nature to leadership that promotes meaningful organizational change and relationships among organization members. He emphasizes appreciating that emotions contribute to the development of dysfunctional groups and organizational dynamics made all the more worse by the dangers of narcissistic leaders.

His work includes critically inspecting the notion that organizations are rationally and logically organized and have carefully engineered processes and methods that make them run like a machine. He finds these perspectives to be aspirational rather than accurate reality testing. Daily organizational life he finds is filled with out-of-awareness and usually hard-to-discuss leader and follower dynamics that contribute to structural conflicts generated by the various parts of the organization, its silos of specialization, developing their own goals, values, and using their unique methods. These kinds of organizational dynamics led him to adapt psychosocial theory to create insights and understanding of the complexities of leading, managing, and working for our organizations. His work informs this book's efforts to adapt psychosocially informed theories so that they are more easily understood, appreciated, and applied in practice in our organizations.

Michael Diamond – Organizational Identity

Organizational identity examines individual, interpersonal, and group dynamics that contain out-of-awareness psychosocially defensive responses to stress. The quality of these dynamics and interpersonal attachments and feelings of connectedness and mutual understanding or lack thereof can contribute to compromising organizational performance. These patterns of interaction within work groups and among organization members are, it is to be appreciated, not necessarily entirely conscious. They may also become defensive in nature providing organization members safety and security by defensively structuring organizational life to manage workplace stress and anxiety. Diamond argues for organization members and leaders ideally being aware that their own internal dynamics can be affected by an operating context filled with distressing experiences. This can lead to dependence on psychosocially shared defensive responses that compromise oneself, others, work groups, and the organization. Organizational identity informs our understanding of organizational life and dynamics and is an important perspective used in this book.

Edgar Schein – Organizational Culture

Organizations have cultures that should ideally contribute to improving organizational life. They are a large part of what it is like to work here. Leaders play a role in creating and managing organizational cultures that provide a comforting predictable framework for understanding and responding to changes within the organization in response to the actions of competitors and regulators. Organizational culture is arrived at by retaining what works and discarding less effective methods. Learning from experience continually refreshes what becomes taken for granted and stable ways for managing organizational dynamics.

Organizations, even under the worst of operating conditions, usually remain sufficiently cohesive, functional, and productive to survive, and in the event culture becomes dysfunctional, leaders help organization members to learn new assumptions to restore stability and predictability. Manipulating organizational cultures implies a deliberate process of leaders changing cultural elements to restore and maintain stress reducing organizational predictability and performance. However, changing well-understood cultural elements can be stressful to organization members and lead to a slow process of change when resistance to change develops about losses of what is familiar and has worked in the past. It is also the case that new organizations usually have dynamic cultural elements where what works is continually being discovered as a part of ongoing innovation and creative change.

In sum, organizational culture provides an important organizing perspective for this book. Organizational culture is an overarching context for understanding leader and follower relationships that are filled with hard-to-understand interpersonal and group dynamics. Equally important is that leaders must deal with their own thoughts and feelings that influence, for better or worse, how they lead and make decisions that, for example, might include manipulating their organization's culture to benefit themselves. Organizational culture shares some similarities with organizational identity in that both are perspectives for understanding the complexities of our lives at work, which is a goal of this book. They will be referred to throughout the book.

Howard Stein – Listening Deeply

Stein's concept of listening deeply focuses not only on what is seen and heard in our organizations but also on the thoughts and feelings of leaders and organization members that are always present but may not be acknowledged. They, however, continually influence what groups and organizations can achieve. Consistent with Bion and Diamond, this lack of appreciation in our organizations contributes to unproductive psychosocially defensive agendas that compromise achieving organizational success. Safely surfacing and exploring these frequently ignored and avoided aspects of work life helps to create a context of awareness and appreciation of the impact that they have on organizational dynamics. This appreciation contrasts to maintaining a cultural context that avoids, ignores, or even angrily rejects considering them. Listening deeply is therefore yet another important psychosocial perspective that, when embraced, can improve organizational life and achieve organizational performance. Stein's approach to understanding organizational dynamics informs this book.

The Thought Leader Contributions – In Sum

This book has as its focus translating the psychosocially informed perspectives of these thought leaders and others into what is hoped to be an accessible, thought-provoking, and meaningful book for all those who are senior-level executives, managers, supervisors, trainers, consultants, and all organization members.

I, as the author, am one of your colleagues and a former senior-level executive in large complex organizations. This book is informed by my management and consulting experience that spans decades starting with managing a small department of a newspaper publisher in high school in the early 1960s that when combined with additional university education led to chief operating officer (COO), chief financial officer (CFO), chief executive officer (CEO), and vice president (VP) roles in five schools of medicine and universities as well as many years of work as an organizational consultant. These decades of management experience included informative challenges for not only managing organizational processes within a dynamic operating setting but also the psychosocially defensively driven organizational dynamics that are always present in our organizations and schools of medicine and universities. What I have learned in terms of adapting these theoretical perspectives into the daily practice of management and supervision and consulting made me more effective in my work. Understanding organizational dynamics in depth contributed to my ability to engage and motivate organization members to turnaround the organizations I worked for and consulted to. In sum, what I learned based on first-hand concrete experience is shared in this book.

THE COMPLEXITY OF UNDERSTANDING ORGANIZATIONAL DYNAMICS

Executives, middle managers, supervisors, and in fact all organization members are confronted with creating their organization every day that they come to work. The buildings and other physical attributes are not what the organization is other than symbolizing the presence of an organization. This perspective emphasizes that organizations most fundamentally are compromised of psychosocial "matter" that is assembled every day. There is a vast array of unplanned and usually underappreciated variables that are continually held in a dynamic tension, a tension that the above-thought leaders are aware of and seek to understand. This book represents an effort to gather many of the ideas that have been created over the past decades, including those of the author, to create insights into these psychosocial dynamics that may include defensive responses to stress that introduce counterproductive psychosocially defensive leader and individual, interpersonal, group, and organizational dynamics.

This book is organized to first engage in Part 1 the problem that many organizations often fail to fully succeed along a range or fail being closed, sold, or merging. These unfortunate organizational outcomes are usually the result of marginally competent and toxic leadership that promotes dysfunctional organizational dynamics that lead to failures to succeed. These are the organizational dynamics that may be avoided by examining in Part 2 the perspective that psychosocial dynamics play a significant role in creating organizational dysfunctions and fragmentation that can make organizations seem as though they are falling apart. Part 3 explores ways to avoid toxic leadership and dysfunctional organizational dynamics and heal our organizations and the lives of their members.

The book is organized around these three themes beginning in Chapter 2 with perspectives for understanding psychosocially defensive organizational dynamics that lead to the organizational dysfunctions discussed in Part 1.

THE ORGANIZATION OF THE BOOK

Chapter 1 – An Introduction to Understanding the Psychosocial Nature of Organizational Life

This chapter provides an overview of the book, its formulation, its organization, and what is to be learned by a better understanding of human behavior in our organizations. The major contributors to the psychosocially informed approach to understanding and managing organizational dynamics are followed by chapter overviews and the implications of this work for managing and consulting to organizations and training and teaching management and leadership.

Chapter 2 – An Overview of the Psychosocial Organization

This chapter recasts psychosocially informed perspectives into accessible plain English to inform supervisors, managers, executives, and organization members as well as trainers and consultants. The question of how best to fulfill leadership roles is always challenging, and this chapter provides insights into how to lead and manage business processes based on a better understanding of the psychological and social aspects of our organizations. Working with and managing people at work includes the hard-to-manage complexities of human nature. Made clear in this chapter is that a deeper appreciation of the human side of our organizations goes a long way toward meaningfully engaging others to achieve organizational goals and objectives.

Part 1 – Destructive Organizational Dynamics

Our hierarchical departmentalized organizations include informal groups, teams, and specialized divisions that dominate our experience of work and "what it is like to work here." These experiences are at one end anchored in uplifting, fulfilling, and positive experiences and at the other end by much darker, punishing, and alienating work experiences that strip away positive self-experience and feelings. The darker side of organizational life is an omnipresent oppressive presence that can be avoided and turned around by a better understanding of the human side of organizations.

Chapter 3 – Oppression at Work

This chapter explores what is often accepted as an inevitable element of organizational life. Oppression can take many forms and is experienced in many ways. Oppression occurs when there are unjust and dehumanizing uses of power and authority by leaders who occupy powerful positions starting with CEOs and a descending array of executive, management, and supervisory positions. The use of this power unfortunately sometimes is unproductive and driven by personal and usually hard to discuss reasons on the part of the individuals holding the powerful positions. The result is feelings on the part of those subjected to their power and authority of being persecuted, subjugated, dominated, and suppressed. If the highest positions in the organization act oppressively, everyone suffers compromising organizational performance. When oppression is resisted, it may well lead to greater efforts by management to control and dominate organization members – doubling down, which is a popular expression. And when failure appears to be an option, ever more toxic leadership dysfunctions may be resorted to such as downsizing and reorganization. Understanding the nature and experience of workplace oppression is a good first step toward improving work life and organizational performance.

Chapter 4 – Autocratic, Authoritarian, and Oppressive Leadership

Toxic and oppressive leaders usually view themselves as self-important and behave in self-serving ways such as feeling the need to be in control of everyone and everything leading to oppressing others to meet their personal needs being admired and failing that feared. Dissenting views and opinions are disregarded. Those who do dissent may find their careers are at risk. There is usually a well-established historical pattern of punishing experiences for resisting the oppression that everyone knows about. These leaders rely on constraining, subverting, and discrediting challenges to their unilateral authoritarian uses of power. These oppressive organizational dynamics become accepted as "boiler plate" cultural approaches to working together when resistance is futile. The organizational culture is one of creating and maintaining autocratic and authoritarian control over everyone that diminishes personal, group, and organizational performance. Better understanding this unilateral imposition of micromanaging authoritarian rule and its toxic and dysfunctional effects within organizations is an essential aspect of creating a more humane and productive work experience.

Chapter 5 – Adapting to the Failing Organization

The chapter explores organizational dynamics that contribute to a failing organization. Organizational failures to succeed can lead to a sense that the organization may not survive. This applies to public and private organizations including non-profits and more threateningly to militaries fighting ground, sea, and air battles. This sense of an impending demise, the sinking ship, is a stressful and anxiety-ridden experience that leads to the development of individual and shared dysfunctional psychosocial defenses that include losses of accurate reality testing enabled, for example, by denial and rationalization.

Acknowledging poor management direction and decision-making that has compromised everyone's ability to achieve at a high level can be threatening and is often usually wisely avoided. This distressing experience of potential failure is underscored many times by the best employees leaving for better and more secure jobs. These organizational dynamics make it important to understand why this is happening. Organizational culture and organizational identity are two ways of understanding how organizations and their members arrive at tolerating toxic leadership and dysfunctional organizational dynamics that make accepting failure as an option. These usually unacknowledged aspects of organizational life help to explain a context where recourse to individual and shared psychosocially defensive dynamics becomes an accepted way to cope with the presence of stress, fears, and anger. Since these dynamics are not particularly open to being discussed, they can be challenging if not threatening to change.

Part 2 – Organizational Fragmentation and Falling Apart

Part 2 is about life at work becoming fragmented and the ability to work effectively together falling apart. Organizations manage complexity by being organized into hierarchical structures that include prescribed roles and role-to-role interactions that it is hoped will provide control and predictability. Organizations members, however, introduce psychosocially based complexity into their role performances that can be hard to understand in terms of the interpersonal, group, and organizational dysfunctions that they create that compromise organizational performance. It is hard to find an organization that operates optimally most of the time and workplaces that are consistently good places to work. Discussed in Chapters 6–9 are some of the fundamentals of organizational, group, interpersonal, and personal fragmentation that can lead to the ability to effectively work together falling apart.

Chapter 6 – Falling Apart: Organizational Fragmentation

Large organizations rely on hierarchical structures with layers of positions arrayed downward from a single position of power and control to the least but most numerous – those on the front lines. The CEO is responsible for the organization's performance to fulfill its mission and create stockholder and stakeholder value. As one descends the management hierarchy, decision-making power and authority diminishes. Employees at the bottom of the hierarchy have little to no formal decision-making authority, and their work is often prescribed in job descriptions and carefully monitored such as in the case of assembly line workers. These controlling organizational structural elements are, however, difficult to maintain in good working order. Maintaining coordination and cooperation among an organization's divisions and the many different organizational roles is challenging. Psychosocially based dynamics and defensiveness frequently contribute to creating operating problems such as conflicts between organization members and the organization's specialized divisions and silos. It is not hard to find instances where these fragmenting organizational dynamics create a sense that the organization's member ability to work together is falling apart at least to some extent. Fragmentation is made even more likely by geographic separation that creates an "us versus them" dynamic and by mergers of dissimilar organizations and cultures.

Chapter 7 – Falling Apart: Group and Role Fragmentation

This chapter explores falling apart from the perspective of workplace groups and roles. Groups are sometimes cohesive like a winning athletic team and at other times less so creating losses of morale, disorganization and chaos, and fragmentation. When different voices and ideas speak to different elements of the group's experience, the result can be the formation of conflicting subgroups with different roles, interests, and methods of work as may occur among specialized organizational silos. These conflicting organizational roles and subgroups can lead to dysfunctional intergroup dynamics where there are, for example, struggles over who has the right to make decisions and who should be in charge. There are many ways that the experience of being together in achieving the organization's work can seem to be falling apart – some if not a lot. Recognizing and trying to correct these ever-changing group and role dynamics is an essential part of the CEO's and management's responsibility in terms of managing the organization's culture to reduce conflict, fragmentation, and stress.

Chapter 8 – Falling Apart: Interpersonal Fragmentation

When it comes to answering a question like "What's it like to work here?" the responses can be confusing. Someone may say "I like my job, but I hate working here." This requires "unpacking" which is what Chapters 6–9 in Part 2 explore. A response like this suggests that the organization or a division or work group may have a toxic leader who generates distressing workplace dysfunctions and a poor work experience. The individuals making this response may, however, like their colleagues and friends and their work, although this valued interpersonal world can also be compromised by a toxic leader or a dysfunctional organization culture. The ability to work together can be lost to interpersonal and role-to-role conflicts resulting in diminished voluntary coordination and cooperation and a shared awareness that we may not be working effectively together. Also, to be explored in this chapter is that those in leadership roles may seek to be admired by loyal subordinates – narcissism is discussed in Chapter 11.

In sum, interpersonal fragmentation underscores that the psychosocial side of the workplace can positively or negatively influence interpersonal relationships between organizational leaders and those they supervise and can lead to dysfunctional organizational outcomes and feelings that our ability to work together is falling apart. Understanding and managing these personal and interpersonal tendencies is a major step forward toward improving working relationships to avoid interpersonal fragmentation and the possibility of unintentionally compromising individual and group work performance.

Chapter 9 – Falling Apart: Individual Fragmentation

Falling apart can happen for more than organizations, groups, and within the interpersonal world. A discussion of falling apart must also explore our awareness of ourselves that influences our relationships with others. We are all faced with the challenge of knowing and understanding our self-experience and managing our thoughts, feelings, and actions. This is made more difficult by the experience of workplace stress. A reflective self-awareness can reveal our personal sense that we and our world seem to be falling apart. There are times we may feel that we are losing control of ourselves, our thoughts, feelings, and actions, as well as our valued relationships with others such as may occur during a downsizing event that ruptures personal relationships inside and outside of work. These losses of self-composure and valued relationships can be profoundly distressing. Finding ways to better understand defensive individual dynamics that arise in response to stress is important and suggests that developing and maintaining an accurate and balanced understanding of ourselves and our relationships with others is important. This chapter explores understanding why our experience of workplace stress is challenging to manage in terms of maintaining our self-integration and intentionality.

Part 3 – Organizational Healing

Healing the toxic and dysfunctional organizational dynamics discussed in this book that create a sense of oneself, work, and the organization is falling apart offers many challenges. Failure is not a good option. Responding to these toxic, fragmenting, and performance-robbing organizational dynamics can be facilitated by psychosocially informed leaders, organization members, trainers, and external consultants who work to discover the underlying often undiscussable elements of the dysfunctions. Organization members should be encouraged to acknowledge the presence of the dysfunctions and their origins. Better yet is avoiding the emergence of these toxic and dysfunctional organizational dynamics by embracing a leadership style that is not only healing but can turn our organizations into good places to work that are highly productive. Intentional leadership can do this. The topics covered in Part 3 provide an understanding of the underlying sources of toxic leadership and organizational dysfunctions. This informs locating ways to create meaningful organizational change that can be embraced by boards, leaders, and organization members.

Chapter 10 – The Psychosocial Dimensions of Roles in Organizations

The interpersonal world at work is filled with complexity. Managers who oversee organization members, all of whom have designated roles, that may not always reflect what those in the roles are doing are encountering a widespread problem. Formal job descriptions and roles represent planned expectations about performing coordinated work based on cooperative role-to-role interactions. However, informal roles worked out among organization members including with superiors are common becoming implicitly accepted as the way we work together. This appreciation emphasizes that human beings bring their life histories, their skills and knowledge, their aspirations, and their hopes and fears to work with them introducing behavioral tendencies that may include acting in ways that are less than functional that compromise organizational performance. We might ask, "So what is really going on in our organizations?" This chapter provides insights for trying to answer this question.

Chapter 11 – Diagnosing Organizational Narcissism

Psychosocially informed perspectives offer a way of understanding complex and diverse organizational dynamics. Explored in this chapter is a framework for understanding harmful organizational narcissistic dynamics that occur with enough frequency among leaders to merit a chapter. This framework informs understanding how narcissistically inclined managers lead and how to make meaningful interventions aimed at limiting performance-robbing out of control narcissistic dynamics.

Chapter 12 – Four Ways to Understand Organizational Dynamics and Leadership

All organizations share the presence of human nature that can become the basis of the authoritarian oppression discussed in Part 1 but also meaningful and caring interpersonal, group, organizational, and societal dynamics. This chapter explores the psychosocial dynamics that disrupt, fragment, and harm people, groups, and organizations. These dark organizational outcomes usually attract a lot of attention because of the harm that they create. These punishing organizational cultures can be understood in several ways. This chapter provides four perspectives for better understanding the dark side of human nature and oppressive, authoritarian, and toxic leaders and the dysfunctional group, and organizational dynamics that they create. Organizational culture, organizational identity, and psychosocially defensive organizational dynamics are used to reveal what is always present in our organizations but seldom discussed and not well understood in terms of how they influence our lives at work.

Chapter 13 – Consultation and Training

Our organizations, large and small, share the complexities that human nature introduces into *what it is like to work here*. The hierarchical nature of our organizations that splits them apart vertically into layers and horizontally into silos of specialized functions like finance, human relations, marketing, and production makes managing our organizations a challenge. These layers and divisions create a complex ever-changing context that dependably generates operating problems that compromise performance and profitability. These problematic organizational attributes are confounded by a range of leadership styles that include toxic authoritarian and narcissistic styles that contribute to everyone's stress and anxiety leading to psychosocially defensive responses. This is the context organizational consultants and trainers are confronted with. To be effective they must make sense of these organizational dynamics to improve operating performance and make the work lives of organization members less stressful and more fulfilling. For example, a dysfunctional executive's actions may be ignored and rationalized away in part because it is felt to be too dangerous to acknowledge. This behavior may have become an accepted part of the organizational culture that locks into place leadership toxicity and the accompanying organizational dysfunctions. Consultants and trainers, to be effective, must find ways to encourage a non-defensive surfacing of these dysfunctional leader and organizational dynamics for consideration as to what corrective actions should be taken.

Chapter 14 – The Intentional Leader

Intentional leadership makes a difference for our organizations. It is characterized in this chapter as a set of values – openness, inclusiveness, transparency, collaboration, and mutual trust and respect. These values are the foundation for creating an organization where innovative ideas and solutions to problems are allowed to emerge and leadership and operating dysfunctions are open to discussion. Intentional leadership locates a balance in providing direction without becoming oppressive, authoritarian, or autocratic – the traditional top-down unilateral command and control form of leadership. Intentional leadership focuses on containing and responding to the stress that organization members experience by first acknowledging the experience and then facilitating organization members to maintain intentional group and organizational dynamics that reduce stress and retreat to dysfunctional psychosocial defenses while improving organizational performance.

This chapter peers inside the "black box" of the experience of leaders and their leadership styles where leaders may develop rigid approaches to using their power and control that are toxic and dysfunctional and compromise fulfilling the organization's mission, vision, and strategic plan. In contrast, this chapter explores the intentional leader's approach to managing that includes self-awareness, reflectivity, and cultural and identity awareness. Reflective intentionality also suggests that achieving perfection as a leader is problematic, and if unthoughtfully and unreflectively pursued, it can lead to feeling stressed out when perfectionistic self-expectations are not met.

Chapter 15 – Looking Back and Looking Forward

This book has taken a hard look at the human side of our organizations and organizational life. The functional, desirable, and admired side of what goes on in organizations encourages everyone to develop themselves and each other creating a fulfilling life at work that is creative and exciting.

This is to be applauded. There is however a darker side to organizational life driven by toxic leaders and dysfunctional psychosocially defensive organizational dynamics that can lead to stress and trauma from extreme cases of organizational and moral violence such as personalized humiliating assaults by those in power and the infliction of mass traumas like a major downsizing. This book, by looking back at dysfunctional leadership and organizations, has revealed that human behavior in our organizations can result in poor organizational performance and the stripping of humanity out of our lives at work. This book, by looking forward, provides insights and ideas for executives, managers, supervisors, trainers, and consultants that can be used in practice to create a valued and productive organization experience for all.

IN CONCLUSION: MANAGING AND WORKING WITHIN ORGANIZATIONS

Toxic leaders and dysfunctional organizations are common. This makes understanding their nature and dynamics important in terms of creating high-functioning organizations that are good places to work for. The dysfunctional side of leadership and organizational dynamics is highlighted by failing or failed organizations that frequently appear in the news and the accompanying job losses that are the collateral damage that toxic, authoritarian, and narcissistic leaders introduce into our organizations. These dysfunctional organizations can be understood to contain individual shared psychosocial defenses to fend off the distress that is invariably present in these types of workplace experiences. These all too human defensive responses, however, also contribute to creating operating problems and stress and a growing sense that failure is an option. The implication of these dysfunctional organization dynamics for managing our organizations is clear. The dark side of organizational life can and must be minimized, remediated, and preferably avoided. Our focus should be on looking forward to creating fulfilling and meaningful work experiences and high-performing organizations.

2

An Overview of the Psychosocial Organization

This book explores how psychosocial perspectives contribute to understanding organizational dynamics that include the individual, interpersonal, group, and organizational workplace. Over my five decades, I came to appreciate that understanding the psychological and social aspects of organizations made me a better manager and leader, and what I learned is shared in this book.

The approach taken in this chapter and throughout the book is to avoid technical scholarly language and references and focus instead on providing insights anchored in everyday life experiences. After all, this is what the many theories about organizational dynamics are trying to explain. The explanations and discussions in this chapter recast these theoretical perspectives to make them easier to understand.

THE PSYCHOSOCIAL PERSPECTIVES

There are different ways to understand our lives at work and how organizations are created, led, and operated. Organizations, large and small, for-profit and non-profit, and private and public are filled with hard-to-understand dynamics. Psychosocially informed perspectives provide a way to understand and manage these dynamics to create work experience that is not only fulfilling and meaningful but also productive. However, if this were easy to do, this book would not be necessary. Organizations are too often led by toxic leaders within hierarchical organizational structures that empower them. Hierarchical organizations and their many

  DOI: 10.4324/9781003464464-2

divisions also create structural conflicts that compromise voluntary cooperation and coordination. The following discussion provides accessible ways of understanding common organizational dynamics that are disruptive starting with an overview of the individual at work.

The Individual at Work

People often see the world in easy-to-understand binary black and white good versus bad terms, especially during stressful times. The world becomes split apart. Our self-image or the image of another individual, group, or nation becomes polarized. There is a good self and a bad other. This simplified binary splitting apart of experience provides comforting certainty that we know what the world is like. In fact, this certainty can so effectively protect us from feeling threatened or anxious that it is not particularly open to our inspection or being questioned or challenged.

For example, if someone suggests another person is anxious or angry the now *bad* person who made this distressing assertion may be responded to by suggesting it is "you" who is anxious or angry, not me. The interpersonal world in this example becomes split apart with no middle ground. Putin's 2022 war in Ukraine to protect Russia, the beloved native country, from the bad and threatening Ukrainian Nazis is another example. In organizations, the finance department and its desire to manage costs may be seen by other departments as creating an oppressive and limiting context when they need more resources to improve their performance. Also, to be noted is that this splitting process operates in reverse. We may see ourselves as weak, ineffective, and bad and see someone else, a leader, or another group as good and acting effectively meriting our admiration and respect. A similar example is a chief executive officer's (CEO's) unexpected presence in a meeting may encourage many of those present to feel threatened and diminished. The executive in our minds becomes bigger than life and we, by comparison, feel less important.

In sum, this split-apart polarizing world degrades accurate reality testing. This defensive psychosocial dynamic is frequently overlooked, ignored, and is not open to discussion because it seems threatening to bring it up especially when it involves the actions of managers and executives. We may hear, for example, different views expressed about someone, an executive or manager, where this person it turns out is "known" by others in diverse ways – some good and some bad. There is also a defensive investment in maintaining this simplified split-apart view of the "other" to meet personal needs to feel good about "us" compared to the bad, threatening, or oppressive "other." These defensive individual, interpersonal, and group needs are not particularly open to self-reflection or discussion, and challenging these dynamics may paradoxically, as mentioned, only serve as proof that the person who is doing the challenging is indeed bad and "I" or "we" are good.

This good and bad splitting of others can become the basis for a *hot button* response when feelings from past similar distressing workplace lived experiences are reexperienced. A supervisor, who looks like, sounds like, or acts like a past supervisor or authority figure who was abusive, manipulative, or oppressive may evoke feelings consistent with this experience that are not necessarily consistent with a manager's or supervisor's self-awareness or actions. The emotional response as a result may be disproportionate. Experiences from the past may, for example, encourage individuals to become fearful, submissive, enraged, or withdrawn when confronted with an authority figure. Everyone may wonder what just happened. And to be noted is that challenging the transference of these past experiences and associated feelings onto the present can be depended upon to be greeted defensively by both the person involved in the transference and those who are targeted further polarizing the situation.

In sum, we all as individuals seek to control our self-experience most often preferring to see ourselves as good and others as bad (or the reverse), and this predictably introduces dysfunctions into our self-awareness, thoughts and feelings, and the interpersonal world as well as group and organizational dynamics.

Group and Organizational Dynamics

There are two especially helpful perspectives for understanding group and organizational dynamics. They provide different but mutually supportive ways to understand our participation in groups and large usually hierarchical bureaucratic organizations.

Organizational culture is one way to understand organizational life with its complex bureaucratic rigidities and the problematic dysfunctions that hierarchically based positions of power and authority introduce into our workplace experience. Organizational culture as a concept speaks to accepted, familiar, established working relationships and methods developed over time by organization members to understand and manage their working together, operating problems, adapting to change, and maintaining organizational integration. These predictable and comforting cultural elements are learned from experience. What does not work is discarded and what works is retained and taught to new members as the accepted way to work together and to problem solve including how to think and feel about their work and their organization and its vision and mission. This process in practice also includes the necessity of having to unlearn cultural assumptions that have become dysfunctional facilitated by executives and managers with the expectation that organization members will embrace the new cultural assumptions.

Leading cultural change ideally involves management decisions that are arrived at intentionally and are open to being discussed before, during, and after their implementation to avoid creating stressful top-down cultural change that can lead to defensive resistance to change. Traditional management styles that autocratically ram cultural change through an organization dependably generate hard-to-overcome resistance by organization members. Resistance is especially likely to occur when it is thought that the changes are self-serving for those in leadership roles or aimed at manipulating stockholder value and not at creating value for the organization's members.

New organizations of course do not have a long-shared cultural history that includes lessons that have been learned and retained. The continual discovery of "new" cultural assumptions is often amplified by planned and unplanned leadership changes that introduce organizational chaos and losses of continuity in terms of developing a stable organizational culture and "who we are." It is also the case that large organizations usually have specialized operating subdivisions that create their own subcultures that are less than compatible with their larger organization's goals and culture. Developing an effective large complex organization is challenging in terms of fusing together these different subcultures to arrive at shared common goals and methods for solving problems and adapting to change. Achieving cultural integration is, however, easier said than done. Organizations often suffer from structural fragmentation between the management layers and silos of specialization resulting in losses of internal integration; compromises to developing shared values and tactics; and problems achieving voluntary cooperation and coordination among organization members. These hard-to-manage organizational dynamics can readily become dysfunctional.

In sum, organizational culture encourages us to think critically about the underlying psychosocial aspects of organizational life that include hierarchically based leadership and defensive organizational dynamics that compromise working together. Adapting to change becomes more difficult reducing organizational performance to the point where failing, it may be thought, has become an option (Chapter 3). In sum, poor and toxic leadership can readily result in dysfunctional organizational dynamics and the loss of a stabilizing and functional culture and organizational identity.

Organizational identity speaks to the psychosocially oriented individual and group dynamics and how they contribute to creating a shared sense of "us" – who I am and who we are as a group and organization. "I" or "we" are good and unsupportive and distressing "others" such as members of other divisions are bad resulting in a binary black-and-white experience of the world as discussed in the above finance department example. Accurate reality testing can become degraded to the point that achieving the mission and goals of the organization becomes of secondary interest to, for example, maintaining a familiar culture of *in-fighting* among the silos of specialization. Outcomes like this are common in organizations fueled at the margins by a lack of appreciation of the psychosocial defenses that reinforce the experience of the *other* as bad and to be defended against.

These defenses are a response to stress that splits us as individuals, our relationships, and our organizations apart. These organizational dynamics are further energized by seeing others as not only threatening but also as familiar figures from prior negative life experiences. Feelings relative to what is going on now may be consistent with this past experience, although these feelings may not be consistent with the nature of a manager's sense of self or the manager's actions. This blurring of accurate reality testing introduces hard-to-understand dysfunctions into the interpersonal world as well as into groups and organizations.

Organizational identity differs from organizational culture by emphasizing the psychosocially defensive nature of individual, interpersonal, and group emotional attachments, feelings of connectedness, and mutual understanding or lack of it as compared to locating what works best to maintain organizational performance. These defenses contribute to the presence of toxic leadership and organizational dysfunctions that contain a hard-won cultural stability that defies easily being changed. Giving up familiar and accepted ways of working together is usually resisted by organization members.

For example, an organization that has an arrogant, aggressive, combative, and dysfunctional leader who is responsible for millions of dollars of lost revenue should be removed and replaced by a new leader who is preferably more intentional, open, and inclusive. A change in leadership like this, however, confronts organization members with stressful changes. A new leader would be faced with a major challenge in terms of turning this organization around and this might be compounded by the former combative leader having created in the operating divisions leaders who are equally aggressive and enjoy the in-fighting. In an example like this, the new leader might wisely avoid getting involved in the combat even though the leaders of the divisions continue their aggression although their aggression may become unrewarding when no one aggresses them back. To be accepted in this example is that changing long-accepted organizational cultural and identity dynamics can be a slow process that requires patience and persistence.

In sum, organizational culture and organizational identity provide perspectives for better understanding the thoughts and feelings that influence leaders, groups, and the actions of organization members that may positively or adversely affect their organization's operations. Changing dysfunctional organizational dynamics like this requires being aware of their presence. This awareness should encourage those in leadership roles to appreciate the importance of creating a safe enough, reflective, and intentional workplace that discourages relying on these defenses.

A better understanding of these psychosocial organizational, group, and individual dynamics is contributed to by another helpful perspective. This framework of defensive individual, group, and organizational dynamics complements the insights offered by organizational culture and identity.

PSYCHOSOCIALLY DEFENSIVE GROUPS AT WORK

Psychosocially defensive groups and their accompanying dysfunctional organizational dynamics frequently occur in our organizations. The reliance on these shared defenses by group members arises spontaneously to manage their stress when threatening situations are encountered. These defenses may include acting aggressively against the threat, seeking dependency and protection from a leader, and retreating from the stressful context. Groups at work can, for example, act aggressively toward each other and against operating threats or withdraw from stressful situations, especially those filled with conflict (fight or flight). Group members may also depend on their leaders to tell them what to think, feel, and do, and if there is a lack of adequate leadership, this group's members may wait and hope that an effective leader will be located to help them. While everyone is waiting, there may also develop a shared interest in being good team members who together try to "hold the fort." This defensive group dynamic also may create a sense that everyone is coequal (an associate), and "we" are working together in teaming up to keep the organization running. These psychosocially defensive group dynamics may lead to the emergence of a stable group culture reinforced by responses to, for example, prior life experiences associated with threatening experiences or losses of personal autonomy and integrity relative to an oppressive leader. The balancing act between the hope of having a leader and submitting to an oppressive leader is made more challenging during stressful times such as a loss of revenue or self-inflicted organizational injury such as reorganization or downsizing.

In sum, the more stressful the work experience becomes, the more likely individual and group psychosocial defenses will emerge. Better understanding these psychosocially defensive group dynamics is important. The discussion of these defenses includes examples that did play out in organizations and can be spotted in most organizations.

THE DEFENSIVE DIRECTIONS OF MOVEMENT

The three directions of psychosocially defensive movement are moving against, toward, and away from leaders, organization members, and the dysfunctional structural elements of hierarchical organizations. These directions of movement are intuitive responses when organization members encounter stressful leaders and organizational dynamics. They also importantly provide a framework for responding to the dysfunctional organizational dynamics that they create.

Moving Against Others – Aggression

This group dynamic has a leader who acts aggressively toward operating problems, some group members, other groups, and various parts of the larger organization that are seen to be an inhibitor, problem, or threat and therefore "bad." This aggressive group implicitly accepts that some members may become "casualties" when attacking the source of the threat as in war. This outcome is made more likely because reflectivity and thinking things through may be lacking in favor of narrowly focusing on acting against the perceived threat. This familiar "fight" response is also reinforced by dependably evoking intense emotions such as fear and anger that fuel the aggression against the "bad" external threat or internal problems generating conflict with other organization members or some of its specialized divisions.

Examples of aggression and conflict between leaders, individuals, and groups especially among the silos of specialization in organizations are common. One example is a new telephone marketing group in the marketing division of a large corporation. This group begins to have remarkable success with its advertising that generates many incoming calls to purchase the organization's products. This success, which was bragged about, attracted the envy of other groups and some senior leaders. This success, however, gradually overwhelmed the initial staffing for the group. Sales were booming but incoming calls could not always be immediately answered leading to the potential customers being asked to leave their number for a callback. Callbacks, however, generated fewer closed sales than the initial calls. Eventually, thousands of callbacks accumulated creating a threatening and overworked situation for the group's members who continued to focus on handling incoming calls to maximize sales. A request by the group's manager to the chief financial officer (CFO), who did not like the manager or the group's well-publicized success, yielded an astonishing response. Since the group's budget had been agreed to, no further funding would be provided to manage the increased sales – passive aggression. The CFO instead ordered the group to focus its time on the callbacks, which led to fewer incoming calls being answered and more callbacks. The group's members were frustrated and felt aggressed by the lack of support as their sales went down. The CFO then decided to cut their budget (more aggression) because of the lower sales volume. The group's members, when asked about this, could only laugh and shake their heads since this decision further compromised what had been successful marketing that added to the organization's earnings.

In response, the group decided to aggress back against the CFO by appealing to the new marketing division CEO who, having just started in the position, preferred to avoid conflict and did not respond to the appeal – a response felt to be once again passive aggression by the group's members. The group, in response to the budget cuts, decided to reduce its advertising budget since answering all the incoming calls that the advertising generated was not possible. This had the effect of reducing revenue – passive aggression once again. In this example, everyone is aggressed and everyone is a loser.

Moving against "bad" others by leaders and organization members is common, and if the resulting conflict is not openly recognized and managed can result in wasted resources and opportunities, losses of morale and profit, and a cultural acceptance of toxic leadership and dysfunctional organizational dynamics. Change in a situation like this can be hard to achieve, although many organization members may hope that a leader will step forward to address the disruptive aggressive movements against others.

Moving Toward Others – Dependency

This defensive group's direction of movement seeks security and predictability by expecting their leader or someone in the group or organization to respond to distressing situations. Group members feel that they are less than capable or not authorized to deal with threatening operating problems, and they fear if they did act that they would not be effective. Under these conditions when someone does take charge, the group's members thankfully accept the person who, in the moment, it is hoped knows what to do and how to do it. This uncritical embrace of a leader can accentuate the person feeling self-competent, powerful, and authorized including expecting group members to assume some of the responsibility that they want to avoid. If a leader is not identified, the group is willing to wait for a leader even when the members continue to be faced with stressful workplace problems and threats. However, if the threats become too hard to tolerate, someone in the group who cannot tolerate inaction any longer may self-identify as willing to try to lead even though this dependent group's needs will be hard to meet. Failure to meet these needs predictably leads to disappointment on the part of the group's members and the likelihood of their leader being rejected and perhaps replaced.

Examples of dependent groups and organizational dynamics are common, especially in large complex bureaucratic hierarchies where major operating problems are not addressed in favor of blaming and scapegoating others. No one may seem to be in charge while the organizational dysfunctions continue to yield suboptimal outcomes that threaten failure as in the above example of the division's CEO not responding to requests for something to be done about the CFO's toxic leadership that compromised sales. It was also the case that the company, in this example, had a culture that accepted many performance-stripping operating problems that no one was responsible for solving or empowered to deal with.

Continuing with the case example, eventually an external consultant was engaged to work with the marketing division. An array of operating problems was presented to the consultant that revealed a gradual systemic failure in leadership in the division but also within the company. Division members held expectations that the consultant would improve operations which were in part fulfilled by facilitating the CEO terminating the dysfunctional CFO. After this change, division members were eager to collaborate with the consultant who guided resolving many of their operating problems by working around a new and poorly designed and implemented information system. Disappointingly it was revealed that little of the system could be changed by the consultant without threatening the chief information officer (CIO) in the home office. The defensive resistance of the CIO to acknowledging the many software problems eventually doomed the marketing division to fail, and it was sold to a competitor.

Moving Away from Others – Retreat

This group's leader encourages group members to *not* engage in resisting toxic and threatening leaders or deal with stressful situations and avoid conflict and risk-taking. There is, however, a sense of hope among group members that the toxicity or threat will dissipate or that it can be tolerated if it does not become too threatening – a wait-and-see strategy. There may also be an underlying fear of what will happen if they do act against and resist a toxic leader such as having their budget cut. There may in fact be noteworthy instances where those who have acted and resisted have been disciplined or even terminated. It is felt that it is safer for everyone to go along to get along. This defensive strategy may lead to hiding out in metaphoric organizational foxholes – cubicles or offices – avoiding the people and groups that are threatening.

The same CFO in the case example had a punishing interpersonal management style and was said by the marketing division managers to make women cry and men mad. This is an attention-getting statement. No one wanted to have to deal with the CFO who presumed to micromanage this division with its hundreds of members. No one wanted to be targeted by the CFO's aggressive questioning and demands. Staying out of the line of fire was achieved by avoiding meetings, not returning phone calls and emails, and withholding and manipulating information flows to the CFO. It was also the case that division members also learned to tolerate the CFO's toxic leadership. As mentioned, the consultant shared with the new division's CEO the toxic effects that the CFO had on operations and profitability, and this led to the CEO accepting responsibility for acting to terminate the CFO.

The discussion of these three directions of defensive movement included mention of additional defensive group dynamics. These defensive group dynamics, when combined with the directions of movement, provide a greater depth of understanding of dysfunctional leadership and organizational dynamics.

DEFENSIVE GROUP DYNAMICS

The three defensive directions of movement implicitly include several group dynamics that merit separate discussion. The intentional group culture is also discussed to provide a contrasting non-defensive perspective to the directions of movement and the defensive group dynamics. These complimentary, sometimes overlapping, and informative ways to understand organizational dynamics will be frequently referred to throughout the book. They separately and together offer insights that are supplemented in some chapters with additional psychosocial perspectives. To begin hope and freedom as defensive responses to stressful and threatening leaders and organizational dynamics were echoed in the discussion of the three defensive directions of movement.

Hope and Freedom

This group's members are attentive and actively participate in discussing problems, but they also take little action. The group hopes a leader, a new idea, or a new strategy is located to respond to threatening operating problems. Organization members stay focused on hope for a better future and ideally a leader will be located who does not hold oppressive expectations for group members to assume personal responsibility for responding to the stressful problems and threats. The hope is that their new leader will save them. However, paradoxically a leader who holds or it is thought may hold expectations for the group's members to act may be resisted. The expectations, it is felt, are coercive and oppressive and will restrict the personal freedoms of the group's members. It may in fact be better that a leader is not located to avoid the threat of being required to assume some personal responsibility for solving operating problems. The operating problems are less threatening than the expectations.

Feelings of hopefulness and the pursuit of personal freedom from oppressive leaders are often present in organizations, especially during stressful times. There may be a pervasive hope that things will magically get better even if no one is willing to assume the risky and burdensome responsibility of taking corrective action. These defensive strategies are common in organizations that rely on bureaucratic norms and culture that can make it seem as though no one is in charge. Those in the management hierarchy may avoid assuming responsibilities outside of their narrowly self-defined roles and job descriptions and therefore "above me pay grade."

Continuing with the above example of a dysfunctional organization, in yet another major section of the CEO's division there was an attention-getting operating problem. This section was assigned the responsibility of contacting employees of large organizations to enroll them in a wellness service program that the division was contracted to provide. Enrollment progress was slow and not achieving the hoped-for results. A close inspection of this group's work revealed that the software they were using made it difficult to find candidates to contact to enroll in the service program. The result was much time was being spent finding people to contact who had not already been contacted. The computerized system did not permit entering the status of the contact – enrolled, to be contacted again, or not contacted.

In this case it was hoped that the consultant could find ways to improve their work but without creating more work or raising performance expectations and without challenging the threatening CIO about the poorly designed system. The consultant recommended a paper-and-pencil approach to tracking the status of the people contacted and yet to be contacted. This design did not require much additional work, was easy to learn to do, and worked very well saving a lot of time. It was also hoped that the CIO would not learn about how the group had worked around the deficiencies of the system which would be threatening to the CIO if the President of the company found out. This fear obliged the group's members to defensively conceal their new method (movement away) to remain free from a punishing and oppressive response by the CIO.

In sum, hope and freedom are all too human expectations although their fulfillment may be problematic in our organizations. They inform the directions of movement in that hope may be a part of moving toward others and seeking freedom from expectations and oppression is a part of moving away from organizational leaders.

Togetherness and Sameness

This group or organization's members respond to toxic leadership, misaligned organizational resources, and stressful organizational events such as downsizing and restructuring by feeling a mutuality in their shared experience. This leads the members to join together for safety since everyone is equally exposed to the threats. Being together and knowing that we are not alone in our shared experience is comforting during distressing times. Group members feel there is safety in being together. The metaphor, "We are all in the same boat." speaks to this.

This psychosocially defensive strategy of feeling together reinforces the feeling that everyone is equally worried and anxious, and this becomes a form of social leveling and coequality. As a result, few group and organization members may be willing to self-differentiate to volunteer leadership. Togetherness and sameness therefore help to maintain a sense of safety and freedom from having to assume personal responsibilities. There may also be present in this defensive group dynamic a tacit understanding that anyone who does step forward to lead will be minimally embraced by the group's members. Volunteered leadership may also lead to the threat of a punishing response from those in senior management roles. The result is that this psychosocially defensive nonthreatening group helps organization members, especially within bureaucratic hierarchical organizations, to cope with threatening workplace experiences. And to be noted is that the lack of leadership and meaningful engagement by group members may also contribute to stressful operating ineffectiveness and at some point organizational failure.

In sum, group members are striving to not set themselves apart from the *crowd*. Will I be the next to be targeted for layoff or obliged to assume personal responsibility for acting? This defensive group dynamic, however, compromises organizational performance. There may develop a growing awareness that the crowd's embrace of sameness compromises their ability to effectively work together. There may also develop an awareness of an underlying quality of group and organizational fragmentation that has a problematic nature not unlike a crowd witnessing a crime or a drowning swimmer on a beach and no one does anything. Who and how will the victim or swimmer be saved? This appreciation may lead to an awareness that our ability to work together is falling apart as can happen during restructuring and downsizing. Who will be left to do the work and take charge? Under conditions like this, groups often focus on locating threatening "others" who are feared and hated (the CEO and leadership group in the case of downsizing) making them targets for everyone to blame for the current distressing situation.

The marketing group, for example, had its new CEO located in the corporate home office hundreds of miles away. This remoteness and the toxic culture of the home office compounded the challenge of repairing the group's dysfunctional operations. The home office and its hundreds of employees who identified with their organization and leaders were sometimes referred to as the snake pit by those in the operating divisions. Their collective mutual suffering was reinforced, in the case of the remote telephone marketing group, by the behavior of the division's toxic CFO who was also located in the home office. Everyone felt that they were all in the same leaky boat together. They did their best to try to overcome the systemic problems in their local operations that had been inflicted upon them by the remote, uninformed, disinterested, defensive, and marginally competent executives in the home office – the snake pit. Efforts made by local managers to deal with their operating problems often linked to the poorly designed information system were at best marginally successful. Everyone began to feel in the marketing group that they were doomed to fail.

Responsibility for this organization's many operating problems was in part managed by bi-directional blaming. The leaders of the telephone marketing group blamed the home office and the executives in the home office blamed the group. These two groups and their interactive dysfunctional and fragmenting organizational dynamics are examples of each group feeling defensively together in their shared work experience that included suspicion and animosity held toward the opposing group.

Yet another common defensive response to stress is to become overly reliant on following bureaucratic policies and procedures (doing it by the book) including accepting hierarchically based autocratic and authoritarian leadership styles that, while fulfilling the hope that an effective leader will emerge, fulfill member fears of having leaders who demand loyalty and submission.

Bureaucratic Control

This psychosocially defensive strategy relies on an impersonal, depersonalized, controlling social structure that, it is hoped, will minimize losses of control reducing the possibility of experiencing stress. This familiar hierarchical leadership culture is invariably accompanied by oppressive qualities and performance-stripping operating and cultural rigidities. Losses of personal autonomy and self-identity are accepted in favor of avoiding feeling anxious about losses of control and not being seen as a team player. Organization members are committed to maintaining coordination and predictability. The organizational cost of this defensive system that is aimed at achieving stability is that it generates the performance-robbing *red tape* associated with bureaucracies. Doing it by the book on the part of everyone is the way to go even though it may not work in all instances.

Bureaucratic organizations are our public organizations and large private and not-for-profit organizations as well. Size and geographic distribution make it a challenge to maintain control over organizational operations. This makes relying on standardized policies and procedures and shared information systems the accepted way to organize to maintain control over the organization's specialized divisions.

An example is a department of state responsible for building and maintaining government facilities and lands. The department hired a new leader who replaced a former retired military officer who had created a military-like chain of command and control throughout the state. Decision-making at the local level required approval all the way up the chain of command with signing off by the commanding officer. Many of those hired into the structure were retired military officers who were familiar and identified with this command-and-control bureaucratic structure and culture. There were, despite all the controls, complaints at the local level that resolving operating problems was being delayed by slow decision-making and losses of critical information regarding the nature of the problems as the information flowed up to the top and back down.

The new leader who was not from the military wanted to decentralize decision-making authority and flatten the organizational structure. This approach to leading and managing did, however, carry the risk of less than adequate local decisions being made that would be criticized in the media. This decentralized approach required flattening the chain of command by removing multiple layers of command and control. The retired military officers were removed from the chain of command but retained for their expertise becoming advisory staff. This new arrangement worked well, although there were predictable local decision-making problems that the new leader was willing to accept and defend. After five years, the new leader left, and a new retired military officer was hired as the leader. The former advisory staff officers were reinserted into the chain of command restoring the former top-down command and control organizational culture and accompanying slow decision-making that created problems at the local level.

Bureaucratic organizations that are large, complex, and geographically distributed are filled with the three directions of movement. In this example, the chain of command approach contains aspects of moving against everyone in the organization by over-controlling organization members and decision-making. At the local level, moving away from the chain of command "them" is also common where some decisions are not cleared up the chain of command. And during stressful times organization members may look to their chain of command to take charge and solve the operating problems without burdening them by having to assume personal responsibilities. Once again, to be appreciated is that the directions of movement and the psychosocially defensive framework provide unique insights into organizational dynamics that contain psychosocial defenses some of which are oppressive, autocratic, and authoritarian.

A Note on Autocratic Authoritarian Control

This approach to achieving control, especially in bureaucratic organizations, relies on an autocratic leader who it is hoped will get control of distressing workplace experiences. Organization members hope that their leader has good management skills, and this may encourage some to think only their leader can save them and the organization. These psychosocially defensive group dynamics (moving toward the leader) encourage the autocratic leader to feel powerful and expected to act authoritatively. Organization members are willing to submit to their leader's power and authority, and this, at an extreme, can result in the leader becoming unaccountable for violating moral, ethical, and social values and developing expansive and overreaching ideas that lead to marginal and costly organizational outcomes. As a result, these leaders may fail to succeed in meeting the expectations of organization members for control and predictability. Members' disillusionment and disappointment may include becoming disloyal and gradually rejecting their leader in the hope a new and better leader will be hired who can get the job done. If replacement happens with some frequency (leadership turnover), the unresolved organizational problems and conflict can become mission-critical. The organization may become fragmented with the ability for organization members to work together effectively falling apart. However, should a sense of failing develop, it can lead to, in bureaucratic organizations with autocratic leaders, doubling down on autocratic and authoritarian efforts to regain control reinforcing this defensive group's strategy with an unthoughtful socially defensive repetition as occurred in the above example regarding the removal and reintroduction of the military officers into the chain of command.

Autocratic leaders and authoritarian control are common, especially in organizations founded by an individual who has, with a strong hand, led the organization's development over the years and decades. Family businesses are an example but so are corporations where one individual holds a controlling interest or takes a former publicly owned corporation private with a leveraged buyout. Autocratic leaders who make all the decisions usually do not accept resistance to their authority. Resistors are disciplined or removed from the organization. These attention-getting staffing decisions, however, can occasionally set an organization up to fail. If overcoming resistance and winning out at any cost is all that matters, these leaders create a cadre of sycophants who move toward their leader combined with many organization members avoiding and moving away from the leader and the sycophant group. There may also be a retreat from participating in the organization that reduces the contributions a creative pool of talent can make.

There are however some benefits to autocratic leadership in terms of running organizations. Autocrats are not all bad. These leaders can make decisions quickly and unilaterally impose the decision on organization members making the organization fast on its collective feet. But, at the same time, these leaders are also often regarded to be only as good as the last major decision and because rapid "shoot from the hip" decisions often exclude contributions from organization members, the decisions are vulnerable to being ill-conceived and poorly implemented. And to be noted, while removing these leaders from their roles is problematic if not dangerous for organization members to consider, the hope may remain that a new leader will be found who frees organization members from the oppressive autocratic organizational culture.

An example of these organizational dynamics is a mid-sized university with a new President who wanted to make all the decisions and set about removing everyone who resisted. A new group of highly qualified upper- and mid-level executives was hired who were, they discovered, not expected to make decisions but rather to be effective at unquestionably implementing decisions made by the President even though the President lacked the experience and expertise to do so in the many specialized academic disciplines. The new deans and senior-level executives were resistant to the poorly conceived decisions resulting in their marginal implementation. This led to another round of removing these individuals and replacing them as near as possible with loyalists who were more junior, less experienced, and less accomplished. Turnover, however, continued whenever resistance was encountered. Eventually, a leadership group of loyalists was hired who understood that keeping their positions required willing submission to the President's control. Most of these individuals were held in low regard by faculty and staff with some being considered to be "spies" for the President who reported any resistance and out-of-bounds thoughts and feelings. This culture of control and domination resulted in organization members moving away into their offices and not speaking up to offer alternate thoughts and ideas in meetings to stay employed.

In sum, autocratic and authoritarian leaders develop a threatening and oppressive organizational culture that works for them but not very well for most of the organization's members or the organization. Regrettably, these psychosocially defensive organizational dynamics are common. There is then to be considered a contrasting way of leading and managing that develops organizational cultures that do not encourage organization members to feel oppressed and rely on psychosocial defenses.

The Non-defensive Intentional Work Group

This group and organizational culture has leaders and organization members who are open, inclusive, and transparent and promote reflectivity and intentionality in working together and making decisions that optimize organizational performance. Dysfunctions, stress, and anxiety are present, but they are openly acknowledged and discussed. Organizational threats do not or minimally evoke psychosocially defensive responses. Members identify their self-interests with their fellow group and organization members and their organization's mission and goals. Everyone is willing to evaluate their assumptions about their work methods, and decision-making adequacy is continually assessed based on the outcomes that are achieved. Learning from experience to achieve group and organizational goals is a valued part of the culture and everyone's identity. Mutual understanding and empathy create an emotional bond between group members that is not threatening and facilitates collaborative and cooperative work. Avoided is over-identification with each other that may lead to a defensive sense of sameness and merger and the accompanying losses of reflectivity, critical thinking, and individuality. Maintaining intentionality is always a challenge in our organizations, especially when there are losses of predictability and safety that are sometimes keyed off by the introduction of new toxic leaders.

An example of an intentional organizational culture is a large corporation where the vice president (VP) of operations hired a new leader of a division to turn its inferior performance around. It had lost many of its managers recently because organization members did not identify with the growing belief that failure was an option. This new leader hired a new group of executives and managers and promoted an intentional organizational culture where decisions and everyone's assumptions and actions were open to inspection. Over a period of several years, this new leader and leadership group achieved an attention-getting organizational turnaround becoming a major profit center for the corporation. Everyone enjoyed working in the division, and recruiting for vacancies was easy since the division had a stellar reputation. The VP also received credit for the turnaround by having hired the new leader and was eventually recruited away by another corporation. The new VP who was recruited turned out to be an autocrat who saw the leadership and culture of the division was inconsistent with autocratic and authoritarian control and terminated the new leader followed by terminating the leadership team that had been recruited. Everyone it turned out was together in the same boat – expendable.

In sum, intentional leadership and an intentional organizational culture can achieve great things. The example also illustrates that there is a problem of sustainability in that autocratic and authoritarian leadership is common, and these leaders will find an open, inclusive, transparent, collaborative, and intentional organizational culture contrary to top-down management command and control.

IN CONCLUSION

It is reasonable to conclude that there are many types of dysfunctional groups and organizational leaders and cultures and that to fully understand them requires developing an awareness of psychosocially defensive responses to stress. The types of defensive group dynamics that have been discussed in this chapter undermine the taken-for-granted belief in stable and rationally managed organizational cultures that optimize organizational performance. The presence of dysfunctional organizational dynamics does lead to spectacular failures such as the global failure of the banking/financial industry during the Great Recession of 2008, General Motors bankruptcy in 2009 or General Electric's decline and break up in 2021. Organizations that fail to thrive may also simply quietly disappear – being sold, merged, or closed. The three directions of defensive movement and the psychosocially defensive framework provide a lot to think about when it comes to working within and managing organizations.

In sum, psychosocially defensive organizational dynamics are common organizational experiences. Better understanding them by using psychosocially informed perspectives contribute to understanding these workplace experiences. Organizational culture as an overarching concept has value but also to be included are subcultures and new organizations that are still in the process of locating what works best. In contrast, organizational identity points out that there are psychosocially defensive individual, interpersonal, group, and organizational dynamics present in organizations that are hard to understand in terms of leaders and organization members managing themselves to achieve operating effectiveness. These two perspectives increase our awareness of the much less apparent side of the workplace by offering ways for understanding, leading, and changing organizations. The three directions of defensive movement and the defensive group dynamics at work provide additional ways to unpack hard-to-understand defensive organizational dynamics to enable changing them by leaders, organization members, trainers, and consultants. The balance of this book will focus on exploring how to apply this knowledge in practice.

Part 1 begins our journey of understanding toxic leaders, leadership, and organizational dynamics by providing perspectives for understanding that form the basis for facilitating change.

Part 1

Destructive Organizational Dynamics

Where we work in our organizations that have layered hierarchies and specialized siloed divisions can lead to many different work experiences. Our experience in an organization, what it is like to work here, can range from being an uplifting, fulfilling, and positive experience to a much darker, punishing, threatening, oppressive, and alienating experience that strips away our sense of self self-worth – who we are.

Part 1 explores toxic leadership that is oppressive, autocratic, and authoritarian creating stressful organizational dynamics that make our workplace experience hard to live with. Oppression and authoritarianism are strong attention-getting words, but ones that suggest that they are also crucial to consider when trying to understand toxic leaders and dysfunctional organizational dynamics. Chapters in Part 1 focus on understanding this dark side of organizational life driven by authoritarian and autocratic leaders who use their power to dominate their organization and its members. Part 1 metaphorically sets the table for the balance of the book by providing psychosocial insights into understanding toxic leaders, dysfunctional organizations, and the darker side of organizational life.

DOI: 10.4324/9781003464464-3

Toxic leaders and dysfunctional organizations are regrettably all too common. This makes trying to understand these organizational dynamics important in terms of fulfilling the hope of developing well-functioning organizations we would all like to work for. The need to develop a better understanding of toxic leaders and dysfunctional organizational dynamics is highlighted by, for example, zombie organizations that fail to succeed but do not fail and those that are failing or have failed. These organizational dynamics are stressful when a valued job is lost in an organizational downsizing. An unfortunate outcome like this becomes the collateral damage of toxic, autocratic, authoritarian, and frequently narcissistic leaders who are abusive and too often unaccountable to anyone especially when they own the organization.

The result of toxic leadership and dysfunctional organizational dynamics is that they lead to organization members relying on psychosocial defenses to cope with their threatening and distressing workplace. These psychosocially defensive responses contribute to creating avoidable and hard-to-resolve operating problems that can reinforce the sense that failure is an option. Understanding these psychosocially defensive dynamics that flow from the presence of toxic leaders and the dysfunctional organizational dynamics that they create is the subject of this book.

Part 1 includes three chapters. Chapter 3 discusses oppressive leaders, organizations, and related workplace experiences for organization members. Chapter 4 continues this discussion by exploring the nature of oppressive leaders and workplaces from the perspective of organizational totalitarianism and its associated autocratic authoritarianism. Chapter 5 discusses dysfunctional organizations that fail to succeed or may well fail due to their toxic and oppressive leadership. This chapter introduces for consideration organizations that become fragmented and have dynamics that compromise coordination and cooperation. Working effectively together may be falling apart, which is explored in Part 2.

3

Oppression at Work

This chapter explores a common experience of life at work that is usually accepted as an inevitable aspect of organizational life. Oppression can take many forms and is experienced in many ways. Oppression refers to unjust and dehumanizing institutionalized uses of power and authority associated with positions and titles in hierarchical organizations that have presidents of boards, chief executive officers (CEOs), and a descending array of executive, management, and supervisory positions and their associated roles of power and authority to manage the organization and its members. The wielding of power, authority, and control by those in these roles may, however, not always be rational and logical. Sometimes it may be wielded for personal and self-serving reasons, resulting in those subjected to these uses of power and authority of being threatened, persecuted, subjugated, dominated, and suppressed. When those in the highest-level roles in the organizational hierarchy act oppressively, everyone suffers, not just those in lower ranks.

Oppressive working conditions compromise organizational performance and when resisted can lead to greater efforts by oppressors to control and dominate everyone including threatening the employment and careers of those who resist being oppressed. Also, to be considered is that tolerating and accepting abusive and dominating uses of power and authority to maintain careers and livelihoods contributes to self-victimization. When you must go along to get along self-compromising choices are being made.

This chapter highlights the nature of workplace oppression in terms of its attributes. A case example is provided to ground oppression in the lived experience of oppression at work. Oppression is then unpacked from the perspective that psychosocial defenses against stress and anxiety lead to oppressive leadership as well as the defensive responses of organization members subjected to abusive repression.

DOI: 10.4324/9781003464464-4

ORGANIZATIONAL OPPRESSION

There are many organizational elements that contribute to oppression. To be noted is the *sense* of oppression is subjective and will vary among individuals and groups both in terms of experiencing the presence of oppression, how punishing and distressing the experience is, and the reliance on psychosocially defensive responses to feeling oppressed.

Being controlled is a common workplace experience, especially when leaders expect unquestioning loyalty and submissive acceptance of their authority. Oppressive leadership is more likely to develop for some individuals in leadership roles than others. For example, narcissistic leaders that are discussed in greater depth in Chapter 11 have an expansive sense of themselves and want to control what others think, feel, and do relative to them including avoiding perceived threats to themselves and their position. Organizations may have a history of *former employees* who offered opposition to their narcissistic leader. Anyone not on "my team" must go. As a result, everyone becomes more attentive to being admiring and supportive of what their leader says and does to avoid offending their leader.

In sum, when leaders abuse their organizationally based power and authority, they may think nothing of intervening in the organizational hierarchy to dominate subordinate executives and managers micromanaging them and their work. These leaders show little respect for the dignity, personal autonomy, and integrity of others. Supporting their subordinates' personal growth and development is not part of this leadership equation, although narcissistic leaders are manipulative and try to seduce organization members into being idealizing and unquestionably loyal and failing that afraid of them. All that matters is what these leaders want. It is *my way or the highway*. The oppressive nature of leaders can be unpacked by inspecting these common organizational dynamics.

Identifying with the Leader

Identifying with the leader and the organization's mission is expected on the part of organization members. These identifications displace to some extent self-identity in favor of becoming a loyal team player who embraces the mission and supports the leaders of the organization. This assumption of an *organizational self* provides a comforting and predictable work experience but at a personal cost. Everyone, by becoming an ideal organization member, begins to self-monitor thoughts, feelings, and actions to avoid scrutiny for not being a team member. These workplace expectations to conform are reinforced within the interpersonal world at work by those who embrace conformity. This dynamic can become pervasive, intrusive, and, when forcefully pursued, a toxic coercive interpersonal presence. Leaders who expect unquestioning loyalty and conformity continually monitor organization members for deviations including encouraging others to report deviations from what is a cultural norm that creates predictability that reduces stress for everyone.

For example, an engineer who invents a unique product and decides to form an organization to produce and market it can be admired for doing this as an entrepreneur. Many of those first recruited to build this new endeavor may idealize their inventive leader who pays close attention to every aspect of the new business to make it successful. However, as the business grows and its complexity increases, this micromanagement eventually reaches limits to its effectiveness. As a result, there may develop a growing number of organization members who are resistant to being continually told what to do, how to do it, and when to do it. For those who joined with the inventor to start the new business, they may feel that they have to not only defend their leader but also reinforce the micromanaging leadership style by adopting it for themselves. Criticism of their leader from within the organizational hierarchy may then be experienced as a personal criticism of themselves having identified with their leader.

Organizational Hierarchy

Large and small organizations are invariably organized as hierarchies of roles in some form. Management hierarchies implicitly include roles that at the top hold most of the power and authority to make decisions and manage operations. These roles, especially in large complex organizations, are readily observed to be desirable for anyone who wants to feel powerful, admired, and idealized. Those in these hierarchical roles are usually willing to use their power and authority to promote themselves and their personal agendas that may, for example, include being admired and loyally followed. Management hierarchies can, therefore, readily be understood to form the basis for oppressive leadership dynamics, especially when these roles attract individuals to fill them who seek the power and control resident in the roles for personal reasons.

For example, the CEO who founded the company in the above-mentioned example used the power of the role to hire and retain those who were unquestioningly loyal and fire those who were not including anyone who opposed those who were first hired into senior management roles when they imposed their power and control over organization members. The use of the power and control associated with these roles, backed up by the CEO, was understood by organization members to be an ever-present threat to their survival in their roles. One senior person offered an attention-getting piece of advice for a consultant. Do not put anything in an email that questioned the decision-making of this senior group or how business systems were designed and operated. There was a well-known history of member deviations and threats that were identified by the original senior leaders and their loyal cadre of direct reports being dependably surfaced to the CEO as disloyalty. This use of a hierarchy of roles by those in the roles proved to be threatening to everyone. Organization members, however, often voiced a hope for positive change but pursued strategies of moving away from these leaders to avoid being singled out for discipline.

Management Recruiting History

Recruiting and retention are essential elements for creating and maintaining an oppressive organizational culture. Those doing the recruiting know that those who have the power and authority do not tolerate anyone who does not embrace their autocratic, authoritarian, and oppressive leadership style. New recruits most preferably are just like "us" and are expected to identify with the culture of oppressive uses of power and authority. Anyone who does not is quickly identified as "not us" and encouraged to leave or become targeted for termination. These threatening and oppressive cultural and organizational identity dynamics are common in our organizations.

For example, a large organization's CEO focused on recruiting for key leadership roles those who identified with top-down management control and loyalty. Not only were these leaders recruited for their willingness to submit to the CEO's authority but also for their willingness to use their authority to dominate others. This cadre of senior leaders, once recruited, bonded with each other having shared prior work experience in a similar organizational culture, in this example, the military. These bonds proved to be strong. They looked out for each other and together defended against those who they thought rejected their leadership style that created oppressive organizational dynamics in their areas of responsibility.

Controlling Information

Controlling information and communications permits leaders to manage what organization members and the public know about what matters and how to work together. Leaders and organizations are described in idealizing terms relative to threatening competitors and government regulation that is said to be limiting and "bad." All threats are defended against. The idealization encourages accepting that only the leader can save "us" and the organization. Defensive measures taken by these leaders may include aggressive and sometimes marginally legal if not illegal activity that is accepted as necessary by loyal organization members. The promotion of an organizational reality using manipulated information including fabrications combined with a constant repetition of the messages is all too common in our twenty-first century organizations and societies. Big lies repeated often enough become believed. Managing information, however, is also a bi-directional defensive activity.

For example, upward flows of information in hierarchical organizations are sometimes carefully engineered to avoid being held accountable for operating problems and inferior performance. A president of a university who reported to a governing board implemented a granular control of all the information the board received. This included withholding, modifying, and making up desirable projections to be retained in role. The board as a result seldom fully understood the organization's performance, toxic culture, and dysfunctional dynamics. The energized oppression of anyone not seen to be supportive of the president and the manipulated information flow to the board, organization members, and the media was noteworthy.

Punishing Workplace Experiences

Bullying, threatening, and intimidating organization members are common in oppressive organizations. These experiences promote fear and anxiety as well as anger that may not be acted on to preserve employment.

Resistance may felt to be futile as evidenced by a history of employees being suddenly and unexpectedly eliminated by the leader including metaphorically being thrown under the bus and blamed for unresolved operating problems. Vindictive actions taken by oppressive leaders to remediate perceived personal injuries to their inflated sense of self-importance become known throughout the organization. Crossing a powerful narcissistic leader can be as it is sometimes said, a career-ending decision. Examples of leaders who have enemy lists and pursue vindication create a punishing workplace experience for the targets and those who witness the harm inflicted by these toxic leaders.

In Sum

These organizational attributes highlight how controlling, manipulative, punishing, and threatening oppressive leaders protect themselves in their roles. Unexpected terminations may be common making it clear deviations from the "script" are not tolerated. This is reinforced occasionally by reorganizations and restructuring that eliminate problem areas and individuals who have not yielded to the oppressive leader. These workplace experiences, although gradually accepted as part of the organizations' culture, can be astonishing to discover for new organization members, external consultants, and even board members if they learn about it.

This discussion of oppressive organizational elements contributes to understanding how toxic leaders gain and maintain control of organizations and their members. Most organizations may develop some of these oppressive attributes at some point. However, when oppression becomes pervasive and regularly relied on by leaders, the organization becomes an oppressive workplace. The degree to which organization members are willing to submit to go along to get along with the oppressive behavior, it should be appreciated, collusively "authorizes" the behavior enabling the oppressor. Those who do not wish to tolerate these dynamics often leave. However, by *selecting out* departing organization members contribute to creating a workplace where oppression is tolerated and even welcomed by those who remain (selecting-in). The following concrete example underscores the significance of these oppressive dynamics and responses to them.

A CASE OF WORKPLACE OPPRESSION

This case example that is informed by actual events builds forward from the above discussion of oppressive organizational dynamics and cultures that regrettably can too often be found in large organizations.

A Chief Financial Officer (CFO) had over several decades gained control of a large complex organization, although recently some executives in operating divisions were challenging this control. A standoff gradually developed with each side of this organizational split introducing performance-robbing competitiveness and aggression toward the other side. The CFO, however, had a major advantage by controlling the financial information for the divisions. This information was weaponized against the division executives who could not access the data in the information system and were therefore at a disadvantage in terms of defending themselves. Their defensive focus became one of trying to manipulate the information going to the CFO. This and other competitive and uncontrolled conflicts gradually led to operating compromises that threatened the organization's financial success.

It was also the case that the CFO's staff were underpaid, although demands were continually being made for higher productivity. Staff, when interviewed by a consultant, sometimes referred to their workplace as a "sweat shop" and a prison where their work was micromanaged and behavior closely monitored. Their experience was one of fear in that the CFO not only treated them poorly but also was threatening and occasionally had outbursts of anger that left everyone feeling fearful and intimidated. Independent initiative, thinking, and problem-solving were to be avoided to remain safe and employed.

The Psychosocial Context of This Case

Oppressive organizational dynamics like these create stress associated with being dominated, overcontrolled, and feeling threatened. Both sides of the split between the CFO and the divisions contributed to the combative bi-directional aggression that was aimed at limiting if not metaphorically destroying the opposing side. In fact, the division executives eventually banded together to advocate for the CEO to ask the CFO to voluntarily leave and take some close associates who were felt to be part of the problem to a new organization. A new CFO would have to meet the challenge created by this devastated organizational "battlefield" with several key open positions that needed to be filled. Staff trust and morale would also have to be restored including adjusting their salaries and adding additional staff as needed. Trying to manage the conflicted but well-established culture with the division executives would be equally challenging.

Toxic leadership case examples like this are regrettably common. They sometimes appear on the front pages of the news where the story is about an organization's operations having become compromised by poor leadership, unresolved conflict, and organizational fragmentation that has led the organization to slowly failing sometimes underscored by announcements of restructuring and downsizing.

Meeting the Case's Challenges

To start, the new CFO should begin by gaining an understanding of the history of the "bad blood" over the past decade. One-on-one and group meetings provide an opportunity for everyone to voice their concerns, describe the history as they understand it, and make suggestions as to what needs to change. This process of respectful listening and learning gradually allows the new leader to develop a sense of safety and respect for organization members that begins to fulfill their hope for a better future free from oppression.

Given the financial data-driven nature of the conflict, the new CFO should also consider opening the financial databases for inspection by the division executives and their staff members. This is consistent with being the open, inclusive, and transparent values of an intentional leader and organization. Continued withholding, manipulation, and weaponization of the data, it would be being signaled, would not be the case going forward. Additionally, the CFO's staff might respectfully be asked to break with the past and stop attacking back when aggressed by members of the divisions. This would contribute to "lowering the temperature" of the antagonistic working relationships and might be expected to gradually reduce the destructive incoming division aggression. The combative culture could also be further healed by the CFO and the staff listening to and engaging members of the divisions in understanding the now transparent financial data to prove or disprove rumors and myths that contributed to the conflict. Action like this can slowly repair this split-apart organization. Healing personal and group injuries created by destructive organizational dynamics like this is discussed in greater depth in Chapter 14.

In sum, healing organizations require patience, persistence, and understanding and to be accepted is that a long history of aggression, conflict, and toxic leadership may take a few years to heal. During this healing process, feelings of having been injured by the oppression, aggression, and moving against each other can be expected to remain accessible to organization members creating hot-button issues.

The End Result

Organizational performance in cases like this can be improved by inviting members from the divisions to participate in recruiting for key positions. This emphasizes that there is a new culture of openness, inclusion, transparency, and respect. The newly jointly recruited staff in the CFO's offices can be expected to contribute to identifying operating problems and developing plans to improve coordination and cooperation with the divisions to, for example, address system problems and their root causes. Accurate reality testing can contribute to gradually changing the past organizational culture that fueled the us versus them split apart combative operating context toward a culture of mutual understanding, trust, respect, and reconciliation. Organizational cultures, like in this case example, can be gradually changed to a workplace where the better-paid and staffed and respected organization members begin to enjoy their jobs. Organizational performance can also be expected to improve as organization members feel free to bring up operating problems for discussion (Part 3).

In sum, dysfunctional organizational cultures can become more intentional, thoughtful, reflective, and collaborative when supported by open communication and transparency. Although there may remain some tensions generated by the division executives in this case example, they can also be managed by focusing on optimizing organizational performance – something everyone can begin to take pride in doing. The case example also illustrates that it is essential that organizational dynamics like this generated by oppressive and authoritarian leaders must be first understood to limit and avoid their toxic impacts going forward and heal organizations and their members.

THE OPPRESSIVE STATE OF MIND

This state of mind potentially resides within each of us as leaders and as followers, when we begin to embrace unquestioned and inflated beliefs about our competencies, abilities, and knowledge. Self-doubts are minimized by avoiding conflicting information and points of views. Denial and rationalization are often relied upon. Others are encouraged to not believe what are self-evident deficiencies – sometimes referred to as gaslighting. Critical thinking is compromised by this streamlined way of "knowing" ourselves, what we accomplish, and how we affect others and our organizations. In sum, oppressive leaders protect their expansive sense of self and confident belief that they should be in control.

This simplified world of self-righteousness can lead to dehumanizing those in opposition including their elimination – *You're fired!* Dehumanization on a global scale has led to ethnic and cultural cleansing, and genocide and in organizations destructive downsizing and reengineering that has laid waste to millions of human beings. Once formerly productive employees suddenly find themselves in the parking lot next to their car with their box of possessions.

Outcomes like these contain a moral void. Everyone is expected to loyally serve their strong and powerful leader. These oppressive psychosocial dynamics result in leaders seeking near-absolute control because they see everyone else as less than capable. Only they can save them and the organization. Their own limitations are projected onto organization members reinforcing this dynamic that leaves the oppressive leader feeling superior and everyone else thought to be inferior. This justifies dominating and controlling organization members to get work accomplished.

In sum, oppressive states of mind become the basis for losses of accurate reality testing. Within organizations, there arises an acceptance of oppression and that *we are all in this together*. Those who do not buy in can opt out or face termination.

Oppressive Mind Sets at Work

When oppression is present, organization members have less personal freedom, autonomy, and self-integrity. This dynamic is reinforced by the imposition of a top-down power and control organizational culture that becomes the way we do things here. Managing the stress and anxiety that is generated by these toxic organizational cultures is a challenge. It is important to self-regulate the degree to which I, we, and our groups conform to an overarching sense of being an ideal organizational member who is rewarded for submission to oppressive authority. Conforming to an oppressive leader's expectations creates sought-after safety and predictability from the leader but at the cost of having to accept sacrifices of personal integrity and autonomy.

What organization members know, and value is of secondary importance when the "will" of the oppressor is encountered. To be expected is that organization members will engage in denial and rationalization of the suppression and their submission to avoid attracting the leader's attention for not conforming to the leader's expectations of what "good" organization members should be thinking, feeling, and doing. These oppressive workplace dynamics, however, create dysfunctions in the form of individuals and groups that, while working on assigned tasks, pursue psychosocially defensive agendas to manage their stress over losing their personal integrity and autonomy to the oppressor's authoritarian organizational control.

In sum, everyone is, it may be appreciated, transformed into an organization member who is expected to submit to the authority of the oppressive leader. Doubts about who to be and what to do and how to do it are absent within this over-controlled context. Everyone becomes dependent on the micromanaging leader. Maintaining personal autonomy, initiative, and self-integrity are of secondary concern. Organization members become self-suppressed out of fear that the oppressor, who has created a hostile workplace, will become aware. Fear and threat are always implicitly present. As a result, organization members find safety in being loyal and devoted to their leader, at least on the surface, offering little to no resistance to oppressive control. This preoccupation with personal survival can become a socially defensive collusion among organization members and groups that unquestioningly embrace their oppressive authoritarian leaders and organizational culture. Everyone knows what is expected of them. Everyone is together in sharing this distressing experience of authoritarianism.

A Note on Authoritarianism

Authoritarian leaders are oppressive leaders as explored in Chapter 4. The wish to command and control without opposition is the goal. Opposition in any form can be expected to be suppressed as is illustrated by the authoritarianism in Russia, Iran, and China. The unconditional submission to authority figures to avoid punishing abusive and disrespectful behavior in our organizations results in the surrender of individuality, self-worth, and personal integrity. These dynamics are enforced by authoritarians who sometimes arbitrarily use their power to remind everyone that they have it and who is in charge. Their ongoing aggression toward anyone who is thought to be resisting their control is to be expected. They may, for example, assert their power because they think others are being disrespectful or aggressive toward them. Blaming others and feeling victimized by malevolent and incompetent organization members translates into never having to apologize for their aggression or admitting to error.

In sum, the combination of toxic oppressive and authoritarian leaders and fearful and anxious organization members leads to the development of a collusive oppressive organizational culture. Those who stay and bond with the oppressive leader feel secure in believing that their leader will meet their needs for dependency, although this is seldom entirely the case. Reality gaps are defensively ignored or rationalized away. These oppressive workplace dynamics that create fear, threat, and distressing anxiety become the basis for psychosocially defensive responses on the part of organization members that can compromise organizational performance.

PSYCHOSOCIAL DEFENSIVENESS AND WORKPLACE OPPRESSION

The psychosocial defenses discussed in Chapter 2 contribute to understanding individual and group responses to stress and anxiety associated with oppression. These individual, group, and organizational defenses simplify thinking and feeling by dividing the world into a binary right way and a wrong way to work. This black-and-white simplification compromises reflectivity and accurate reality testing. For oppressive leaders, this defense can lead to more effort on their part being directed at controlling others and events to allay their anxieties about losing control. Organization members who are being dominated may also feel less than capable of dealing with stressful operating problems preferring to submit to a controlling leader who it is hoped will provide safety and predictability. Better understanding these oppressive leaders and group dysfunctional defensive responses is important.

Leader Psychosocial Defensiveness

Many who aspire to roles of leadership are not well prepared to deal with the anxiety-ridden aspects of these roles. Narcissists, for example, may experience the power, control, and status resident in their organizational roles as exhilarating. They may also become disillusioned and defensive when confronted with hard-to-resolve operating problems and the unintended consequences of their decisions and actions. Using their power to gain and maintain control to reduce their stressful experience can become a self-defeating strategy when achieving sufficient control over problematic organizational dynamics and their own anxieties promotes resistance to their control. These leaders can feel that no matter how much effort they put into mastering an operating problem, they are not going to succeed. Denial, rationalization, and blaming others may then become the go-to defensive strategies. When this happens, organization members feel vulnerable and defensive.

It may also be the case that organization members feel dependent upon their oppressive leader and hold unrealistic expectations that their leader will manage threatening problems. Oppressive leaders, because of their use of power to maintain control, are often subjected to a constant press of expectations on the part of organization members – expectations they may fail to meet creating more stress and a greater reliance on psychosocial defenses on their part and the organization's members. There exists in this a psychosocial collusion that creates an idealized, admired, powerful, and controlling leader and loyal followers who hope that they will be saved by their leader. This leader and follower relationship offers the leader and the organization's members comforting predictability and stability. Everyone is committed to it or at least accepting of it and the accompanying oppressive culture. Everyone has something to lose if it is changed by, for example, their leader being replaced with a new leader.

There are two ways of understanding this collusion between bigger-than-life charismatic leaders who may know few self-limits and followers who are submissive and feel dependent. The leader's defensive expansive sense of self provides insights into oppressive narcissistic leaders (Chapter 11) who are easily threatened by others and unexpected operating difficulties. Their response to these threats may well be a willingness to vindictively punish others who, it is felt, have failed to do an excellent job. Criticizing the leader may also lead to these individuals being dehumanized, scapegoated, attacked, and restructured or downsized out of their jobs.

In sum, these defensive organizational psychosocial dynamics contribute to explaining the submissive and dependent roles organization members are willing to assume to maintain their affiliation with their leader to retain their jobs. They must continually compromise, accommodate, and submit to the leader's actions. The ideal organization member becomes someone who is unquestioningly loyal to the leader (a sycophant) where personal integrity, self-efficacy, and autonomy are sacrificed to keep one's job. Oppressive and threatening leaders can also be understood from the perspective of a failure on the part of organization members to contain their fears that leads to relying on individual and shared psychosocial defenses that encourage accepting oppressive leadership and organizational cultures. And also, to be appreciated is that these leaders often promote fear by pointing out that there are many threats to the organization which encourages organization members to continually rely on psychosocial defenses.

Organizational Psychosocially Defensiveness

Organization members can be expected to experience stress about their organization's performance since they are dependent on it for their careers and compensation. Our large impersonal hierarchical organizations promote anxieties about what is going on and how decisions are being made that result in creating dependent psychosocial defenses. Organization members can develop a sense that *we all stand together or hang separately*. This retreat to a shared togetherness encourages a counterproductive self-defensive stance that leads organization members to withhold ideas out of fear of being criticized and rejected as well as not stepping forward to assume personal responsibility for problem-solving. For example, in stressful situations, the low-hanging fruit, the easier to solve problems and solutions, are often get picked foreclosing more extensive research and analysis into the root causes that may include locating their oppressive leader as part of the problem.

Idea generation is avoided when innovative ideas and critical thinking may overshadow or threaten the leader exposing organization members to being criticized by group members and punished by their leader. No one, as a result, may be eager to self-differentiate by questioning dysfunctional aspects of the organizational dynamics and culture. If someone in authority agrees to the low-hanging fruit solution, everyone is relieved. Anxiety about what to do is reduced at least in the short-run even though the solution may also be known to be less than optimal and possibly promote future problems resulting in yet more stress and conflict that may include organization members being blamed and scapegoated if the results of corrective actions are less than those expected by the leader.

Unresolved conflicting and stressful situations in oppressive organizational cultures often lead to blaming others, "other" departments and divisions, that are said to be the problem. Blaming and scapegoating become an accepted defensive strategy especially because it usually seems to work. As a result, avoiding assuming stressful personal responsibility and offering innovative ideas in an organizational context like this may become accepted by many organization members. Predictably organizational dysfunctions like this promote distorted working relationships and losses of critical thinking benefited by listening to opposing points of view and innovative ideas. These types of defensive psychosocial strategies break down cooperation and coordination across group and organization boundaries leading to organizational fragmentation (Part 2). Organizational fragmentation reinforces the need for oppressive leaders who take charge to fill the void left by the defensive movements away from each other and away from assuming personal or group responsibility.

In sum, individual, group, and organizational forces like these must be acknowledged to be present to avoid and remediate them. This must include the hazards of dealing with the oppressive leadership culture. Denial, rationalization, and distorted communications perpetuate what may be well-known but also paradoxically unacknowledged. The elephant in the room is ignored. These undiscussable collusive defenses are not open to discussions, and this forecloses the possibility of meaningful change.

ORGANIZATIONAL REPAIR

Organizational change especially when it comes to changing oppression by powerful leaders who are willingly supported by organization members can be threatening to consider and a career-ending decision on the part of organization members aspiring to create change. Part 3 discusses in greater depth the notion of *organizational healing*. It is, however, worth noting that collusive failures by leaders and organization members to address dysfunctional oppressive organizational dynamics and reliance on psychosocial defenses can become an accepted workplace culture that may well have existed for years if not decades. Endeavors to create organizational change in these circumstances may require hiring an intentional leader (Chapter 14) who can develop a safe enough workplace that addresses the powerful leadership toxicities and organizational dysfunctions as in the above-mentioned case example. The removal of the toxic oppressive leader and replacement with an intentional leader, in the case example, opened the door to meaningful change by promoting a new safer and welcoming culture that valued thoughtful, non-defensive, reflective inquiry in support of change.

An outcome like this however is not likely when the oppressive leader remains in role. A long history of oppression makes clear to organization members that at best coaching their leader into being less oppressive, threatening, dominating, controlling, micromanaging, and dysfunctional is the only alternative but one that usually can only be pursued with patience and tact. The hiring of an external psychosocially informed consultant (Chapter 13) can also be a viable strategy if supported by enough subordinates of this leader. The engagement, however, must be described in a non-threatening way relative to the oppressive leader such as focusing on organizational analysis and strategic planning.

In sum, there are no easy answers when the oppressor has been in the role for many years and has acquired significant power, authority, and control in the organization. The result may be that some organization members may have selected in and some may have selected out, creating a large group of organization members who identify with this leader's oppressive leadership and accept the oppressive organizational culture.

IN CONCLUSION

Oppression creates organizational toxicity and dysfunctions that compromise performance. There are also frequently underlying collusive defensive psychosocial dynamics that serve to facilitate the oppressive workplace culture. Hierarchical organizational structures that invest ever more power and control in roles at the top of the organization are also enablers of oppressive leadership. This chapter has discussed these oppressive organizational dynamics from a psychosocially informed perspective. These perspectives are a way to understand in greater depth oppressive leadership and the effects of oppressive workplace cultures on their members who end up losing valued parts of themselves. Their reflectivity, creativity, and meaningful contributions for achieving better organizational performance are sacrificed if not lost.

Chapter 4 continues exploring toxic oppressive leadership and organizational dynamics by examining autocracy and authoritarianism in organizations but also within societies and nations.

4

Autocratic, Authoritarian, and Oppressive Leadership

Chapter 3 explored toxic oppressive leaders and the dysfunctional workplaces that they create from the perspective that these leaders who are self-important and self-serving and feel free to oppress others to meet their personal needs to feel in control. They can also be understood to have personality disorders like narcissism discussed in Chapter 11. Dissenting views and opinions are suppressed or disregarded and those who do dissent may well find their future employment is at risk. These leaders, whether of public or private organizations, constrain and discredit challenges to their use of their power and authority. They are willing to bully, threaten, and intimidate those who do not voluntarily submit to them. These oppressive organizational dynamics are what toxic leaders rely on to maintain their power and control over others and their organizations as well as their societies and nations. This makes better understanding autocratic and authoritarian workplaces filled with oppression and suppression essential if meaningful change is to be achieved.

Autocratic, authoritarian, and oppressive leaders are hardly limited to global politics. Corporations and most organizations are not democracies. Their structural design relies on hierarchies of ever more powerful organizational positions to manage and control their operation. The result is the power at the top of the hierarchy can be used unilaterally with few limits sometimes cloaked in language that conceals and obfuscates the intentions of these leaders. This compromises accurate reality testing by organization members. The power and authority permit the top-down taking of action that, for example, can result in unexpected organizational pronouncements of restructuring and downsizing – the language of reengineering organizations. An example is Albert Dunlap's (Scott Paper,

 DOI: 10.4324/9781003464464-5

Sunbeam) being labeled as Chainsaw Al for his ruthless and fraud-laden organizational change methods that rewarded shareholders with greater stock value. The more people he fired, the higher the stock prices became. For leaders of organizations like this getting rid of *them*, the *organizational fat*, and resistors to their autocratic authoritarian control is a winner. Neutron Jack Welch at General Electric (neutron bombs eliminate the people but leave the buildings standing) also relied on similar unilaterally imposed destructive management methods to create stockholder value. These leaders and their shared use of fad-like methods such as downsizing, restructuring, and reengineering are harmful to organizations, their cultures, their people, and to the larger society. They pump up shareholder value and their reputations by asserting that these methods create *lean and mean* high-performing and more profitable organizations. Toxic organizational dynamics like this make it essential to better understand the nature of hierarchical organizations that form the basis for autocratic leadership and authoritarian organizational cultures. Defining these concepts is the first step toward creating this understanding.

DEFINITIONS

Words like autocratic and authoritarian are strong and threatening words that have readily understood meanings in that they are forms of leadership that are common in families, our organizations, and especially globally regarding nations ruled by dictators. These words also have meaning based on our firsthand experiences of having encountered them and the accompanying oppression in our lives. Autocratic is used with authoritarian in this chapter to describe leaders who make unilateral top-down decisions many times with little or no input from organization members and then proceed to forcefully impose the implementation of their decisions. Resistance, if encountered, is overcome with aggression by moving against anyone who stands in their way.

Autocratic Leaders

Autocratic leaders can be expected to make most if not all the decisions for their group, specialized division or silo, organization, or country. They frequently do not solicit the ideas, expertise, and opinions of those whom they manage, and if they do, they feel free to modify what is offered sometimes transparently selecting only those elements of the ideas of others (cherry-picking) that support their predetermined decisions. Autocratic leaders are usually described as self-driven and highly motivated to be in control. They drive everyone and their organization forward to achieve their self-defined goals. Resistances, which may take many forms, when encountered are not acceptable. When organizational problems resulting from their decisions are encountered, others are blamed. Those blamed by the autocrat may be subjected to punishing scrutiny and to being bullied, threatened, intimidated, and metaphorically thrown under the bus. These organizational dynamics fit with the description of Al Dunlap and Jack Welch as well as leaders who choose sweeping organizational downsizing and restructuring that imposes their will on everyone and their organization. Our experience of autocrats is present throughout our lives including when we encounter family members, friends, and colleagues who presume to control and dominate and who are highly motivated to do so including overcoming resistance on the part of others. These interpersonal, group, and organizational dynamics are authoritarian forms of control that require organization members to be loyal and submit to being dominated to keep their jobs.

Authoritarianism

Authoritarianism results when a leader autocratically makes decisions for others, groups, and their organization. Everyone is expected to blindly follow their orders and dictates and submit to the authority of their leader. This concentration of power and control in the hands of the autocratic leader who is enabled by having a role at the top of the organizational hierarchy is expected to be accepted by loyal committed followers and sycophants creating an authoritarian culture and organizational dynamic. Autocratic leaders who create these oppressive cultures can be expected to occasionally reinforce their control by using their power and authority arbitrarily and perhaps without regard for cultural norms, values, and even laws. These tendencies make this leader unpredictable, threatening, and unaccountable magnifying the authoritarian culture of fear and submission. Organization members who do not go along to get along will be held to account including being terminated. The power and control of these leaders are maintained by repression, oppression, the removal of potential challengers and rivals, and restriction of everyone's ability to act without approval (micromanagement). Close attention is paid by these leaders to exceptions to the expected willing submission on the part of all organization members. This leadership dynamic may also include a network of loyalist "spies" who report deviations on the part of organization members to their leader to demonstrate their loyalty and to receive rewards. This dysfunctional organizational dynamic sometimes includes reporting people that these individuals simply do not like or who have offended them in some way to get even. This makes these fellow organization members threatening to anyone who might consider questioning or challenging them.

These descriptions of authoritarian organizational cultures run by autocrats should resonate with anyone working within an organization with a culture like this or as a citizen residing in a national context like this. This combination of leader and follower dynamics readily leads to complex dysfunctional organization dynamics and reliance on psychosocially defensive responses to these alienating, oppressive, dominating, and threatening workplace experiences.

THE PSYCHOSOCIAL NATURE OF AUTOCRACY AND AUTHORITARIANISM

Autocracy and authoritarianism are a part of the psychosocial reality of American organizations but also around the world. The organizations that we know have their roots in psychosocial dynamics and our self-experience. The underlying nature of autocratic and authoritarian organization cultures and oppressive leadership split apart the workplace (further explored in Part 3) into polarizing good and bad leaders, decisions, others, departments, and events. Autocrats expect loyalty and submission to their authority, power, and control. Those who are not team players may find themselves marginalized in dealing with the autocrat who holds them in low regard and suspicions that they are not loyal enough. This is to say, "You know it when you *feel it*."

This easy-to-understand black-and-white binary good versus bad experience informs understanding workplace dynamics, especially during stressful anxiety-ridden times when threats from competitors, government regulation, and self-inflicted operating problems abound. Autocratic authoritarian leaders often put forward imagery of a world filled with bad others and threats that will harm and victimize us, the good people, and our organization. It is also often thought during stressful times that only the autocratic leader can save us, and this is reinforced by the fact no one may be authorized by the leader to make decisions and act.

This dependence on an autocratic leader serves to rally organization members around their leader who will lead them in fighting back against the threatening and bad "other" identified by their leader. This movement against threatening others may target anyone such as leaders of less-than-submissive organizational silos, members of the organization, and the sources of external threats. The result of this dependency-oriented psychosocial response to stressful and threatening workplace experience encourages willing submission on the part of organization members to their leader to be "saved" no matter how demeaning and oppressive their leader becomes. Work life is reduced to an ultimate simplicity – us versus them. We are all in the same boat together as organization members and willingly give up our personal autonomy to identify with our idealized leader who will defend us and our organization. These aspects of autocracy and authoritarianism are frequently present in our lives. Several examples serve to highlight this.

EXAMPLES OF AUTOCRATIC AUTHORITARIAN ORGANIZATIONAL DYNAMICS

These two case examples are drawn from organizational dynamics that did occur. They illustrate what autocratic authoritarianism is in practice. The following meeting with all the administrators of a large organization during a period of financial challenges is the first example.

The Meeting

A meeting of all the senior and middle managers was scheduled to discuss an already announced downsizing to reduce operating costs that was to be led by an external consulting company incentivized by how much they could cut from the budget. The meeting started with the chief executive officer (CEO) stepping forward to provide an image of how the downsizing change process would happen. The CEO explained there were three choices. Everyone in the room was metaphorically standing on a train station platform. They could choose to get on the train that was leaving (the downsizing process) and go where "I" am going. Some who were not sure could wait on the platform for a brief time to decide whether to board my train or not. Everyone else could get on a second train that was leaving the hospital to seek employment elsewhere. And to be noted this imagery shares much in common with the trains and loading docks that played a prominent role in the Nazi Holocaust.

This meeting underscores the significance of authoritarianism where what is being said is framed in such a way as to both make clear that top-down unilateral decisions are being made that will fragment the organization and split apart its members from each other in the process. Who will survive? Who has a target on their back? Life at work was suddenly falling apart as everyone looked around the room to see who might be laid off, hopefully not themselves. The *good people* will board the train and the *bad people,* the organizational fat will leave. Valued long-time relationships and friendships were to be lost. There was now the sobering and oppressive ever-present threat of, will I be next?

The autocrat's embrace of authoritarianism in this example suddenly and irreversibly restructured work experience into the good and idealized *us* and *bad* disposable others. The resulting fear and shared anxiety can be expected to lead to individual and shared reliance on psychosocially defensive measures to defend against their oppressive threatening leader.

For example, dependency, as a shared psychosocial defense, is usually paired with accepting a strong, powerful, and authoritative leader who can save us from, in this case, a fiscal crisis, although for many organization members, the question may be who will save us from the leader's self-defined fiscal crisis and solution to it. This defensive reliance on dependence on the leader for protection from financial failure (or from the leader) limits individual, group, and organizational reflectivity and the possibility of creative change. This loss of intentionality becomes the basis for unthoughtful attacking and moving against the *bad* threatening inferior *other,* the organizational fat, by the leader who pursues an aggressive response (downsizing) in the hope of overcoming the financial threat that is asserted to exist.

In this case example the loss of friends and colleagues and former valued organizational leaders was stressful for many who had to mourn their losses. Additionally, those who remained had to absorb the work of those who were downsized to the unemployment line. Being overworked was stressful, especially for those who valued meeting their own self-expectations to achieve excellence.

In sum, this embrace of an autocratic authoritarian leader came at the expense of the loss of what those in the room might have contributed to resolving the fiscal crisis. Learning from experience, critical thinking, and self-differentiation to lead had to be avoided in favor of seeking the safety of identifying with this new transformed organizational culture. Charismatic narcissistically inclined leaders who are willing to act authoritatively expect organization members to dutifully follow their direction by getting on their train. This willingness to follow unquestioningly and loyally also serves to reinforce the leader's narcissism, grandiosity, and use of autocratic organizational authoritarianism. And to be noted these leaders also promote fear by locating threats and enemies and this increases anxiety and reliance on a psychosocially defensive response such as dependency on a strong and powerful charismatic idealized leader. Organizational dynamics like this lead to the development of a comforting sense of safety that we are all together in this experience and on the same team.

A second example drawn from the internet further highlights the dysfunctional nature of autocratic authoritarianism in organizations.

I Am the Organization

Corporate authoritarianism and the autocratic suppression of dissent was Tyco's culture under Dennis Kozlowski's leadership. Kozlowski used people to achieve his personal goals. He expanded Tyco by acquiring organizations that included healthcare products, security systems, electronics, disposable diapers, and fiber-optic cable. To increase profitability in 2001, he downsized Tyco laying off 11,500 people to cut $350 million of costs. This extreme measure put him on the cover of Business Week under the headline, *The Most Aggressive CEO*.

As CEO his personal interests became identified with those of Tyco. He stole millions of dollars and granted himself stock options. He was so powerful as to become unaccountable. He authorized for himself bonuses and forgave his corporate loans. Questioning actions like this were suppressed. Unquestioning submission to his leadership was expected. He hired loyal supporters to work for him and promised them that he would make them wealthy to bond them to him. Their dependency, submission, and sycophancy were expected.

His leadership style was autocratic and oppressive. He publicly humiliated organization members to keep everyone focused on making a profit. He set salaries low, and bonuses were tied to making a profit. He also sometimes presented awards to the best managers but also sadistically to the worst. Oppressive autocratic authoritarian leaders rely on bullying, threatening, and intimidation (management by fear) to motivate organization members creating a toxic organizational culture. His followers, who were bonded to him, were looked out for by him as members of his management team. Everyone else, however, might be dehumanized as *them* and humiliated, ignored, and made expendable. He aspired to be remembered as the world's most aggressive business executive who was highly compensated for creating profit and stockholder value.

Ironically, days before he was indicted for tax evasion he, during a commencement speech at Saint Anselm College in New Hampshire, spoke of doing the right thing and not the easy thing. His distaste for runaway executive compensation in the speech contrasted to his high compensation that included receiving 3.3 million in self-awarded stock options. Similarly, he extolled the virtues of an austere workplace with few executive perks, although he built himself palatial offices. The split between these public pronouncements and his behavior and between the ethic of producing stockholder value and his ethic of unrestricted self-aggrandizement is hard to ignore. In interviews, he often disavowed his own well-publicized excesses – gaslighting the media. He also felt that he had not intended to do anything wrong and had a tough time believing that he was indicted.

Kozlowski is an example of someone who has an expansive sense of self. He fused his personal interests with those of his organization. I am the company. When he acted for himself, he was in his mind acting on behalf of the corporation. Also, to be noted is that Kozlowski was supported by the collusion of organization members, lawyers, accountants, and a board of directors who enabled him. As an oppressive autocratic authoritarian leader, he was also enabled by a cadre of dependent, compromised, unquestioning, and willing sycophants. Kozlowski's toxic oppression combined with his excessive narcissism and expansive sense of self created a profitable but dysfunctional organizational culture. His arrogance and willingness to punish those who were not sufficiently loyal combined with his striving for personal wealth, title, and prestige are all attributes of narcissistic autocratic authoritarian leaders. The result is a toxic leader who creates a dysfunctional organization that may be successful by Wall Street standards but is split apart into good and bad members becoming a dysfunctional organizational culture. And to be noted for perspective are the palaces of authoritarian autocrats around the world.

In Sum

CEOs and other executives who practice organizational autocracy, authoritarianism, and oppression terrorize everyone's lives at work thinking they are achieving an organizational good (for themselves). Dissent is prohibited in favor of organization members keeping the CEO feeling strong, powerful, admired, the center of attention, and most of all in control. Organization members join together for safety by accepting an overarching organizational culture that puts the CEO in charge.

The Tyco example is a reminder that American-style autocracy, organizational authoritarianism, and oppression generate thousands of casualties from the use of what has become standardized forms of organizational violence such as restructuring and downsizing. Those who survive a downsizing or similar organizational trauma and spiritual injury even if they find other jobs after being rendered as organizational fat are harmed. These types of workplace experiences are filled with fear and loss. These organizations and their toxic leaders with their self-identified and sometimes generated operating threats that are used to authorize implementing stressful organizational dynamics like downsizing encourage organization members to rely on individual and shared psychosocially defensive responses to cope with their distressing lives at work.

This presence of personal harm and sacrifice during and after an event like downsizing must be recognized. The "survivors" are left with more responsibilities and work to do to meet the incessant oppressive demands for more productivity underscored by Elon Musk's acquisition of Twitter in 2022. This paradoxically suggests that those who do not survive and are laid off to find new jobs might in fact be the "winners." Feeling victimized may then paradoxically occur regardless of whether you end up taking the leader's train or taking the train out of the organization to the unemployment line or globally migrating to somewhere else to escape their toxic leaders and dysfunctional national cultures.

Autocratic authoritarianism and the accompanying oppression are common attributes for leaders of nations. Their citizens are subjected to power and control and failing that imprisonment, execution, or for Russian oligarchs falling to their death to send a message that resistance is futile. There are many nations ruled by dysfunctional leaders who seek power to fulfill their self-interest to acquire great wealth, as was the case for Kozlowski. They embrace political ideologies that are opposed to liberal democracy creating ill-liberal outcomes if not dictatorships. The first half of the twenty-first century promises to be a constant struggle between autocratic authoritarian rule and liberal democratic values. A brief overview of these global dynamics provides more insights into autocratic authoritarian leadership.

AUTOCRATIC AUTHORITARIANISM AND NATIONAL POLITICS

Managing large organizations and corporations that are not democracies shares much in common with leading and governing states and nations around the world. Liberal democracy is in the twenty-first century considered to be threatened in the United States and globally. The rise in the number of autocratically ruled authoritarian countries including aspects of how the United States and its states are governed has attracted much attention. Democracies are being undermined from within, resulting in countries that have ill-liberal democracies with many being taken over by autocratic authoritarian leaders such as in Russia, China, and Iran. And to be appreciated are authoritarian countries and regimes such as in North Korea, Syria, Saudi Arabia, the United Arab Emirates, Hungary, and Venezuela. A better understanding of geopolitical autocratic authoritarianism and its persistence provides additional insights into understanding these same cultural organizational dynamics.

The Decline of Liberal Democracy

Authoritarianism has been gradually increasing over the first decades of the twenty-first century with only a fifth of the world's population living in democratic societies. It has been assumed that authoritarian systems will fall, but this view underestimates how authoritarian governments persist by limiting meaningful participation by their citizens in their own governance. This is illustrated, for example, in the United States by those on the right suppressing left-leaning voters. It is also the case that democratic and authoritarian forms of government ebb and flow over time, suggesting there is a dynamic psychosocial setting that oscillates based on a leader's performance which is equally true for nondemocratic organizational dynamics.

Liberal democratic societies encourage their members and organized parties and special interest groups to participate. This active participation contrasts to authoritarian societies which have leaders who serve their own financial interests and seek to maintain their power. The participation of their citizens is suppressed. They are expected to submit to their autocratic leader who claims to be the true voice of the people. In the United States, during the first quarter of the twenty-first century, Donald Trump's approach to politics has been labeled as a populist authoritarianism. This perspective describes many populist right-wing as well as left-wing political parties that oppose the liberal elites and oligarchs who are said to dominate national interests. Popular authoritarians often claim that only they represent the interest of the people of their country. And to be noted is that the willingness on the part of most of a portion of the population of a country to embrace autocratic authoritarian leadership can obligate everyone in the country to submit to the power of their leader who controls the state.

The Rise of Populist Authoritarianism

Populist authoritarian leaders are usually anti-establishment and promote polarization between the self-serving super-wealthy elites and the good and ordinary people. These leaders feel empowered to dispense with traditional political constraints to combat control by the left-leaning liberal elites. Increasingly, social and political polarization gradually splits the national identity apart highlighted in the United States by the culture wars. Similarly in other countries, national identities may develop around ethnic, religious, or tribal interests that include the shared psychosocial dynamics of being joined together to fend off threats from an enemy.

For example, combating demographic, social, and religious change in the United States combined with the outsourcing of valued industrial jobs and the promotion of fear of non-white outsiders has become an accepted social identity for Republican voters in the twenty-first century. Populist authoritarian leaders globally advocate for building walls that are physical or legal to stop the threatening growth of cultural diversity represented by those who are "not the real people" such as immigrants, racial and ethnic minorities, lesbian, gay, bisexual, transgender, and queer (LGBTQ+) social deviants, and those opposed to their populist ideology and populist authoritarian autocratic leaders. Attacks on their leaders are an attack on "us."

Threatening social, demographic, and economic changes are used to encourage societies to embrace authoritarian leaders who, it is hoped, will preserve the status quo, and minimize the threat of change. This psychosocial retreat toward autocratic authoritarian leaders is also encouraged by these leaders who promote fear by continually speaking out about threatening change. It may also be the case that they assert only they can save everyone from the threats that they, for example, may have created by attacking a group that is expected to fight back. Why then do a substantial portion of the US population as well as citizens of other countries around the world seek strong and powerful leaders to protect them from threatening and unpredictable change? The hope for a powerful take charge leader suggests that a better understanding of the psychosocial aspects of populist authoritarianism must be included when trying to understand autocratic authoritarian organizational leadership that may be resisted by organization members. However, they may also rely on their leaders to take charge during stressful times in the hope that they will lead them out of harm's way and reestablish their safety and wellbeing. And as mentioned, autocrats dependably spot many threats that evoke member fears to make their resort to autocratic authoritarian leadership seem essential.

In sum, national and international autocratic authoritarian populism is a powerful force in our daily global lives. These powerful psychosocial dynamics inform our understanding of similar organizational dynamics where, for example, powerful competitors and government regulation represent pervasive threats that require strong organizational leadership to fend them off to save the organization and its members from failing.

THE IMPLICATION OF GLOBAL AUTOCRATIC AUTHORITARIANISM FOR BETTER UNDERSTANDING AUTOCRATS AND AUTHORITARIANS IN OUR ORGANIZATIONS

The comparison of autocratic authoritarianism in organizations and governing countries is informative. Autocratic authoritarian populism suggests that, when used as a lens to view organizations, there are times when organization members and those on the governing boards may feel the organization is threatened with failure either from dysfunctional organizational dynamics such as leader turnover, poor decision-making, or from competitors and regulators. Threatening and dysfunctional organizational fragmentation may also have been promoted by powerful leaders of specialized siloed divisions who are a source of unresolved ongoing conflicts that sap organizational time and resources and compromise coordination and cooperation. As a result, the organization and its ability to function may be felt to be falling apart (the subject of Part 2).

It is during stressful times like these that citizens and organization members often seek a charismatic, strong, and powerful leader who can save their nation or organization by providing firm direction – the new sheriff in town. Some in senior management roles may be terminated, the organization restructured and downsized, and new ideas, products, and services introduced to regain profitability but often without sufficient planning and marginal management of the unintended consequences of the rapid change. The new leader is not only depended upon to lead change but is also fully empowered to do whatever it is thought is necessary to achieve the change. This may include self-enrichment as was the case at Tyco. These organizational dynamics may also mirror autocratic authoritarian leaders of countries who take charge eliminating all opposition and creating a country that is identified with their own self-interests. National and organizational dynamics like this are all too commonly welcomed by those who feel anxious, threatened, and dependent on others for protection and caretaking.

There is, however, another way to create organizational turnaround that involves leaders who, rather than overpowering and dominating organization members and dictating organizational goals and objectives and work methods, engage organization members in a process of collectively turning things around. This form of intentional leadership, as discussed in Chapter 14, does not use crises to seize power and authority but rather authorize and empower organization members to improve the organization's performance. These leaders calm the fears of organization members by engaging them in locating the root causes of and solutions to the operating problems and threats. Everything – whoever, wherever, and whatever – is open to non-defensive inspection to improve performance. There are *no sacred cows* within this safe enough workplace.

In sum, the comparison of these two types of leaders and their leadership offers important insight into the psychosocial nature of toxic leaders and dysfunctional national and organizational dynamics. Autocratic authoritarian leadership is, it should also be appreciated, not an all-bad form of leadership and it may have its place, especially under extreme circumstances where national and organizational failure is imminent and where there is a lack of time and local expertise to be recruited to join in achieving a turnaround. In the near term the leader must act and if necessary unilaterally implement decisions. If the turnaround is achieved and the organization restaffed if necessary with capable members, there should wisely be a change from this leadership style to one that is more open, inclusive, transparent, trusting, and respectful of others. Regrettably, this often does not happen often. Those who are recruited discover they are going to be dominated and controlled by their leader and may choose to leave to find another position (selecting out).

Organizational dynamics like this can become a self-fulfilling prophecy where there is always chaos and threat being generated by the autocratic authoritarian leader who it is paradoxically felt is needed to restore comforting predictability and control. It may be the case that only this leader can save the organization from the leader's own actions where sometimes the more things change, the more they remain the same.

IN CONCLUSION

Workplace autocrats rely on the power and authority of their roles at the top of organizational or nation hierarchies to dominate and oppress those around them. They can become destructive toxic leaders who introduce dysfunctional organizational dynamics that harm people and their organization or country. Readers may well find that these organizational experiences are familiar and feel some sense of personal validation in knowing that you are far from being alone in this experience.

In sum, this chapter has presented the case that these types of toxic leadership and dysfunctional organizational dynamics are not only common but also harmful and lead organization members to rely on individual and shared psychosocial defenses. There may be, for example, a strongly felt need for a leader who takes charge and takes no prisoners to achieve organizational or national turnaround and defend against all threats foreign and domestic. The underlying psychosocial nature of this experience and its accompanying problematic national and organizational outcomes is further explored in Chapter 5. Oppressive and dysfunctional organizational dynamics can lead to failure to achieve good outcomes (failures to succeed) and, at an extreme, lead to an emerging awareness that failure is an option.

5

Adapting to the Dysfunctional Organization

This chapter explores dysfunctional organizational dynamics in oppressive poorly led organizations that are less than successful (failing to succeed) or failing. Toxic organizational dynamics and cultures may be present in public and private organizations including corporations, non-profits, armies fighting in ground, sea, and air battles, and athletic teams. The sense of not succeeding is stressful and encourages organization members to rely on individual and shared psychosocial defenses to relieve their anxiety including sometimes leaving the organization for new positions. Those who remain must defend themselves from what their leaders may do next such as cutting budgets and downsizing to restore profitability and increase stock value. These organization members are left to manage their fears as best they can including avoiding interacting with their leaders by moving away from them and retreating to the safety of their offices or working from home.

Dysfunctional organizational dynamics like this make it important to consider the effects of toxic leadership on what it is like to work here. The psychosocial elements of organizational culture and identity offer a way to understand how an organization's members arrive at tolerating toxic and oppressive leadership and dysfunctional organizational dynamics that can seem to make failure an unwelcomed but imaginable option. Understanding these distressing and usually undiscussable aspects of organizational life that lead to depending on psychosocial defenses that can become accepted as a part of the organizational culture is the focus of this chapter. Changing defensive organizational and cultural dynamics like this is challenging. Change is threatening to organization members and their leaders, especially when they are partially aware that they are responsible for the organization's compromised performance.

DOI: 10.4324/9781003464464-6

A case example is provided that highlights these powerful psychosocial dynamics where threats are not successfully dealt by leaders and organization members and create a fragmented cultural context that leads to uncertainty, fear, anger, and unresolved conflict. The emerging awareness, in the following case example, of accumulating failures that are driven by a compromised ability to effectively work together gradually leads organization members to appreciate that their organization is not succeeding and going to fail unless, of course, their organization is too big to fail. This understanding combined with relying on psychosocial defenses helps to explain the dysfunctional organizational dynamics and the growing sense that cooperation and coordination are lacking. This fragmented work experience in organizations is often underscored by infighting and blaming rituals that diminish trusting each other compromising organizational performance and a recent history of corrective actions making them worse.

THE CASE EXAMPLE

General Services (GS) is a major division of a much larger organization, National Products and Services (NPS) with a home office in another state. The size and complexity of NPS have led to a rigid reliance on a bureaucratic organizational structure to manage operations and achieve integration with all the accompanying advantages and disadvantages. GS has, in the opinion of the chief executive officer (CEO) of NPS, gradually lagged in achieving superior results and profits. This has led to an intervention by the CEO and the Board aimed at making GS more efficient, effective, and profitable.

A new visionary GS CEO has been recruited to turn around the division's marketplace competitiveness and profitability including addressing significant morale problems. The Board is supportive of this new leader and is willing to commit additional financial resources to upgrade facilities and purchase a new computerized information system. These changes have led to rising expectations and a sense of hope among GS organization members that operating success and improved profitability is possible.

The new CEO was from the start an omnipresent autocratic micromanager intruding into operations throughout GS insisting on complete control and not sharing information about operations beyond a small loyal inner group of advisors. Organization members were, however, willing to give their new CEO the benefit of the doubt during the usual metaphoric honeymoon period. Grand plans were soon announced further raising expectations for a more secure and profitable future.

There, however, developed after a year a problematic nature to the grand plans as their implementation began to set in. There were unintended consequences generated by the rapid changes to operations and services that were not being successfully managed. The resulting rising levels of stress gradually led to turnover in middle management that was explained away by the CEO as "old-timers" leaving who, it was said, created the operating problems in the first place. They could not be expected to have meaningfully contributed to the turnaround. However, some of the new hires also left within a year. They were, it was said, not "team players." Despite the churn in middle and upper management, there was support for the new visionary leader who continued to dominate all aspects of GS often relying on an authoritarian autocratic command and control leadership style that marginalized everyone in management and the organization's members creating a pervasive *sense of* dependency on their leader.

The Emerging Organizational Destruction

The costs and manner of the rapid change process, organizational expansion, and the hard-to-resolve collateral damage of the unintended consequences gradually led to financial shortfalls. The CEO's response to the lagging performance indicators was to rely on layoffs and resource cutbacks that eventually spread throughout GS except for the CEO's visionary projects. As GS performance lagged and despite the ongoing layoffs and budget cuts, profitability continued to decline returning GS in the eyes of governing board members to its former unacceptable status prior to the hiring of the new CEO and the new investments into the division.

There was a growing feeling on the part of GS organization members of being abandoned by their new CEO, the CEO of NPS, and the board. Morale declined once again as management turnover continued and low salaries led to staffing shortfalls and recruiting difficulties that compromised the ability to achieve higher levels of performance. The hope of becoming successful and achieving excellence was being lost as was the new CEO's rising star status in NPS signaled by NPS leadership's decreasing engagement in seeing GS succeed. GS members felt powerless and vulnerable in addition to being overworked. They were being betrayed by their new CEO as well as NPS's leaders. They had worked hard to succeed, but now there was a growing sense that no one seemed to care about GS succeeding. They were being left to manage on their own the stressful challenges of making the best use of their diminishing staffing levels and operating resources. Failure, it seemed, might be an option.

In sum, organization members tried to compensate for what gradually emerged as marginal leadership by the new CEO and top management at NPS. Up to a point they were successful at keeping GS running but not well enough to overcome what was their disruptive CEO's leadership style, decisions, and change implementation methods that gradually overwhelmed their best efforts. The honeymoon period was long expired. There was a growing awareness of impending failure caused by losses of coordination and cooperating and organizational fragmentation that could not be denied or rationalized away. The visionary plans had overextended the division's resources and the ability of organization members to cope with unresolved problems and conflicts that were being continually generated by unrealistic and poorly planned change. Everyone was beginning to feel burned out from being overworked. These dysfunctional organizational dynamics were aggravated by the micromanaging autocratic leadership of the CEO combined with upper and middle management turnover and chronic staffing shortages, all of which contributed to creating hard-to-resolve internal conflict. It also turned out GS was not the only NPS division that was having this experience suggesting that the Board and NPS leadership contributed to the unresolved operating problems that GS members sensed might lead to failure.

Adapting to Dysfunction and Failure

GS organization members had to learn to cope with the stressful organizational dynamics. Organizational dynamics like this can be found in many organizations that encounter toxic organizational leadership and operating dysfunctions. Examples of dysfunctional organizational dynamics are as follows:

- Increased infighting, factionalism, and losses of voluntary cooperation.
- Development of a gap between self-expectations to achieve high performance and the ability to fulfill the expectations.

- Organization members individually and in their work groups experience distressing feelings of apprehension, self-blame, helplessness, hopelessness, resignation, and anger.
- Periodically morale may improve when new staff and managers are hired that increases the hope that they might improve upon what is happening.
- A perverse sense of pride arises from being able to achieve satisfactory work even though everyone is aware of being hobbled by toxic leadership and organizational dysfunctions.
- Losses of accurate reality testing develop when psychosocially defensive responses to the stresses are relied on such as denial and rationalization and splitting that fragments the organization where we feel "we" are good and other parts of the organization and in particular its leaders are bad.
- Some in management as well as some organization members are known to be discreetly looking for new jobs.
- Organization members fear losing their jobs as the organization seems ever more likely to eventually fail or at least not achieve success that could lead to raises and promotions.
- Rumors, myths, and misinformation are increasingly present as everyone begins to watch for signs of what is to come next including budget cuts, downsizing, and restructuring to fend off impending failure.

This list of outcomes can be found in many organizations. They are interactive and mutually reinforcing and promote reliance on psychosocial defenses that have feedback loops that increase dysfunctions, stress, and anxiety. Avoiding these types of organizational dynamics and repairing the organization may regrettably be a hope that gradually fades leading to accepting the lack of operating success and that failure is an option.

Analysis

The lack of transparency and inclusion in hierarchical top-down autocratic authoritarian bureaucratically managed organizations encourages their members to feel disempowered and relegated to the impersonal status of a human resource. Those located in remote home central offices (NPS) may also be felt to be judgmental of "us" in the divisions (GS). Is our work creating profit? This "us" versus "them" context can readily become the basis for organizational dysfunctions and fragmentation causing mutual respect, voluntary cooperation, and coordination to fall apart.

In the case example, the uncertain if not threatening future resulted in a gradual retreat to individual and group psychosocial defenses as a response to feeling that their CEO and NPS leadership did not care if they were successful. Accurate reality testing and what became a foreboding sense of impending failure began to compromise their culture of achieving good work despite the challenges. Staffing and resource reductions further lowered morale. These organizational dynamics and the loss of their aspirational cultural identity added to the fragmenting split between GS and NPS that threatened the survival of GS.

The possibility of failure arising from the CEO's toxic leadership and the lack of support from NPS made accepting this emerging reality of failing a challenge for GS members. Finding a way to meaningfully embrace this distressing organizational dysfunction and the potential loss of one's job meant relying on individual and shared psychosocial defenses.

In sum, dysfunctional psychosocial dynamics like this arise during stressful times. Members of both organizations, in the case example, began to see the "other" as a threat if not an external enemy "knowing" themselves to be good, dedicated workers or providers of financial support while also feeling victimized by each other. GS was bad for not measuring up, and NPS was bad for ignoring and marginalizing GS. GS members also felt that they had been set up to fail by the CEO's grand vision that led to ill-advised, expansive, costly, and unachievable goals for the division. Time-tested ways of working no longer achieved acceptable results. Failing to fulfill the vision eventually threatened organizational survival. As a result, organization members began to focus on alleviating feeling angry and fearful about the self-defeating organizational dynamics and hard-to-resolve operating problems. Attempts to cope with the emerging threat by relying on psychosocial defenses also had the unintended consequence of introducing coordination and cooperating challenges and organizational fragmentation. The ability to work together was falling apart further exacerbating the stress and encouraging greater reliance on psychosocial defenses such as splitting, denial, rationalization, and withdrawal from active engagement. GS managers and staff had gradually entered an information vacuum where the CEO withheld and manipulated information marginalizing organization members in favor of maintaining unilateral control and avoiding personal accountability. NPS was similarly opaque. Information flowed in but not out – what were they thinking? This paranoid dynamic was magnified by filling the void with rumors and myths that accentuated the sense of a growing threat and failure. The experience of being marginalized and failing to succeed divided organization members from their leader, each other, and NPS. Something had to change.

An External Intervention

An external consultant was engaged to try to help turn things around. Initially, the leadership groups of GS and NPS were at best minimally open to discussing their individual and collective defensive responses to their failures to succeed. Most GS members were aware of their leader's mercurial, toxic, oppressive, micromanaging leadership and the resulting dysfunctional organizational dynamics. However, they were not ready to acknowledge that they shared a growing awareness of the possible failure of GS. With time and facilitation, the consultant was able to develop some acceptance among the leadership group and GS's members that failure was on the table and that there were limits to what could be done to avoid the demise of GS. Getting this out in the open was critical if failure was to be avoided. GS continued to linger for years in the twilight zone between being marginally successful and failing. NPS's leaders were also willing to accept reduced profitability and a slower recovery of their investment in GS. Many organizations like this end up being sold to other organizations that have leaders who believe they can turn them around or want to acquire their assets and customer lists. And to be noted many governmental organizations also often survive in the twilight between achieving successful operations and marginal performance.

INTERVENING IN THE DYSFUNCTIONAL DYNAMICS OF FAILURE

Intervening in organizational dynamics like these whether by an external or internal consultant or new leader or by organization members is challenging, as discussed in Part 3. There are multiple levels of analysis. A good place to start is listening to everyone, such as executives, managers, and organization members, to better understand their stories and the organizational culture that may include avoiding acknowledging failure might be an option. Listening in the form of individual and group interviews and orientations to administrative and operating processes can raise member expectations for positive change simply by the fact someone cares enough to listen. Listening is a good first step toward rebuilding trust and cooperation. Listening to the stories may also encourage organization members to locate once again how to effectively work together, solve problems, and make informed collaborative decisions reducing some of the conflict and stress and their reliance on psychosocial defenses. Listening begins the process of minimizing mistrust, suspicion, blaming, and withdrawal from work by actively engaging organization members about their work experience. This begins to diminish some of the defensive dysfunctional organizational dynamics. Recovering a sense of "us" as individuals and work groups, and our productive identity as an organization that can be effective and respond to challenges contrasts to unacknowledged but shared feelings of despair about the future. In sum, acknowledging the organizational story by those leading the change efforts encourages reflectivity on the part of leaders and organization members that facilitates the rebuilding of organizational resilience and feelings that we can do this.

Several more examples of toxic leadership and dysfunctional organizational dynamics are provided to make clear that organizational leadership and culture can have profound effects on achieving success.

EXAMPLES CUT FROM THE HEADLINES

There are many examples of failures to succeed when it comes to corporate mergers. Two prominent examples are the 2000 AOL and Time Warner merger and the Amazon and Whole Foods merger of 2017. Both are examples of failures to capture synergies because of conflicting organizational cultures.

AOL Time Warner

The failure of this merger is considered to be the result of conflict between two different organizational histories and cultures sometimes described as old versus new. The synergies that were thought to be achievable such as opportunities to exploit internet search-based advertising and business promotion by Time Warner were compromised by each organization continuing to operate separately. The unresolved cultural conflict was compounded by AOL delaying its move from a dial-up service to cable-based broadband connectivity to compete with new search engine companies like Google. The loss of tens of millions of AOL paid subscribers during the dot com recession also stripped away plans to increase income from advertising. Little effort was made by the leaders of the two organizations to promote cross-cultural understanding and organizational communication to coordinate business processes and technology. The promised synergies gradually dissolved into mutual disrespect, contempt, and conflict that compromised their ability to capture the promising synergies. Organizational fragmentation won out. In sum, the leaders of these two organizations did not sufficiently consider the differences in their histories and cultures.

This merger that failed might have been avoided if greater attention had been paid to the psychosocial nature of the merger from the start. Avoiding failure, as will be discussed, is achievable but only if those responsible for planning and implementing mergers assume responsibility for assessing the impact of different histories, cultures, and value systems on achieving success. Failures like this are common enough that it might be thought that these assessments would be a part of any merger analysis and due diligence. But these dysfunctional management outcomes continue to happen as illustrated by Amazon's merger with Whole Foods.

Amazon and Whole Foods

The Amazon-Whole Foods merger in 2017 also had a synergy that could be captured. It would allow Amazon to sell its online groceries and Amazon Prime membership in Whole Foods stores and extend its e-commerce grocery selling to hundreds of stores. Amazon would also improve Whole Foods operations that would permit lowering its prices to enlarge its market share. The outcome, however, created marginal outcomes that arose from their conflicting organizational cultures, employee identities, and values. Amazon's culture focused on efficiency and uses of technology but lacked the personalization and idealistic values of Whole Foods. Whole Foods' culture had led to financial issues due to its "high touch" and less efficient operations. Whole Foods' employees became disillusioned by the merger feeling that they were being overworked in part due to reductions in staffing levels. They were also alienated by Amazon's culture of closely monitoring employee performance which was not part of the culture of Whole Foods. The implementation of a technology-enabled stocking system that allowed for price reductions led to more time being spent on inventory control and stocking store shelves that, when combined with downsizing, led to less time to interact with customers who were valued as a part of the Whole Foods culture that employees identified with and was their customer's expectation.

In sum, Amazon's efficiency-oriented computerized and standardized controls over operations and the marketing of Amazon-centric products conflicted with the more open, decentralized, collaborative, creative, and less rigidly organized, controlled, Whole Foods organizational culture that focused on interacting with vendors and customers on a personal basis. Capitalizing on each organization's strengths was compromised by this culture clash.

Underappreciated mismatches of cultural and identity values, like the AOL Time Warner merger, can cause merger failures that can be avoided by an organizational "diagnostic" that identifies the areas of cultural conflict and locates ways to avoid the culture clashes. Avoiding and responding to these challenges should be, based on these examples, an important goal for acquisitions or mergers.

AVOIDING TOXIC LEADERSHIP, ORGANIZATIONAL DYSFUNCTIONS, AND FAILURE

The NPS/GS case as well as AOL/Time Warner and Amazon/Whole Foods are examples of CEOs who held expansive and unrealistic organizational expectations that failed to materialize. In the GS example, the new CEO's expansive ideas were first supported by the parent organization (NPS), but resources were withheld as performance expectations were not met. This and the other examples highlight the role toxic leadership and dysfunctional organizational dynamics play in creating organizational failures to succeed. The examples also make clear that an inability to accept potential organizational demise forestalls meaningful acceptance of the threat and organizational change. The question, however, remains, if it is problematic to create meaningful organizational change in a context of gradual failure, avoiding it in the first place is a good strategy. So, what can be done? Part 3 provides insights into how to do this that will be briefly overviewed to provide an immediate response to this question. There are ways to avoid toxic leadership that creates dysfunctional organizational cultures that can lead to a growing awareness of failure being an option.

The Organizational Diagnostic Process Opens the Door to Change

As has been mentioned, taking a time out to listen to better understand what it is like to work "here" for an organization's members is an important first step toward more intentional leadership and meaningful management of organizational dynamics and culture. This diagnostic listening work can be accomplished by an external consultant or by organizations members such as human resource professionals who learn to do an organizational diagnosis and are fully authorized to do this work. A new leader might also take the time to listen although the role itself may be an inhibitor to hearing from organization members what is really on their minds. Established leaders should preferably depend on others to do the diagnostic listening that should include what organization members think of the quality of leadership they receive at all levels in the organization.

The diagnostic work involves interviewing throughout senior management and randomly down through the organizational hierarchy covering all the locations, divisions, and shifts. The interviewing process should preferably begin with an open-ended question – What is it like for you to work here? The range of responses suggests follow-up questions to further elaborate key points being made, and as the interviewers gain more insight, asking more questions to achieve a better understanding of the emerging trends in the responses. This interviewing process leads to gradually locating "thematic data" that explains what it is like to work here. Recommendations based on these findings can be developed including what those interviewed believe will improve their organization. For example, incorporating the findings into a planning process to locate and implement organizational change can create a systemic change process that, having begun by listening, can be expected to be more readily accepted by organization members since it is a response to having been heard.

Organizational Recruiting

The diagnostic assessment can also be adapted to inform recruiting and selection processes for leadership positions as well as all positions based on listening to stories about past recruitment problems gathered during the diagnostic process. The diagnostic process of conducting confidential interviews throughout the organization surfaces history, thoughts, and feelings about the organization; its leadership; and the recruitment of senior-level leaders and organization members. This listening process surfaces for inspection recruiting themes about what is needed, what has worked well, and what has stood in the way of recruiting and retaining outstanding leaders and organization members.

For example, leadership turnover combined with a financial future for the organization that may be thought to be problematic can generate a strong desire on the part of organization members to be saved by a new leader. There may be stories about a lack of clear and consistent management decision-making and direction that have created organizational vulnerabilities in an ever-changing competitive and regulatory landscape. There may also be reactive themes of compelling feelings that the next leader must heal the organization after the previous one "tore it apart" or that a strong leader is needed because the last one was weak and ineffective. Other themes might be that some influential people in powerful positions are dominating recruiting and this organizational dynamic may not be openly contested to avoid putting careers on the line. Other key individuals may feel indifferent and disengaged, uncaring about who is recruited because it is felt meaningful change is not likely due to a toxic autocratic authoritarian CEO. Themes like these will emerge from the listening diagnostic process that must be thoughtfully shared back with organization leaders to be non-defensively heard.

In sum, the challenge for the organizational interventionist(s) is to return the knowledge gained by listening to the organization's leadership which can be challenging when the top of the organization's hierarchy is found to contain dysfunctions and a history of avoiding receiving feedback that is critical of their leadership. Similarly, there may be a deeply felt sense the organizational fragmentation both vertically (members of the hierarchal layers do not work well together) and laterally (among the silos, centers, departments, and divisions) that has created well-known dysfunctional organizational culture that is problematic and makes working together stressful. Information like this signals that there are problems

in the overall leadership of the organization which will inform developing recommendations for organizational change including recruiting new
leaders and staff able to work within, manage, and change the revealed
dysfunctional themes of the organization's culture.

CREATING ORGANIZATIONAL CHANGE

The case examples demonstrate that planning and implementing organizational change requires developing an in-depth understanding of the organizational dynamics involved including the psychosocial defenses that are
present to cope with stress. The cases remind us that human nature is not
always logical and willing to accept carefully engineered workplace designs.

Diagnostic listening by consultants and internal interventionists provides the insight to understand the underlying organizational psychosocial
dynamics that must be addressed to respond to organizational fragmentation and unresolved conflict to improve individual, group, divisional,
and organizational performance. Psychosocially informed organizational
change emphasizes organizational leaders and members should seek to
develop a culture that is open, inclusive, and transparent to create an organization that is a good place to work. This culture can also be modeled by
consultants and interventionists who facilitate meetings to discuss their
diagnostic findings and engage the organization's leaders and members in
an open, inclusive, and transparent process of planning change to address
the themes, issues, and trends in the listening data. Engaging managers and
executives in facilitated group discussions of the findings of a diagnostic
assessment creates a context where everyone is encouraged to listen to each
other to better understand their organization's dysfunctional dynamics. By
encouraging a critical listening focus at the start of the meeting, the group
culture can be shifted to locating mutually agreed-upon ways to create
change, respond to the identified operating problems and, just as importantly, avoiding creating new dysfunctions going forward.

Facilitating Meetings

A logical extension of sharing the organization's themes, issues, and
trends that may be dysfunctional in facilitated meetings recruits those
present to being open to working in groups to heal dysfunctional

organizational dynamics. Given the findings and discussion, it may be asked what should be done, when, how, and by whom. This process of knowledge transfer and proactively locating the next steps avoids the diagnostic work of the consultant or internal interventionist ending up in a binder on a bookshelf – remembered, seldom consulted, and minimally acted upon. This "shelving" is an especially regrettable outcome if organization members, having been heard, developed a growing sense of hope that meaningful change might be forthcoming.

For example, conflicts often arise between specialized divisions and individual organization members. Each side may see what needs to be done differently such as finance, marketing, and manufacturing, each having potentially conflicting goals. These hard-to-resolve conflicts sometimes take on a life of their own creating avoidable errors and problems such as last-minute changes to a product that cause it to not fit in the shipping department's specially ordered boxes. A facilitated meeting that avoids finger-pointing and blaming (no fault change) is a way to calm everyone down and locate both how to avoid problems like this in the future and to resolve the problem at hand. In sum, facilitation is important especially when the magnitude of the problem involves serious avoidable costs and historical conflict. Regular meetings of all the stakeholders that are proactively coordinated by a facilitator are also a way forward to heal the organization and avoid more dysfunctions going forward.

Promoting Meaningful Board Engagement

Depending on the type of organization, its form of ownership, and its history, the governing board may be effective at providing overall guidance and suitable levels of accountability. Board members should ideally receive sufficient communication to understand how well their organization is performing. Examples of information are internal auditing financial, operating, and management reports, reports from external consultants, and financial reports and updates from senior executives regarding performance and future plans. These types of information flows help governing board members to proactively assume any number of responsibilities that may include:

- Establishing policies.
- Making strategic decisions and overseeing the organization's operations.

- Contributing to making sure management decisions are consistent with the organization's mission and vision.
- Establishing budgets and maintaining oversight of the management of costs and revenues to minimize avoidable financial risks.
- Participating in establishing the organization's vision, mission, and purpose and guiding the organization toward achieving them.
- Recruiting and evaluating the chief executive starting with developing the CEO's job description and performance expectations and how these align with the organization's needs.
- Ensuring the organization's operations have adequate resource allocations to optimize performance by overseeing how resources are allocated.
- Overseeing the development of strategic plans, goals, and objectives that guide the organization toward achieving success.
- Ensuring compliance with organizational policies and the organization's legal requirements including paying attention to avoiding issues that could put the organization at risk.

Consults who develop organizational diagnostic analyses should consider requesting a meeting with the Board to discuss their findings. This can be important when there are considerable leadership and organizational dysfunctions, although to be appreciated is that those in senior management may oppose this. However, a meeting with the Board is an opportunity to encourage the board's members to become engaged with their CEO and senior management group by overseeing how the organization responds to the findings. Changing dysfunctional organizational dynamics and culture is always challenging even when everyone joins in the change process.

IN CONCLUSION

This chapter has explored the psychosocial organizational dynamics of work life in toxically led and dysfunctional failing organizations. Developing an awareness of the sources of threats to organizational performance and how to respond to them is stressful and can make organization members feel anxious, encouraging them to rely on individual and shared psychosocial defenses that make it more problematic that operating successes can be achieved. Organizational culture and member identity are organizing concepts that provide a way of understanding how organization members tolerate toxic leadership and dysfunctional organizational dynamics. The example of marginal success achieved by a visionary CEO who was recruited to turnaround a division supported by the commitment of additional financial resources by the organization underscores the importance of understanding how toxic leaders create dysfunctional organizational dynamics. There was initially hope that achieving operating success was possible, but an emerging stressful sense of dysfunction and failure gradually developed. Performance-robbing internal splits, competition, and conflict led to a growing awareness of a gap between achieving the hoped-for higher performance levels and an inability to fulfill these expectations. Feelings of apprehension, helplessness, hopelessness, and resignation resulted in anger and conflict that promoted internal splits. The ability to work together effectively to achieve the division's goals fell apart and anxiety about the spiraling sense of failure made clear organizational fragmentation threatened everyone.

Healing this or any organization is a challenge for a new leader or external or internal consultants. Listening to everyone, however, is a great place to start, and to be expected listening usually raises expectations by the fact someone cares enough to hear what organization members have to say. In sum, there are many ways defensive organizational dynamics and fragmentation at the individual, interpersonal, group, and organization levels compromise organizational performance. These outcomes of toxic leadership and organizational dysfunctions that lead to organizations falling apart are explored in greater depth in Part 2.

Part 2

Organizational Fragmentation and Falling Apart

Part 2 explores organizations that become fragmented to the point that there are losses of effective direction, losses of work on the mission, and a lack of meaningful planning and implementation combined with diminished coordination and cooperation among their members and operating divisions. These outcomes adversely affect organizational performance and life at work. Organizational fragmentation can lead members to feeling that "things" are falling apart and that they are losing their ability to work together underscored by the ongoing presence of hard-to-resolve conflict.

Large organizations are usually bureaucratic hierarchies and rely on prescribed but also often not well-defined role-to-role interactions among organization members to provide coordination and predictability allowing organization members to work together. However, the complexities that people and human nature introduce into organizational dynamics inevitably suboptimize this "engineered" operating performance. It is in fact hard to find an organization that operates optimally most of the time (all the time is too much to be expected) and that is felt to be a good place to work (most of the time). Discussed in Chapters 7–10 are the fundamentals

DOI: 10.4324/9781003464464-7

of organizational fragmentation and why this also happens for groups, interpersonal relationships, and individuals.

These four levels of analysis, organizational, group, interpersonal, and individual, provide a framework for understanding the complexities of managing our organizations. They also provide insights into our experience of our world at work that is influenced by many different forms of fragmentation such as the structural conflict that arises between specialized workplace silos. These silos, by their presence, can introduce defensive "us" and "them" polarization that compromises voluntary cooperation and coordination. The accompanying losses of performance from organization fragmentation like this can lead to an inability to effectively work together and the organization falling apart.

The presence of unresolved conflict and losses of coordination and cooperation are distressing experiences for organization members that can lead to relying on individual and shared psychosocial defenses to cope with their organization's stressful dynamics. These defenses complicate overcoming organizational, group, interpersonal, and individual fragmentation.

In sum, the four levels of analysis provide a way to understand performance-stripping organizational dynamics and fragmentation and a sense the organization's ability to accomplish work is falling apart. Understanding these levels of analysis is also a good starting point for intervening in organizational fragmentation, toxic leadership, and dysfunctional organizational dynamics. Understanding these work experiences and how to manage them is challenging, but a psychosocially informed approach can reveal underlying elements that when addressed can help to again optimize organizational performance and improve life at work.

6

Falling Apart: Organizational Fragmentation

Large organizations invariably rely on hierarchical structures that date back millennia. Their many layers of positions are portrayed in organizational charts that array positions downward from a single position of near absolute power, control, and authority to the least but most numerous – those on the front lines and in metaphoric trenches producing, cleaning, repairing, delivering, and meeting customer needs. The single position at the top in corporations and other large organizations is usually the chief executive officer (CEO) who may also be the Chair of the Board or the owner of the enterprise. This individual is responsible for the organization's performance and profitability or for nonprofits and public organizations fulfilling their missions. As one descends the hierarchy decision-making power and authority diminishes to the point at the bottom there is little to no formal decision-making power or authority with everyone's work being prescribed and carefully monitored (assembly lines are an example).

Hierarchical organizations, however, are more than multi-layered structures with power and authority distributed on a *vertical* axis. They are also divided up on a *horizontal axis* that encompasses specializations, such as finance and accounting, marketing, legal, information services, research and development, production, and human resources. Within these many divisions, there is also sub-specialization that breaks them up into manageable work groups doing the same or similar work or subspecialties such as recruiting within the human resources division. These organizations with their logically designed, regulated, and monitored workflows are usually referred to as bureaucracies.

Large hierarchical bureaucratic organizations rely on policies and procedures manuals, position descriptions, work schedules, specialized

DOI: 10.4324/9781003464464-8

training, and supervision to standardize the work by their members. Predictability, coordination, routinization, and control are the sought-after goals of bureaucracies. Unfortunately, in addition to providing these, bureaucracy also creates operating rigidities that challenge the organization's ability to adapt to changing internal and external operating environments.

This chapter explores the vertical layering of power and authority in organizations and the horizontal silo-based specialized divisions as contributors to organizational fragmentation that compromises the ability to work effectively together. Understanding the psychosocial dynamics that the vertical and horizontal axes contribute to operating dysfunctions and organizational fragmentation is important.

THE ORIGINS OF ORGANIZATIONAL FRAGMENTATION

Organizational fragmentation is created by vertical hierarchies and horizontal specialization. The imagery of the layers of power and control and the familiar organizational silos is represented in organizational charts and more concretely in organizational features such as office space and plant designs where space is allocated based on function but also based on the hierarchy of roles. These different functional organizational and geographic spaces are a part of our experience in organizations, and they can lead to frustrating losses of planned and voluntary vertical and horizontal cooperation and coordination. These common experiences of organizational fragmentation and not being able to work together are often only overcome by organization members working around the "system" to voluntarily cooperate and coordinate their work. These organizational dynamics are sometimes referred to as the informal organization that makes things work.

In sum, the description of bureaucracies as rigid, slow to change, and inhibiting communication, coordination, and cooperation between layers and specialized silos is the basis for the development of stressful operating dysfunctions that compromise operating efficiency and effectiveness. These dysfunctional organizational dynamics can be better appreciated by "unpacking" their psychosocial nature.

ORGANIZATIONAL FRAGMENTATION GENERATORS

Vertical organizational fragmentation arises within and among the layers of hierarchical power, control, and authority. Position titles and well-appointed executive suites are the symbols associated with differentiating among organization members working within the layers of hierarchy. They also form the structural basis for turf battles over who is authorized to do what compounded by silo cultures of specialization and hard-to-recognize and discuss psychosocial defenses. Being unexpectedly called to the boss's office can be an anxiety-ridden experience for those who work in cubicles, warehouses, on production lines and who drive delivery trucks. And to be noted is that coordination and cooperation up and down within the silos are just as stressful as working together across the silos within the larger hierarchical organizational structure.

For example, organizational fragmentation can be unpacked by inspecting the technology and layout of buildings for their contribution to *horizontal organizational fragmentation*. The knowledge and expertise of divisions, which have work methods, technical language, and uses of data that differ across an organization, promote fragmentation. How easy is it to understand a complex engineering problem for an accountant or marketing professional? This specialization creates the basis for a shared sense of silo culture reinforced by technical expertise that leads to the creation of us versus them organizational dynamics.

The silos and their cultures can readily become inhibitors to organization-wide thinking, coordination, and the embrace of a unifying vision for the larger organization. They can function as barriers to efficient and effective coordinated and cooperative organizational performance becoming the basis for what can be hard-to-resolve organizational conflicts and dysfunctions. When organization members participate from their unique perspectives and especially when there is a history of blaming, unresolved conflict, and interpersonally competitive silo leaders, organizational fragmentation becomes a reality.

In sum, vertical and horizontal organizational fragmentation include cultural and identity-based psychosocial dynamics that are the experience of *what it is like to work here and who we are*. The presence of these workplace elements is usually simply accepted normalizing the hierarchical culture of organizational power, control, and silo-based specialization. Getting everyone on the same page is invariably challenging for organization leaders.

ORGANIZATIONAL FRAGMENTATION AND ITS CULTURAL ELEMENTS

Horizontal and vertical organizational fragmentation create communication, coordination, and cooperation barriers that contribute to problematic and stressful organizational dynamics that are usually accepted as part of an organizational culture. Work experience that is organized into management roles in hierarchies as well as within specialized silos creates challenges for vertical integration and horizontal linking. Also, organization members can become their own personal silos of self-interest and specialization as a way to fulfill their needs for autonomy, recognition, and achieving meaningful personal goals. These individual pursuits are, however, frustrated by being a member of a group, a silo, and the organization, and these frustrations must be defended against introducing fragmentation.

Organizations and societies are structured around the tensions that exist among these structural organizational elements and personal needs. Hierarchical organization structures are the basis for organization members feeling powerless and stuck deep inside of their organization losing their individuality and autonomy. These experiences form the basis for self-fragmentation where parts of the productive self are lost (Chapter 9). Organization members can also experience losses of interpersonal affiliation, collaboration, collegiality, and mutual respect and trust (Chapters 7 and 8). Following the chain of command that delays timely decisions makes protecting our silos, our work groups, and our interdisciplinary teams, "our turf," from organizational dysfunctions is a common contributor to organizational fragmentation. Work experience can become a *us versus them* mindset and accepted as a part of the organizational culture. Operating problems that arise are blamed on *them*. This finger-pointing protective psychosocial dynamic readily generates conflict between the layers and among the silos. Suspicion and aggression are also often present, especially when power and authority are misused from the perspective of those being subjected to their toxic uses. Being dominated and controlled is invariably an oppressive, alienating, and distressing workplace experience that splits organization members apart.

Vertical Organization Fragmentation

Dominance and submission are a fundamental aspect of hierarchical top-down, vertical relationships where power and control are held by senior-level positions and those who are managed and supervised in lower-level positions are expected to willingly submit to those who have the power, authority, and control. Dominance and submission are blunt terms that highlight the implicit nature of vertical hierarchical power and control over others.

It is common for organization members to experience feelings of oppression, helplessness, and sometimes hopelessness, especially when threatening operating challenges arise that make a management response to regain control necessary. The expectation for submission on the part of organization members to receiving direction, however, can promote feelings of being minimized, disregarded, angry, and relegated to a dependent child-like status. These feelings may also be accompanied by hostility toward the chain of command when their leaders act autocratically and seem to be out of touch with life in the trenches. And to be noted is that these feelings usually lack ways to be constructively expressed in organizations leading to hard resolve interpersonal and organizational resistance and conflict. As a result, organization members who find themselves locked into toxic autocratic, authoritarian, and oppressive vertical relationships can feel frustrated with their work experience. Coping with this stressful experience results in organization members relying on psychosocial defenses that tend to split themselves, others, their work groups, and their organization apart.

The vertical dimensions of organizations with their explicit and implicit levels of power and control contain many stressors that can evoke psychosocially defensive individual and shared responses. Power wielded by remote authority figures makes it easy to feel uncertain about their motivations and what they know and are thinking and feeling. Remote figures near the top of the hierarchy are also usually made up in our minds since we seldom interact with them or know them. These defensive psychosocial processes include, as discussed in Chapter 2, mindful splitting, projection, and the transference of feelings from past experiences with authority figures that may range from positive and idealizing to feared and despised. These all too human psychosocial dynamics contribute to senior-level executives being known to organization members based on the sum of the projections placed onto them by organization members which makes these remote leaders less of a mystery. We "know" them because we in part created them. The outcome is that they are experienced as "more or less" friendly and supportive or threatening, oppressive, and autocratic.

In sum, these defensive psychosocial complexities are going on all the time in our organizations. They become accepted as who we are, our identity and how we work together, our organizational culture. These cultures, however, frequently include *structural conflict* created by organizational fragmentation and reliance on dysfunction inducing psychosocial defenses that split everyone apart.

ORGANIZATIONAL FRAGMENTATION AND STRUCTURAL CONFLICT

The specialized skills within and among the layers and specialized silos often lead to organizational fragmentation, structural conflict, and the accompanying problems of not being able to work well together. When organization members are asked to describe their workplace experience they often directly or indirectly speak of a seamless mix of the psychosocial dynamics that combine the vertical organization dimension with the horizontal dimension. These two structural organizational elements and how they operate in practice are experienced as mutually reinforcing, confusing, and stressful. Everyone is aware of the organizational dysfunctions that fragmentation creates, and it may seem as though little can be done to avoid them. The compromised communication, cooperation, and coordination vertically and horizontally are simply accepted even though the fragmentation contributes to problematic outcomes. The case examples emphasize that organizations that have dysfunctional organizational fragmentation are a challenge to manage.

Fully understanding the meaning of fragmentation to organization members requires appreciating that people experience vertical relations within their organization and their silos in unique ways. For example, interpersonal competitiveness for promotions within silos as well as within the organization's vertical layers can become a zero-sum competition that disrupts voluntary cooperation, coordination, and operating effectiveness. Winning out over others can become all that matters for some organization members. And to be noted is that vertical and horizontal organizational fragmentation are not mutually exclusive structural contexts. They are being discussed separately but they also unavoidably overlap to create the experience of what it is like to work here.

The phrase promotion by death morbidly underscores the nature of the hierarchical organizational fragmentation as there are ever fewer senior-level positions as one approaches the top of the hierarchy in silos and the larger organization. A second important organizational dynamic, other than receiving promotions, compensation, and organizational perks such as large offices and company cars, is the experience of the loss of power, control, and autonomy over ourselves and our work. Submission to higher-level positions is expected and of equal importance is that the submission is expected by those who hold the senior level positions. These expectations can become the basis for ill-advised interpersonal uses of power and control and resistance to these toxic leadership dynamics. For example, individuals who may not be well suited to assume the responsibilities of powerful roles can feel anxious and defensive about their responsibilities, especially during stressful times. This can lead them to act oppressively and autocratically to maintain feeling in charge and in control. These individuals may also use their power and control with malignant intent such as pursuing interpersonal and interdivisional vendettas to vindicate never-forgotten transgressions. In these cases, these leaders may be said to have fragile egos and that they are thinned-skinned and easily offended. The result may be that they are willing to move against those who offend them by any means available to get even.

In sum, vertical organizational fragmentation has concrete, institutionalized, and commonly accepted elements. These organizational elements influence organization members who live their lives within this vertical structure of power and control and the pressing need to maintain horizontal integration, coordination, and cooperation across the specialized silos. Creating a well-functioning organization is challenging. This is illustrated by the following two case examples.

CASES OF ORGANIZATIONAL FRAGMENTATION

These case examples of vertical and horizontal organizational fragmentation highlight that there are out-of-awareness psychosocial elements in the workplace that create our experience of what it is like to work here. The cases make these dynamics apparent and included are short analyses of the organizational dynamics described.

Vertical Organizational Fragmentation

Vertical fragmentation is often the result of the unilateral, autocratic, authoritarian, and top-down management styles discussed in Part 1. These two case examples, micromanagement and a merger, are common organizational dynamics.

Micromanagement refers to an oppressive leader who presumes to manage everyone and everything much of the time by directly subordinating organization members to command and control. Their knowledge, skills, and abilities to act autonomously are compromised. Micromanagers impose their points of view on how to run the organization, and they are sometimes not well-informed of the facts on the ground. Micromanagers focus on achieving control over most operating details including how organization members live their lives outside of work such as monitoring their postings to social media.

The obsessive nature of this toxic leadership style alienates organization members by monitoring their thoughts, feelings, and communications. No aspect of the workplace may be too small to ignore. Organization members may have their work frequently checked in detail. Minor errors when found may be weaponized as grievance lists that are mentioned when new errors are discovered. This partial list of typical micromanaging attributes suggests there is a compelling need on the part of these leaders to be in control and this alienates organization members from their leader, each other, and their own self-experience, such as feeling competent and respected. In sum, micromanagement that is imposed top down is most fundamentally about controlling others, work, the workplace, work products, and more profoundly the thoughts and feelings of organization members. Micromanagement's toxicity is frequently encountered in our organizations, and the following example of this toxicity illustrates its effects.

The new CEO of an organization over a period of a year hired a new cadre of executives, managers, and silo leaders. Prior to these new hires arriving, the CEO directly managed most of the operating areas. After this new group got situated in their roles, it became clear that the CEO had hired them not to make decisions or manage their areas of responsibility but rather to be effective at carrying out the many decisions being made by the CEO often with minimal consultation and without sufficient operating knowledge across the various divisions and disciplines of the organization. One leader of a large silo commented that the CEO was micromanaging 120%, leaving this leader no authority to do anything other than follow orders. The result of this wave of recruiting of capable people was their departure within a year or two. The CEO learned from this experience and proceeded to hire replacements focusing on individuals who were less experienced and accomplished and who would be loyal to their CEO for giving them higher-level positions. Even so turnover continued with more departures until eventually a group was hired who accepted being dominated and micromanaged sometime referred to as becoming sycophants.

Mergers are also a common organizational dynamic. They can readily generate organizational dysfunctions and fragmentation and leave organization members adrift as to what to do about their growing sense that their ability to work together is falling apart.

Mergers with acquired organizations can take many forms where some are pursued as a good business decision to those that are less voluntary, and the organization is spun off as a losing entity to another organization. Regardless of whether there is goodwill or not, mergers translate into one organizational hierarchy taking over and dominating the acquired organization's hierarchy such as the merger of AOL and Time Warner announced in 2000. The value of these companies that were eventually split apart was reduced to one-seventh of their worth at the time of the merger making this a worst-case example of a failed merger.

This failure tells the story of capable technology and media professionals failing to successfully collaborate. There are two views of how this happened. What happened many think was that their cultures were too different and merging them was doomed to fail. Mergers invariably create conflicts between organizational cultures and member identities, business systems, and operating models. Some in leadership roles as well as organization members may become redundant and must depart for new positions elsewhere.

There are then winners and losers when mergers happen leaving members of both organizations wondering "Will I be next?" These types of organizational dynamics are most fundamentally a story about power, authority, and control being used to create a new merged organization. A second example is an organization assembled from three mergers.

The three merged local organizations had each encountered difficult financial times, and it was argued that together they would improve their financial viability by attracting new talent to improve product development and the marketing of their three product lines. Each of these three had a long local history, well-developed cultures, and dedicated board members many of whom had worked for the organizations. The merger fatefully included deciding to merge the three separate boards into a single board. This emphasized that the formerly separate organizations would retain their individual identities for decades to come. Good faith efforts were made to accommodate the different organizational cultures and dynamics of the three organizations. There were no major layoffs, and no immediate reorganization was undertaken although new products, services, and marketing programs were developed for each. These expanded programs eventually helped to create a more viable financial outcome. However, tensions remained in the board that were hard for the president of the board to manage. There were *sacred cows* that each of the three sets of board members faithfully defended to safeguard elements of the former organization's culture and the well-established workplace identities of their members. The newly merged organization's horizontal fragmentation proved to be hard to overcome.

Vertical organizational fragmentation is often accompanied by performance-limiting horizontal fragmentation. The combination of the two increases the complexity of trying to limit and overcome organizational fragmentation.

Horizontal Organizational Fragmentation

Horizontal fragmentation between specialized silos and their disciplines can lead to the development of competition for resources and recognition and hard-to-resolve conflict that compromises coordination and cooperation and organizational performance. The two examples provided may also be familiar and highlight how organizations become horizontally fragmented which can make it seem to organization members that they are having a progressively harder time cooperating and coordinating and that their ability to work together is falling apart.

North American Manufacturing

A vice president of operations of a large national organization, North American Manufacturing, reported to a consultant that his company was being confronted with major challenges. There had been a major organizational and geographic restructuring, and several hundred employees quit rather than accepting being relocated to a new site. These voluntary separations were unusual. The organizational culture had been stable for decades having been managed by the founder of the company, a conservative patriarch. However, adjusting to globalization and new technology required joining in e-commerce and this required some restructuring.

Two major divisions, marketing and sales and manufacturing, came into conflict. Sales and marketing had been seen as the key to success for decades selling a limited line of dependable quality products. The sales force in the field combined with the home office's telephone marketing division was beginning to be displaced by a new successful online e-commerce marketing division located near the plant producing the products. Adapting to an e-commerce marketing strategy translated into the need to continually create new products. This expectation placed demands on the manufacturing division. Responding to these expectations required more resources to be allocated and more control over the product line expansion to avoid manufacturing problems. Better integration and coordination between the new e-commerce group and plant management required structural, strategic, and cultural shifts. Changing some of the historical lines of specialization, responsibility, and authority proved to be challenging. These two organizational silos had to better understand each other to achieve successful organizational change. However, the founder, who was seen by employees as friendly and benevolent, was a marketing executive who identified with those in sales and marketing to the disadvantage of everyone in the plant.

Historically silo-thinking had promoted a workplace culture where sales and marketing were seen as the keys to success and the usually well-managed and controlled plant operations were of secondary concern. Marketing had to sell what they made more so than they had to make what could be sold. These dynamics reinforced the fragmented culture by promoting an "us and them" culture that led to blaming plant manage-ment for mistakes, product problems, and not innovating new products to be sold. Overcoming this organizational fragmentation proved to be a multi-year challenge.

In sum, organizational dynamics like this that include turf battles, egos, and differences in professional and cultural values among specialized silos can undermine working effectively together. Being aware of the root causes of these dysfunctional outcomes of organizational fragmentation can lead to better-managed cooperation and collaboration and a sense of "we are all in this together."

Fragmented organizational cultures and their dysfunctions that have become accepted as how we do business here must be called into question especially when operating problems arise that preferably should include everyone (the stakeholders) in solving them. The split apart polarized "us and them" organizational culture in the case can be found in many large complex organizations where there are professional silos such as fiscal management, human resources, and information systems that dependably generate hard-to-resolve conflicts and a defensive reliance on blaming and finger pointing when operating problems develop. These types of organizational dynamics are illustrated by Global Enterprises.

Global Enterprises

The leaders and staff of Global Enterprises seem to not understand or at times respect other divisions and groups, "them." Global is a major marketing company that distributes computer games and entertainment disks from a remote automated facility and a remote mass mailing division that sends out tens of millions of mailings to past, present, and future customers. The mass mailings require a lot of control over what is mailed, when, and how, including the sizing of the advertisement to fit the ordered envelope stock. A sudden unplanned change in the size of a mailing resulted in a rushed order to acquire several million more new envelopes. The millions of unused envelopes were stored for future use. This lack of coordination drove up operating costs and created avoidable mailing delays undermining the sales and marketing group's goals in the home office. The marketing executives were creative and frequently envisioned new marketing concepts and felt free to make last-minute changes in their advertising plans. They also expected their plans and changes to be immediately implemented without appreciating what it took to manage their remote mailing division. These hard-to-respond to expectations and delays invariably resulted in blaming each other. This organizational fragmentation was aggravated by the geographic separation and the development of unique subcultures that readily created misunderstandings, distrust, and hard-to-resolve conflicts between the marketing staff and those managing the mailing operations.

Members of each division felt blamed and mistreated by the members of the other division. Bridging these conflicted views of each other required finding a way for both sides of the organizational split to safely share their thoughts and feelings with each other and transcend their local silo thinking, culture, and psychosocial defenses.

The CEO and senior leadership group tried to facilitate overcoming these costly operating problems by holding an unsuccessful retreat that aggravated the conflicts. They turned to external facilitators who conducted a listening organizational diagnosis that revealed the cultural conflicts, the frequent use of psychosocial defenses, and the related operating problems. This intervention based on the diagnostic work created a safe enough organizational context, as discussed in Part 3, to do the important work of getting everyone "on the same page."

In sum, vertical and horizontal fragmentation can easily compromise organizational performance. Defragging these organizational dynamics requires understanding the group and organizational psychosocial dynamics to allow both sides of the conflict to safely explore finding mutually agreeable solutions to their shared dysfunctional organizational dynamics. Avoiding the creation of organizational splits that are the basis for operations falling apart and healing them when they occur is a worthy challenge for organization leaders and consultants.

DEFRAGGING OUR ORGANIZATIONS

Defragging a computer hard drive is analogous to the challenge of repairing fragmented organizations. The challenge for leaders, trainers, and consultants is not to remove organizational layers and the silos of specialized knowledge, but rather to facilitate building bridges between them to develop a cross-functional organizational culture. Organizations that have their members focusing on their narrow specialized areas of responsibility and are rewarded for this contribute to the fragmenting dysfunctions that inhibit achieving effective levels of coordination and cooperation. Developing interdisciplinary groups that include a cross-section of the hierarchy to explore and understand how the parts of the organization fit together is one way to keep organizations from falling apart.

This chapter has directed our attention to hierarchical and siloed organizational landscapes. Creating a *safe enough* organizational context (Chapter 14) where imagining change that can be explored by everyone is a good beginning for achieving better organizational integration. The performance-compromising nature of silo thinking and cultures paired with the psychosocial defensive complexities and barriers that develop within hierarchic command and control organizational structures including toxic leadership must be open to inspection. Improving integration and collaboration across disciplines and professions, specialties and sub-specialties, and between management layers in our public and private organizations defrags them.

Healing Organizational Fragmentation

The acceptance of unquestioned organizational fragmentation that includes psychosocially defensive dynamics creates a context that must be open to non-defensive inspection to create meaningful change. Locating the potential for organizational change starts with acknowledging that the hierarchy and the specialized silos promote organizational fragmentation. These familiar vertical and horizontal organizational boundaries must also be acknowledged to serve psychosocial defensive purposes in that they reduce uncertainty and stress. Acknowledging the defensive attraction of hierarchical structures and silos that promise predictability that minimizes individual, interpersonal, and group membership anxieties is important. It is this paradox, coordination and cooperation versus psychosocial defenses, which is so challenging to deal with for executives, organization members, and consultants when leading organization change to reduce the negative effects of organizational fragmentation.

An example of a successful effort to manage organizational fragmentation was a major retreat that included representatives from all the major divisions and layers of an organization. The retreat was organized around the theme of strategic planning and facilitated by external psychosocially informed consultants who paid close attention to the subcultures of the divisions and hierarchy of layers informed by diagnostic interviewing. The first challenge was to assign the new CEO, who contributed to some of the dysfunctions by micromanaging, the role of listener which was accepted. The retreat began with an overview of the findings from the many interviews followed by developing a SWOT-like (where SWOT is Strengths-Weaknesses-Opportunities-Threats) analysis to better find what was on everyone's minds. These two parts of the first day of the retreat gradually developed a consensus of the history, current operating problems, business sustainability challenges, and some ideas as to how to improve the organization.

The second day of the retreat involved the silo divisions meeting separately in the morning with senior-level executives assigned to the various groups to find what ideally they wanted to do to plan for change. In the afternoon, each group presented its work to everyone with sufficient time allowed for open facilitated discussion. Day three involved ranking the many ideas in terms of their cost to implement, how long it would take, and the benefits of making the changes. There emerged a matrix of low-cost, easy-to-implement, and profitable changes along with those that were more costly and would take more time and resources to implement. Those that were more problematic and thought to be too costly, too difficult to do, and would generate unknown benefits to the organization were kept for future consideration. By the end of the retreat, the various divisions and layers of management felt as though they had been heard and that by working together they had accomplished good work and that they could start to implement the agreed to changes immediately. The organization's members also felt that they were now more joined together in this work and more understanding and respectful of the work of the members of the specialized divisions.

In sum, organizational success in the twenty-first century hinges on the ability of organization leaders to provide sufficient organizational structure and predictability to allow organization members to tolerate stress associated with collaboration, creativity, and the development of productive relationships among the silos and layers of hierarchy. At the same time, they must avoid defensive uses of organizational structure and control that contribute to fragmented organizational defensive routines and rigidities that split the organization apart and stifle organizational performance.

IN CONCLUSION

Organizational fragmentation is a common stressful experience for organization members, especially when there are clashes within the hierarchy of power and control between strong personalities that generate ongoing unresolved conflict that makes coordination and cooperation a tension-filled experience. The metaphor of walking through a mine field is sometimes applicable. The silo is also a distinctive feature of large complex organizations that must be understood to contain a defensive psychosocial construction that helps their members to cope with their stressful work lives. Organizational change that acknowledges the positive nature of silos and management hierarchies must also address their use as psychosocial defenses. Developing insight into these organizational features in a facilitated setting of safety can lead to problem-solving, as well as greater job satisfaction, collaboration, mutual respect, and understanding among organization members.

In sum, better appreciating the psychosocial dynamics of silo thinking and organizational hierarchies that create barriers to collaboration and organizational change is an important first step toward reducing the organizational fragmentation among the layers of power and control and the tunnel vision of silo thinking. Organizational fragmentation and the losses of cooperation and coordination that lead to a sense that effectively working together is falling apart can also be understood from several more perspectives in Part 2. Each perspective contributes to a more holistic understanding of toxic leadership and dysfunctional organizational dynamics.

Chapter 7 continues our unpacking of organizational fragmentation that can lead to the organization's members feeling that their ability to work together in their groups is falling apart.

7

Falling Apart: Group Fragmentation

This chapter explores falling apart from a group perspective. There are many kinds of groups in our organizations. They are sometimes cohesive, and their members work together effectively and at other times much less so. Group dynamics can develop varying degrees of fragmentation based on group members speaking to various aspects the of group's work and the organization's dynamics. Those voicing different perspectives may develop a subgroup of followers who agree with what is being said. These types of subgroups may successfully cooperate with other subgroups and with the membership of the group as a whole to achieve success. They may also create dysfunctional group dynamics that lead to struggles over who has the right idea and who should be in charge. Group and subgroup dynamics are also ever-changing because of hard-to-understand leader, group, and interpersonal psychosocially defensive dynamics.

A group and its subgroups may change direction, leaders, and members as well as merge with or challenge other groups within the layers and silos. Sales and order fulfillment are two subgroups in the marketing silo that may find common cause against the accounting and budgeting groups in the finance silo that are limiting their work by not providing adequate financial resources. They may also challenge manufacturing or service operations to provide the products and services they need to rack up a high sales volume by pleasing customers or clients. Other organizational stakeholder groups such as purchasing, supply chain management, inventory control, warehousing, shipping, and repair and maintenance, all in their own silos and subgroup, may have their own goals that compromise working with other organizational siloes and the organization's overall performance.

Discussed in this chapter are the psychosocially defensive group dynamics outlined in Chapter 2 and how they are applied in practice to better

DOI: 10.4324/9781003464464-9

understand groups at work. These defensive group types are noticeably different from one another, but together they provide complimentary insights into how members of groups and subgroups work together or do not work together. This framework makes defensive group dynamics more open to inspection and better understood and managed as illustrated by these case examples that are informed by actual events.

CASE ONE – A LEADERSHIP PROBLEM

A large organization with a long history in the community has experienced frequent leadership turnover punctuated by interim leaders. In part, this has been the result of not recruiting ideal leaders some of whom have used the position to move onto higher-level positions in national organizations. Some have also self-destructed and had to leave. This leadership turnover has resulted in dysfunctional changes in the organization's direction including stopping, changing, and reversing projects that were being implemented by prior leaders. An example was a large area being developed into cubicle space to decompress existing office space. Organization members in this specialized silo had to sit so close to one another that it was difficult to walk to their cubicles or even back up their chairs to stand up without bumping into the person behind them. As a group, they felt neglected and oppressed. A new leader stopped this project and reallocated the space for a "pet" project. This necessitated finding space in a remote location for half of this silo's members complicating communications and coordination. In addition to this change being confusing, there was also a history of this silo being marginally managed at critical times leading to poor performance and decreased organizational profitability.

The leadership vacuum and losses of consistent direction and coordination were accentuated by disruptive competition and unresolved conflict among the silo leaders and centralized operating units such as marketing, finance, and information systems administration. In several instances, interim leaders also pursued attention-getting self-serving actions that enhanced the funding of their former silo and their position. Organizational morale suffered. Relationships with political and business groups in the surrounding community deteriorated. Many in the organization and the community felt that there was an uncertainty about the continued well-being of the organization.

Despite the leadership difficulties, organization members in their work groups did their best to keep the organization functioning. They hoped at some point that a capable leader would be recruited who was not self-serving or oppressive and capable of providing affirmative leadership to turn the organization around. However, the series of new leaders proved to be disappointing with some oppressively pursuing extensive central-ized control combined with micromanagement. Anyone who stood in the way was forced out or terminated.

CASE TWO – REGIME CHANGE

A chief financial officer (CFO) has had near absolute control over all mat-ters of business and finances and has dominated this multi-million-dollar organization with over a thousand members. No aspect of the operation was too small to not be subjected to micromanaging control. Interventions were swift, unilateral, and disregarded what others thought. Organization members were fearful of their CFO who had a long history of punishing anyone who resisted being overcontrolled. Some organization members who questioned the decisions being made became targets of highly visible and unrelenting bullying and intimidation. This made it clear that anyone or any group in the organization could be next. No one including the chief executive officer (CEO) or governing board was willing to step in to stop these toxic leadership dynamics. No one crossed the CFO.

Survivors of this toxic leader who had not voluntarily left felt exhausted and unsure of themselves and their future in the organization. When a new CEO was hired, this CFO was forced to leave. The CEO, however, assumed the role of micromanaging and intimidation. This toxic leader-ship style with its oppressive, autocratic, and authoritarian features was immediately recognized as familiar by organization members who felt their hopes for better leadership were dashed. Organization members found themselves even more dominated, oppressed, overcontrolled, and threatened since it was now the CEO doing this. Some in hierarchical administrative and silo management roles responded by identifying with the new CEO. This group supported the toxic leadership culture, and its members secured promotions and raises by doing so. They were, however, held as a group in contempt by their colleagues who worried that they were reporting to the CEO what they heard and saw, especially when resistance to being micromanaged was occurring.

These higher levels of oppression and intimidation led many organization members and groups to retreat as near as possible from actively engaging with the CEO and the group of loyal supporters. An example of these dynamics was a strategic planning process commissioned by the CEO to locate new directions for the organization. The planning group that included the leaders for all the specialized silos gradually developed a well-integrated and thoughtful plan. However, the CEO did not follow the plan preferring to pursue a process of spontaneous changes in direction and imposing them on the organization. Autocratic and authoritarian leaders can readily feel limited by planning and bureaucratic administrative processes preferring to simply make decisions and have them implemented.

CASE THREE – LIFE IN THE TRENCHES

This southern statewide service organization had for many years suffered from turnover in senior leadership positions. Historically open leadership positions have been filled through upward promotion of those eager to take charge. However, few of those selected had the leadership and managerial skills to become effective leaders. The result was a chaotic sense on the part of organization members of top management direction and oversite, and planning and the implementation of change.

The resulting operating problems threatened the organization with losses of customers. Lapses in managing and quality controlling the services were apparent. A listening diagnostic review by an external consultant (Chapter 13) revealed that it was the organization members and their silo leaders who identified with the organization's mission who had kept the organization running well enough to survive. Everyone had filled in for the ineffective leadership and management failures. This taking of leadership initiatives, however, had not gone unnoticed by those in senior positions. They, at times, took exception to organization members, some of whom were members of a union, stepping up to provide leadership to keep the organization running. They occasionally unilaterally imposed their power and authority to make sure everyone knew who was in charge.

The pride that hundreds of organization members had in fulfilling their mission was further compromised by a poorly planned annual meeting held at the central office. Not only had sufficient space not been scheduled requiring last-minute changes to meeting locations, but there was also present as part of the organizational culture racism. The union members who were mostly black found themselves being criticized by derogatory comments consistent with aggressing unions but also consistent with southern racial stereotypes such as union members being lazy and always taking breaks.

The consultant tried to coach the leaders to not use this language during the meeting, and the meeting successfully ended with an afternoon of testimonials by some of those who had benefited from the organization's services. However, subsequent regional meetings included the use of anti-union (racist) language despite more coaching by the consultant to avoid the language. Organizational cultures can be hard to change.

There are several ways to understand these three cases and their group dynamics using the typology of group dynamic perspectives in Chapter 2.

THE DEFENSIVE GROUP TYPES

Defensive group dynamics arise as a response to shared group stress associated with working within dysfunctional, oppressive, autocratic, and authoritarian hierarchical organizations. Relying on individual and shared group psychosocial defenses reduces the ability of organization members to work together creating fragmentation and the sense that the organization is falling apart. When defensive group dynamics become a part of the accepted culture and who we are changing these cultural and identity-based dynamics is challenging.

A Note on Organizational Culture and Identity

Groups that have a temporary status do not usually develop a culture about how we work together, but they can have a shared identity with some out-of-awareness dynamics. Groups rapidly develop boundaries around themselves where us versus them binaries make understanding the group and its work relative to the organization much easier. For example, a problem-solving task group might be formed by drawing members from several different specialized silos – the stakeholders. This interdisciplinary group preferably has a clearly assigned task. The group may, however, modify the task based on its learning process to add consideration of systemic workplace elements – sometimes referred to as mission drift. The group members not only embrace their mission but also identify with it in terms of doing an excellent job of solving the problem. This makes anyone who questions the mission and group's purpose a threat to be defended against. It is this shared identity that makes "us" different, unique, and important. However, groups that do not have a long life associated with long-term problem solving and management do not usually end up developing their own culture that guides working together which can be stressful for their members in terms of how to work cooperatively together. This problematic aspect of temporary groups is compounded by bringing across the group's boundaries the cultures of their member respective specialized silos.

It is also common to find organizational leaders who do not support the groups that they create. This may include a group's work being felt to be threatening to, for example, several silos leaders who feel that it is they who should oversee the work. The defensive response may be to cause the group to be disbanded or assigned a new direction. Similarly, task groups may be formed without sufficient coordination and oversight leading to the groups to develop conflicts about who is doing what and how it is to be done.

In sum, a better understanding of group dynamics like this is helped along by exploring the contribution of the framework of the defensive groups. It is briefly overviewed before applying the defenses in practice to understand the above group-based case examples.

Moving Against Others – Aggression

This group's leader and some of its members have tendencies to spot threats and express aggression toward the source of the threat leading the group against the threat. The group's members may not be too concerned about some of its members becoming casualties by, for example, being disciplined by some in senior management positions because their actions are filled with a sense of urgency that creates a group that may not be particularly reflective or thoughtful. Group members are focused on act-ing, which is a familiar response to threatening situations. Fighting back against perceived aggressions and threats is a common human response at work and outside of work. So is retreating and withdrawing from the threat or problem – flight.

Moving Away from Others – Retreat

This group has a leader and members who feel threatened by other lead-ers, groups, and organizational dynamics. The threatening situation is accepted or at least tolerated to avoid entering into stressful conflict and resistance – movement against others. Passivity and submission may include the belief that the threat will simply dissipate (hope is discussed below) or it may be thought to be tolerable and not too threatening. There may also be an underlying fear of the threat growing worse if they do resist or fight back. There may be, for example, a history on the part of manage-ment of punishing resistors who have been publicly disciplined or termi-nated. Hiding out in one's metaphoric foxholes in cubicles and offices and avoiding the area where the threatening person or group is located also creates a sense of safety. Moving away is often accompanied by ignoring and denying what is going on is threatening.

Moving Toward Others – Dependency

This group seeks to be protected by its leader or a group member(s) to attain individual and group security. Group members feel that they are not particularly able to respond to threats. Tolerating this stress is easier than the imagined stress associated with stepping up to assume personal and group responsibility for acting. Group members prefer to wait for someone to take charge. When their leader or someone in the group is identified to take charge, this person is much appreciated and admired for doing so and readily followed. Projection onto the leader of personal com-petencies by group members contributes to seeing their leader as capable. This psychosocially defensive dynamic also encourages the leader to feel competent and empowered, and in some instances, this may include feel-ing that there are few limits in terms of acting illegally, immorally, and unethically.

If a leader is not readily identified, the group is content to wait for one to emerge. This group dynamic of waiting may however gradually increase everyone's anxiety about not responding to the threat. This can result in a group member who cannot tolerate inaction any longer self-identifying to lead. And to be noted, this self-authorized leadership role includes the possibility of being undermined by management and there is also the probability that the dependent group members cannot have their dependency needs met eventually resulting in being rejected if not replaced.

Hope and Freedom

This group hopes a leader will emerge to save them or a new idea or strategy will emerge to resolve the stressful threats. Group members are attentive and participative, but not proactive. They are focused on the hope that change will occur even if they do little to create it. They prefer to be free from oppressive risk-taking expectations to act. If their hope is fulfilled and a leader or an idea is located, they paradoxically may fear that they will lose their freedom from having to assume personal responsibility for acting due to the leader's stressful expectations for group members to act. Being expected to act and assume responsibility is felt to be coercive and oppressive and to be avoided leading also to new ideas not being embraced. The undiscussable group preference may, as a result, be that the leader or new idea remains unlocated and unthought to avoid the threat of becoming responsible for taking actions. Hope is a "good enough" response in terms of coping with the threats and stress.

Togetherness and Sameness

This psychosocially defensive group is a response to stressful organizational work experience that encourages organization members to feel that they are all in the same metaphoric boat. This experience of being together levels the playing field with group members feeling coequal when faced with a major threat. Knowing that "we" are all in this together is comforting. Few in the group may be willing to self-differentiate by volunteering leadership. It may be tacitly understood that the volunteering of leadership will be marginally accepted by the group's members and perhaps rejected by those in senior management roles.

These group and organizational dynamics result in a lack of leadership and initiative taking that leads to operating ineffectiveness. Increasing awareness of unresolved operating problems and losses of coordination and cooperation can make it feel like the ability to work together is falling apart and that failure is a possibility.

In sum, organization members are striving to not set themselves apart from the *crowd* and they are worried about not being supported by the group's members and targeted by organization leaders who may respond punitively if leadership is volunteered. And, while everyone is together and coequal in this experience, it is apparent it contributes to group and organizational fragmentation making effectively working together a problem. Dysfunctional group and organization dynamics like this can lead to the feeling that the organization is falling apart, which is more likely to be experienced during restructuring and downsizing as a response to unresolved operating problems. Organization members in these cases will easily feel vulnerable and that they are all in the same boat together. Who will be next?

Bureaucratic Control

This group relies on hierarchical structure, layers of management, and policies and procedures to achieve control over distressing experiences at work. This reliance on a bureaucratic hierarchical organizational structure and its familiar overarching culture makes clear who we are and how we work together. Losses of personal autonomy and self-identity (and freedom) are accepted in order to avoid feeling stressed out about losses of workplace control and predictability. Doing it by the book on the part of group and organization members, it is hoped, avoids stressful group and organizational dynamics.

Bureaucracy is a familiar experience in large organizations that depend on prescribed role descriptions and performance monitoring to regulate working together. When organization members encounter threatening operating problems, the response is to reinforce dependency on the bureaucratic culture. We have this problem because "we" do not have enough control. However, this response usually includes slow and cumbersome decision-making processes within the vertical hierarchy of roles and horizontally among the specialized organizational silos. The result may be less than optimal responses to the threats compounded by the proverbial performance-robbing red tape that does not allay member stress perhaps leading to accepting more assertive and autocratic leadership.

Autocratic Authoritarian Control

This approach to achieving comforting control relies on an autocrat who assumes an authoritarian leadership role. It is hoped that this leader will get control of the distressing situation and feelings that the organization has become disorganized, dysfunctional, and the ability to work together is falling apart. The organization and its group members want to believe their leader can make all the right calls. This expectation and dependency encourage the leader to feel fully authorized to act. This authorization can result in the leader becoming unaccountable and willing to violate moral, ethical, and social values including abusing the group's members. Overreaching grand ideas may also arise that generate marginal group and organizational outcomes that are then blamed on their members.

If this leader fails to succeed in meeting the needs of the group or the organization's members there may develop disloyalty, especially among those who have been injured by the leader. Rejection may develop along with the hope that their leader will be replaced and free organization members from the oppression and incompetence. It is also hoped that a new leader can get the job done without holding stressful expectations for organization members to assume personal responsibility for dealing with threatening problems. However, leadership turnover can also result in persistent and hard-to-resolve organizational problems and conflicts that can become mission critical. Organization members may feel their ability to be effective is gradually falling apart and that failure is a possibility or at least that they are failing to succeed at a high enough level to have a bright future together. Outcomes like this, it should be noted, are prominent in countries ruled by autocratic dictators.

In sum, reoccurring psychosocially defensive and toxic leadership dysfunctions that include leaders seeking power and authority over organization members can be depended upon to result in dysfunctional psychosocially defensive group and organizational dynamics. Organization members can end up feeling together and locked into what seems to be socially defensive repetition where operating problems and threats are seldom resolved, and everyone is left with the hope that the next leader will save "us." Working together and improving organizational performance may seem like a remote possibility.

The Intentional Work Group

This group has members who, in contrast to the psychosocially defensive groups, embrace a thoughtful and reflective stance. Group members are willing to assume personal responsibility to work together to solve operating problems. They are willing to nondefensively evaluate their reasoning, decisions, and actions paying attention to learning from experience to ensure success. This group dynamic regrettably is not common in bureaucratic, autocratic, and authoritarian-run organizations and when stressful leadership turnover is present. The intentional group culture, if achieved, may also not be sustained across time because it is always subject to being compromised by stressful and threatening dysfunctional leaders and organizational dynamics that lead to the emergence of the psychosocially defensive group dynamics that compromise intentionality.

In Sum – The Defensive Psychosocial Framework

The descriptions of psychosocially defensive group dynamics make us aware that these dysfunctional ways of coping with stressful times do develop and can inhibit organizational performance and problem-solving. Leaders and bureaucracy are often relied on to provide reassuring direction and control to deal with problems and threats. Autocratic and authoritarian leaders who take charge encourage organization members to depend on them. This is accentuated by the leader withholding and manipulating information and resources (rewards and punishments) heightening distressing feelings among organization members who are expected to be passively dependent and view themselves as marginally informed and competent. Feeling oppressed by autocratic leaders, however, is also often resisted. Resisting oppression and moving back against the leader is to be expected. There may also arise a hope that a better if not revolutionary intentional leader will be found and, if not, it may simply be hoped the threatening operating problems will self-resolve making doing nothing a good option.

The framework of defensive group dynamics provides insight into the three case examples. Keywords are italicized in this chapter to link the cases to the defenses and encourage spotting them throughout the book.

CASE ONE – LEADERSHIP PROBLEMS

Frequent changes in leadership have led to a leadership vacuum, unresolved operating problems, and some feel that the organization is falling apart because of the lack of clear direction and timely, consistent, and effective decision-making. Interim leaders have changed direction disrupting organizational continuity, predictability, and the ability to work together. The limited direction and changes in direction have created a distressing experience of organizational fragmentation. Group members have *retreated* from identifying with the organization and its dysfunctional leadership culture. During the leadership gaps, there have been losses of *bureaucratically* controlled coordination and sometimes noticeably *aggressive* power struggles have developed among the leaders of the specialized silos. This chaos seems dangerous at times and encourages many to seek the personal *freedom* of pursuing self-interests and personal goals including staying in their jobs. Some feel that they are being subjected to the same repetitive dysfunctional leadership dynamics and that everyone is *together* in their shared experience.

There is nonetheless also *hope* that an effective leader will be located who will solve the operating problems even though when new leaders are hired, they do not stay. The reality is that the turnover in leaders has sometimes led to the hiring of leaders who are *oppressive*, and many organization members have been resistant and *moved against* these leaders. Some have also *moved away* from these leaders seeking to be *free* from their *autocratic and authoritarian* leaders and changes thought to be in their own narrow self-interest. Under these conditions, efforts *to join with each* other to hold the fort have been compromised. The status quo of accepting the organizational dysfunctions that no one seems to be able to control has become the default culture. Threats and operating problems are not being dealt with or at best minimally so.

In sum, the *hope* of effective leadership remains unfulfilled and yet the wish remains for a leader who will allow organization members to retain their *freedom* and *avoid* having to accept stressful personal responsibility for maintaining organizational performance. And to be noted, this dynamic conserves the power and control of the leaders of the specialized silos, subdivisions, and work groups. This case is then an example of why organizations become fragmented and may seem to be falling apart into what sometimes is referred to as empire-building strategies.

CASE TWO – REGIME CHANGE

In this case the organization's culture is dominated by *autocratic and authoritarian* organizational and silo leaders who unilaterally control everyone and everything including overriding established *bureaucratic* processes and cultural norms. These punishing leaders have instilled feelings of powerlessness, vulnerability, and *dependence* that encourage organization members to feel *together* in their shared experience of helplessness to achieve good work. Feelings of being alienated from each other and their organization are common. As a result, organization members have *moved away* from these leaders hiding out in their metaphoric organizational foxholes keeping out of the line of fire. Personal *safety* and *freedom* in the form of remaining silent, *avoiding* contact with the leaders, and saying little to colleagues who may share critical remarks with the leaders are the norm. The occasional leader of a group who has stepped forward to oppose these leadership dynamics has been conspicuously neutralized by being publicly humiliated, marginalized, transferred, or terminated. Over-identification with these leaders has also resulted in the willing submission of some organization members to keep their jobs. The result is the leaders feel fully empowered to control and dominate the organization and its members with few restraints on what they do including some glaringly unethical, immoral, and unjust actions.

In sum, organization members feel that they are *together* in sharing their distressing experience of these toxic leaders and the organizational dysfunctions that they create. This has compromised everyone's ability to achieve sought-after high-performance levels. At times, some resistance to and *movement against* the leaders has arisen but more often organization members have relied on retreat and *moving away* from unrewarding and sometimes punishing interactions with them. A successful focus on overcoming resistance and expecting submission has led these leaders to think that they are fully empowered to take charge and micromanage. This *oppressive* workplace culture has created an overarching sense of *organizational identity* of being *together* in being victimized and little hope is held for positive change. Organization members have to accept the out-of-control toxic and dysfunctional organizational and leadership dynamics and group and organizational fragmentation to feel safe and keep their jobs.

CASE THREE – LIFE IN THE TRENCHES

In this case organization members, when confronted with a dysfunctional senior leadership group, have successfully stepped up to run the organization sticking to what has worked in the past – their *bureaucratically* oriented organizational culture. They also strongly *identify* with their mission that they are devoted to fulfilling. Members of the specialized groups have tried to *avoid* the toxic senior leadership group by *moving away* from them while *moving respectfully toward* their silo leaders who have compensated for the tendency toward organizational fragmentation. Organization members feel that they are *together* in achieving their mission and operate as a coordinated multidisciplinary team to accomplish their work. This defensive dynamic resembles federal, state, and local governments that keep running through changes in elected leaders with differing ideologies and leadership styles. Employees get the work done and *resist* making changes that they believe will compromise their work to achieve their organization's mission. Reliance on policies, procedures, and their silo leaders has compensated for their marginal senior-level leadership.

In sum, the organization has run itself avoiding falling apart and not accomplishing its mission. However, the leaders at the top of the *hierarchy* in this case have not entirely ignored what is happening and have at times acted *autocratically* to challenge and *move against* the silo leaders for taking "unauthorized" leadership roles that do not seem to acknowledge their official status at the top of the organizational hierarchy. Despite these interventions, the organization's members have successfully compensated for their less-than-effective senior leadership group to keep their organization running. This case illustrates that the need for effective leadership can be reduced by relying on silo leaders and an established *bureaucratic culture* that coordinates work among the specialized work groups. These defensive organizational dynamics all too often are what keep public and private organizations running.

In Sum, The Defensive Group Framework

The case examples and discussions illustrate that the framework of defensive group dynamics can be recognized in organizations and that their presence will vary over time based on changes in leadership. New leaders can range from being effective and welcoming to instances where they are toxic, micromanaging, and authoritarian and autocratic oppressors of organization members. The defensive group dynamics should for many readers be familiar from the perspective that they describe common organizational experiences. The framework of defensive psychosocial dynamics offers "usable" perspectives that make undiscussable group cultures and their accompanying dysfunctional workplace experiences understandable and open to inspection by leaders and organization members within their silos and work groups. However, using the framework to intervene in toxic and dysfunctional organizational dynamics by leaders, organization members, and internal and external consultants is, as has been discussed, a challenging proposition. However, this challenge can be best managed by having first gained insights into an organization's history and culture by conducting a listening diagnostic process of interviews throughout the organization as explored in Part 3 and briefly highlighted here.

THE DEFENSIVE GROUPS IN PRACTICE

These cases have provided an appreciation that the belief in stable and rationally managed organizations that optimize performance is problematic. Toxic leaders and dysfunctional organizational dynamics are common and often lead to spectacular failures such as the global banking/financial industry meltdown starting in 2008 and the bankruptcy of General Motors in 2009. More common is that organizations slowly end up falling apart dooming them to not succeed in fulfilling their potential resulting in their sale, merger, bankruptcy, or closing.

The defensive group framework provides a way to understand how organizations fragment and how coordinated and cooperative work can fall apart. A good starting point for changing toxic leadership and dysfunctional group and organization dynamics is revealed in a listening organizational diagnostic. However, also to be appreciated is that these defensive dysfunctions are difficult to change with each type of psychosocially defensive group offering its own unique challenges.

For example, if attacking a threat or operating problem is the goal, which is expected in organizations, organization members will seek out someone to lead them to victory. Member dependency pulls CEOs, the leadership team, and consultants into care-taking roles that, if accepted, reinforce organization members feeling dependent. Another example is that autocratic and authoritarian leaders tend to create organizational cultures filled with a combination of resistance to their leadership and submission. Organization members may seek freedom from these leadership dynamics by hiding out in the organization and reducing their level of engagement and commitment to each other, their groups, and their organization.

In sum, these psychosocially defensive group responses to stressful and anxiety-ridden work experiences underscore the problematic assumption that organizations are purposefully and intentionally operated to optimize everyone's experience at work and the organization's performance.

IN CONCLUSION

The framework of defensive group dynamics has provided insight into what are often out-of-awareness and undiscussable aspects of organizational life. This framework offers leaders, workers, and consultants a basis for understanding and changing psychosocially defensive, dysfunctional, and fragmented groups and organizational dynamics. The complexity of these individual, group, and organizational psychosocially defensive dynamics also suggests that there is no one right way to understand organizational life and that maintaining critical thinking and reflectivity is challenging when immersed in dysfunctional organizational dynamics. Chapter 8 continues our exploration of the psychosocially defensive workplace by directing our attention to the challenges of understanding the interpersonal world at work and how we work together. These interpersonal dynamics often include hard-to-appreciate complexities that can make it difficult to work together.

8

Falling Apart: Interpersonal Fragmentation

When it comes to answering the question "What's it like to work here?" the responses can be confusing. Organization members may say something like "I like my job, but I hate working here." This problematic response requires "unpacking." Responses like this surface for consideration that the organization as a whole and one's silo and immediate work group may have toxic leaders and distressing dysfunctional elements. What they may like is their interpersonal world at work – their friends, colleagues, and working relationships. These compensate for the less-than-desirable organizational and group dynamics. However, the interpersonal world can also include toxicity and dysfunction leading to the feeling that the ability to work together is falling apart.

Topics like leadership and followership are two of the key elements of the interpersonal world at work. Examining the workplace from a psychosocially informed perspective that includes out-of-awareness and hard to explain and manage interpersonal dynamics is a challenge and requires understanding them from a perspective of defensive responses to stress and anxiety.

This chapter explores the psychosocial defensive side of the workplace that influences interpersonal relationships between organizational leaders, managers, organization members, and consultants. These defensive dynamics can impact everyone leading to dysfunctional organizational outcomes that include toxic leadership and less-than-desirable actions by organization members relative to each other. Leaders and organization members may, for example, seek to attract preferred idealizing and admiring projections that foster favorable emotional attachment to them. And the opposite may also occur when leaders and organization members avoid drawing

DOI: 10.4324/9781003464464-10

positive or negative projections from organization members who may then transfer their feelings, positive or negative from prior life experience, onto them creating hard-to-understand interpersonal dynamics. Those in leadership roles may also selectively identify with some of the projections such as embracing idealizing projections that can make them feel "bigger than life" and reject projections that are less desirable. Interpersonal dynamics like this make a better understanding of them essential to managing and working within the interpersonal world at work.

THE INTERPERSONAL WORLD AT WORK

The interpersonal world at work is often filled with a kind and caring sense of humanity that includes reflective and intentional working relationships that draw everyone together. This workplace contrasts to defensive and dysfunctional interpersonal dynamics that split organization members apart and by extension split apart the organization's departments, divisions, and specialized silos. "Unpacking" this psychosocially defensive interpersonal world is essential if the ability to effectively work together is not to become dysfunctional and fall apart.

Unpacking the interpersonal world at work and how it becomes split apart and fragmented requires exploring psychosocial concepts that help to explain our defensive responses to what is happening around us that is stressful. These defensive responses are discussed using concrete examples of splitting and projection and their influence on those who are the targets of the projections who may or may not identify with the projections. These defensive responses also include the transference of emotions consistent with the projections that are drawn from similar prior life experiences. This process invests in knowing the person who is the target of the projections with positive or negative emotions. These interpersonal dynamics are sometimes referred to as "hot buttons" where the emotional response is disproportionate to what someone else said or did.

Splitting

Splitting, as discussed in Chapter 2, is a defensive thought process that divides oneself or another individual or group into most often a good self or group and bad others to defend against stressful experiences. We may, for example, deny that we are anxious and angry about what is going on but believe another person (or group) is, which serves to promote calming self-experience. The distressing self-experience is denied and split off allowing it to be projected onto others in our thoughts.

Splitting can become a shared experience when other group members also experience the leader and interpersonal world as distressing. Others may not only be thought to be anxious but also to be *bad* and potentially threatening our *good* selves. I or we are good and are being attacked by bad others or a group. These all too human defensive dynamics are common and fade into the background out of immediate awareness. We feel we are being victimized by a bad individual or group that we know is bad because we made it so in our thoughts. For example, valued approval for funding a project may be withheld by a chief financial officer who is thought and felt to be bad for doing this regardless of the reasons provided. Interpersonal dynamics like this fill our organizations with black-and-white binary imagery where there is little to no middle ground. In sum, at an interpersonal level individuals in other groups, departments, and organizational layers may be thought and felt to be oppressive and punishing and limiting our good self-experience for doing the organization's work.

Splitting may also occur in the reverse. We may experience ourselves as not being effective at our jobs, but another person is thought and felt to be doing a good job and acting effectively meriting our admiration and respect. This dynamic is common relative to leaders who are "known" to be powerful and effective. This encourages organization members to feel, for example, anxious when a powerful and authoritative leader is present, especially when the presence is one of being closely supervised. It is only human to feel diminished, threatened, and anxious in their presence who, in our minds, is bigger than life.

Splitting, as discussed below, usually occurs with projection. These defensive splits and projections are durable defenses that distort self and other awareness. Because they are defensive, they are not usually open to being questioned unless a substantial reality gap calls them into question.

In sum, defensive splitting is common and degrades accurate reality testing. Splitting combined with projection creates a context that is not accurate but is comforting in terms of coping with stressful relationships with others. At an extreme, splitting and projection promote thinking, feeling, and actions that can be personally and interpersonally destructive, especially when others become the enemy. When this happens, the enemy may merit destruction as happens in political, international, ethnic, and religion-based relations with a distressing frequency. This defensive dynamic also contributes to the aggressions seen in hostile takeovers where interpersonal dominance and submission and cultural dislocations occur.

Splitting an Example

The psychosocial dynamics discussed about a leader selectively attracting preferred projections (of competence) from others where organization members split off their self-experiences of being competent and capable and project them onto their leader are common. At the same time, the leader rejects undesirable projections of being less competent than the organization's members. This interpersonal dynamic emphasizes that splitting and projection can be driven from either side of the interpersonal context.

The owner of a large company, North American Manufacturing, has engaged a consultant to improve organizational performance. Immediately noticed by the consultant is that the owner who founded the company is admired by everyone. The owner designed a product that no other company has. This safe market niche with no competitors allows everyone to feel safe and secure in their jobs. The pay is good, and their work is rewarding.

Everyone thinks and feels that their chief executive officer (CEO) is a superior engineer and leader compared to themselves. The owner fully embraces this warm glow of employee admiration and approval although the new consultant is not joining in on this organizational dynamic remaining suitably skeptical. Is all this admiration merited based on observations of the owner's leadership and decision-making? The consultant's skepticism has been noted by organization members who have interpersonally pressured the consultant to conform to their culture of idealizing the owner who it is observed also actively draws these positive projections. This has created a leader who is bigger than life in the hearts and minds of organization members, and this is reinforced by an omnipresent micromanaging presence by their leader who feels authorized to make interventions anywhere at any time.

Projection

Projection accompanies splitting. Projection rids us of the split off and distressing "bad" self-experience by placing it in our thoughts onto those we work with. This allows us to "know" these others with some sense certainty in a way consistent with the projected content. This can create, for example, an awareness that "I" am good and the other person(s) is bad. The result may be that we are fearful of the other person's potentially aggressive intent that we have attributed to them. We may then feel that the person is devious, incompetent, or uncaring and comfortingly that we are not. An outcome like this is an all too human response to stressful organizational experience that influences how we relate to those we work with. We often hear, for example, different views expressed regarding the same person – some good and some bad.

We may also reinforce this interpersonally defensive strategy by rejecting information contrary to our mindful creation. For example, bad others may have good qualities that are ignored. We pay selective attention to only what we want to believe sometimes referred to as confirmation bias. This bends reality to meet our personal defensive needs to feel good about ourselves and that others possess the undesirable personal attributes we have.

Mindful splitting and projection do, despite being something we have privately made up in terms of how we know, think, and feel about others in our minds, leak out into the interpersonal world and we act in ways relative to others consistent with our mindful creation of them. The person who is targeted may become aware of being thought to be a certain way (as a bad aggressive or a withholding victimizer) that is not consistent with the individual's self-awareness and intent. This indirect and hard to pin down interpersonal awareness contaminates and fragments interpersonal relations at the margins of awareness. There might be said to be a "tension" between the two individuals over who each is and who "we" are. Challenging the leaked projections by the targeted individual paradoxically may reinforce this defensive interpersonal dynamic of being "bad" consistent with the defensive "bad" projections.

Projection an Example

Continuing with the North American Manufacturing example, everyone is encouraged to see the owner as an entrepreneur and inventor as well as a superior leader who has all the answers. By comparison, organization members feel less capable and depend on their leader to manage their organization, something that the leader does not discourage. It is hoped their idealized owner will continue to provide organization members with rewarding careers and good salaries.

The consultant's "objectivity" has occasionally questioned these idealizing and dependency-oriented dynamics of organization members by challenging them to think for themselves. They, however, have remained committed to idealizing their leader and sometimes see the consultant as bad for raising questions about some of the plans and decisions made by their leader. The organization's members remained committed to encouraging the consultant to join with them in idealizing their leader. This constant press of influence, to be noted, might gradually alter the consultant's thoughts, feelings, and actions creating personal fragmentation on the part of the consultant (Chapter 9).

These idealizing dynamics are accompanied by self-conceptions on the part of the organization members that are created by projecting their sense of themselves as competent onto their leader. They do not think of themselves as competent or capable as their leader and must depend on their leader to manage their organization. This interpersonal process results in the organization member's fragmenting losses of valued parts of themselves. This dynamic has gone unacknowledged even when the psychosocially informed consultant suggests that there is more going on here than meets the eye.

When the consultant has spoken to these defensive interpersonal dynamics relative to their leader, it has threatened the shared collusive splitting and projection dynamics. The owner, their leader, because of this collusive interpersonal culture, maintains an expansive self-conception that fulfills organization member expectations that their leader will take care of them because they cannot manage the organization themselves. No one wants to disturb this collusive idealizing culture and their individual and shared identities that they are less than capable and must depend on the leader.

In sum, both sides of the interpersonal splitting between organization members as individuals and their leader are committed to maintaining their familiar shared culture of dependency on their leader. This cultural imperative allows organization members to identify with their leader as well as with each other. We are all in this together. This cultural dynamic also allows the leader to identify with the organization's members who feel dependent and must be taken care of, which frees them up from having to assume stressful personal responsibility for decision-making.

Identification with the Projections an Example

Identifying with the projections by those subjected to them takes the discussion of splitting and projection one step further. Identification encourages the target to feel, think, and act in accordance with the projections. This self-fragmenting invasive interpersonal process encourages the target(s), which may include other groups, silos, and even countries, to accept the projected content and act them out. "If everyone seems to think I know everything, maybe I do." This interpersonal pressure confirms the "accuracy" of the splitting and projections and relieves organization members of feelings of uncertainty. The target has become as we desire. This interpersonal dynamic also, however, further compromises accurate reality testing, and the sum of these compromises forms the basis for interpersonal working relationships falling apart.

These fragmenting interpersonal dynamics usually occur outside of immediate awareness. For example, a mother wants to see her daughter as sweet and innocent fulfilling her preferred way of knowing her daughter. She wants her daughter to feel this way and continually nurtures this self-experience in her to become the perfect daughter completing this fragmenting interpersonal contracting. The daughter desires to fulfill her mother's vision of her by acting as desired to avoid being rejected for being resistant and nonconforming. This interpersonal response in turn shapes how the mother experiences herself as being accepted by her daughter as a caring and loving mother and encourages her to be less expectant of how her daughter should experience herself. All is well between them. Each has gradually shaped the other to fulfill how they want the other to be. Outcomes like these are what amount to collusive interpersonal contracts resulting in mutual adjustment to maintain the relationship. This process can also be understood to include each side of the split losing parts of self (self-fragmentation) that are not consistent with the projected content that has been accepted. The result is each person may gradually become someone who is not "who I am."

In sum, interpersonal dynamics like this are common in organizations, especially between leaders and followers where a conforming mutuality reduces pressure and stress about who everyone is while at the same time splitting everyone apart. This subtle interpersonal dynamic leads to a loss of some parts of oneself and the acceptance of parts that are foreign in the process of becoming the "perfect" group and organization member. The outcome of these interpersonal dynamics leads to a fragmented sense of who I am and who we are. We have fallen apart as discussed in Chapter 9.

Identifying with the Projections an Example

Organization members idealize the founder, owner, and leader of North American Manufacturing. Why not? Having created the company within a protected marketing niche has made some of the first employees wealthy and the rest secure and well-paid. Thinking, feeling, and acting like others imagine and expect reduces a lot of stress on everyone's part. Everything and everyone are safely under control – predictable and coordinated. Anyone who does not join in this dynamic is ignored, marginalized, encouraged to leave, or terminated for not being a team player.

Organization members, by waiting for decisions to be made by their leader, actively encourage their leader to make them and receive admiration (rewards) for doing so. Organization members, by coaching their leader to call all the shots, free themselves from having to assume risky decision-making responsibilities. This interpersonal dynamic meets their dependency needs so that their work experience is comfortingly controlled and not stressful. Having encouraged their leader to accept these projections, however, has the effect of coercing their leader into experiencing the many stresses associated with being singularly responsible for organizational success.

The counterpart of these coercive interpersonal dynamics is that leaders, who embrace being powerful and in control, project their imperfections and limitations onto organization members who are then known to be marginally capable. They must be closely supervised fulfilling everyone's expectations that their leader is in charge which minimizes stressful workplace experience. The outcome of this interpersonal collusion is that their leader meets their dependency needs to be free from making stressful decisions and assuming responsibility for managing the organization. Organization members, by accepting the leader's projections regarding their competencies, view themselves as being marginally capable. This reinforces their expectations that their leader should make all the decisions perhaps resulting in authoritarian and autocratic leadership.

In sum, this collusive interpersonal dynamic creates a balance within an undiscussable shared echo chamber. The employees feel less than capable, and their leader, feeling more than capable, must step forward to accept the responsibility for operating the organization.

The new organization member or consultant who encounters interpersonal dynamics like this must be careful to not make the leader and organization members anxious by, for example, holding their collusive culture up for inspection directly or and even indirectly. Asking questions about unresolved operating problems may suggest that the leader is not in fact so effective. Even though organization members may be threatened by anyone who does not support their collusive interpersonal cultural dynamics, consultants who encounter this type of organizational dynamic should not abandon finding nonthreatening ways to help the organization's members to overcome the defensive splitting and bi-directional projection and energizing transferences from past experiences that fragment their interpersonal relationships.

Transference

The workplace is filled with thoughts and feelings from everyone's past. Their transference onto the present not only changes self-experience in the present but also how organization members understand their interpersonal world and group and organizational dynamics. A manager, who it is felt resembles a past authority figure that was abusive, manipulative, and uncaring may evoke similar thoughts and feelings consistent with this past experience. These past thoughts and feelings contribute to making the manager a familiar experience but one that may not be consistent with the manager's self-awareness and the decisions and actions taken. This interpersonal and all too human response to others may include, for example, feeling fearful, enraged, submissive, admiring, or withdrawn. The manager may wonder about what just happened since the emotion-filled response seems to be inconsistent with what was said or done – a hot-button response.

In this example, there is not only a blurring of reality by splitting and projection but also an introduction of past interpersonal experience consistent with the mindful creation of the manager who resembles a past abusive authority figure. The revisiting of the experience in the present may encourage moving against or away from the manager as might have been the response in the past.

In sum, these enduring familiar interpersonally defensive experiences and responses from the past are often unwittingly present in relationships in distorting accurate reality testing to reduce stress by making the interpersonal world more familiar. The outcome is, however, that splitting, projection, and transference together fragment and disrupt the interpersonal world at work.

Transference an Example

North American Manufacturing's admired innovative leader is someone who knows how to make decisions sometimes under stressful conditions. Organization members approve of this even though the idealization may not be consistent with accurate reality testing as the consultant sometimes points out. These out-of-awareness collusive interpersonal dynamics, however, allow everyone to feel good about their leader, themselves, and each other. This caretaking culture has created a soothing happy family like experience. The transfer of positive thoughts and feelings by organization members onto their leader, their father, and authority figure fulfills the collusive interpersonal dynamics. It should also be noted that similar psychosocially defensive dynamics can create a leader who, it is thought and felt, is bad. Organization members may then experience themselves as good and being dominated and abused by their autocratic and authoritarian leader consistent with a past family, social, or organizational experience. Also, to be considered is that idealized leaders and positive transferences can lead to a collapse in these collusive interpersonal dynamics resulting in the leader being resisted or rejected. Organization members may then move against their leader who has failed to meet their dependency needs to keep them safe and their organization performing well. Should this occur these leaders often leave to take position elsewhere, retire, or they are terminated for creating a toxic dysfunctional organizational culture.

In sum, managing splitting, projection, and transference in organizations is especially important during stressful times. Denying and looking away from the presence of these individual, interpersonal, group, and organizational dynamics should preferably be avoided to maintain a high-functioning intentional organization.

HOW TO AVOID FALLING APART

Human nature and its accompanying psychosocial defenses pervade the workplace introducing reality-distorting, disruptive, and fragmenting experiences of ourselves, the interpersonal world, and our groups and organizations. Leaders may act in ways that promote psychosocially defensive outcomes. This may include encouraging favorable projections and transferences onto them that magnify everyone's perceptions of their power, knowledge, and ability. This magnification may lead to increases in the leader's vulnerability in that everything the leader says or does is closely scrutinized by organization members and investors. This appreciation suggests that avoiding idolizing organizational dynamics may make the executive less of a threat to organization members including themselves. And to be considered is that intentionally avoiding and resisting being idealized may also paradoxically make the leader more vulnerable to being rejected and moved against by organization members who seek dependency and a strong and powerful leader. A better understanding of how positive projections and transference are encouraged by leaders is a good starting point for examining how problematic avoiding them is.

Drawing Positive Perceptions and Feelings

CEOs often are bigger than life appearing on the covers of popular management magazines and becoming cult-like figures such as Steve Jobs (Apple), Jack Welch (GE), and Sr. Richard Branson (Virgin Group). These CEOs have a personal grandiosity that may compromise their critical thinking and their realistic self-assessment of their and their organization's performance. There are also, in contrast, many less-than-grandiose organizational leaders who achieve outstanding organizational performance and are suitably admired for their achievements. These intentional leaders promote critical thinking that makes their decisions and work and everyone else's decisions and work open to inspection in the service of achieving excellence. In contrast, idealized CEOs who are seen as in charge, powerful, and authoritative may have achieved this lofty status by eliminating everyone who has not been suitably supporting and admiring. Actions like these magnify their organizational presence to the point that they become micromanagers who make or participate in all decision-making and who are willing to intervene far down in the organization to impose their ideas overwhelming any resistance.

Leaders who are bigger than life may be present at all levels of organizations. Toxic leaders, for example, are also often found to have held onto their position for many years if not decades supported in their role by having acquired inordinate power and control by moving against resistors and weaponizing information systems to defend themselves. Many elements of the hierarchical bureaucratic organization structure may have been deployed to limit, control, and dominate those who resist their decisions, plans, and directions. The level of organizational, group, and interpersonal destructiveness can be attention-getting.

An example of overcoming resistance is the outsourcing of a silo's functions such as security or major elements of information technology which is said to be necessary to reduce operating costs. The elimination of an entire function and its members who are resistant avoids having to justify individual terminations. Taking an action like this also provides the rest of the organization with a signal that resistance is not a good idea. Similar outcomes are achieved by declaring a downsizing which can screen removing anyone who is resistant along with, if necessary, those who are supportive of this individual's resistance.

Downsizing is so common an event that it is accepted as a reasonable way to manage an organization. Downsizing is also often linked to managing stockholder share value and perceptions of the leader as being in charge and effective. Equally threatening are reorganizations that subordinate resistant individuals or groups to new leaders who are expected to bring them into line stifling the resistance. There may also be instances where a valued but resistant individual who has a position of some authority is reorganized to an advisory role to reduce the resistance enabled by the role's authority.

There are countless ways charismatic, idealized, strong, and powerful organizational leaders who have few limits on what they do can feel free to impose their will one-on-one in the interpersonal world or relative to groups as well. Keeping one's job may require accepting an organizational culture of unquestioning submission to the leader – no questions asked.

In sum, these organizational dynamics make clear that the interpersonal world at work may include idealizing or denigrating a leader accompanied by the transferring of feelings from past similar experiences onto the present. Effectively responding to these interpersonal dynamics can metaphorically open the door to developing a high-functioning and safe organizational culture that everyone identifies with – who we are. Accomplishing this, however, is challenging.

HOW TO AVOID THE INTERPERSONAL WORLD FROM FALLING APART

Individuals in leadership roles ranging from supervisors to CEOs are authority figures that invariably draw projections that may be selectively accepted and even encouraged. These interpersonal dynamics alter the self-experience of these leaders and that of organization members who may be reminded of past authority figures. These workplace experiences raise for consideration how to be more aware of them especially regarding how leaders act and are thought of, for example, as supportive, paternalistic, maternalistic, authoritarian, dominating, or threatening. Leaders may encourage submissive responses on the part of organization members and their moving toward their leader in the hope of having their dependency needs met. Organization members may also be resistant to their authority figures moving against them including withholding sought-after admiration or failing that not fearing them.

In contrast, when leaders are self-aware, self-reflective, and insightful, they can intentionally set about drawing fewer projections – idealizing or less so. The bi-directional nature of projections and transference is invariably present contributing to distorting the interpersonal nature of leader and follower dynamics. For example, in the case of new leaders, organization members may think it is only a matter of time before the leader's actions will fulfill their worst expectations such as the leader becoming autocratic and authoritarian or conversely risk averse to making tough decisions and not available to provide caretaking guidance. The best of leaders, even those who are intentional and attuned to psychosocially defensive interpersonal dynamics, will unavoidably reinforce some positive and negative projections onto them by making decisions and providing direction.

Leaders in all types of roles can, however, benefit from trying to minimize positive idealizing and negative autocratic projections and transferences although their best efforts may not entirely succeed. For example, executives, managers, supervisors, and consultants may inadvertently encourage organization members to think of and experience them as powerful, authoritative, and competent. The use of language and office locations sends a message that encourages projections and transference consistent with being competent, expert, and an in-charge authority figure. Being aware of these unavoidable outcomes is important in terms of responding to unintended consequences associated with toxic leadership.

These same inadvertent dynamics are also relied on by toxic leaders to impose power and authority reinforced by the making of unilateral decisions without consulting organizational stakeholders and not receiving accurate and timely information – shooting from the hip. Jargon-filled language is also often relied upon by executives and consultants to impress everyone with their authoritative knowledge. Public shaming rituals and the ever-present threat of discipline and termination are sometimes relied on to make clear who is in charge and promoting psychosocially defensive responses. In contrast, and equally dysfunctional are leaders and consultants who want to be friends with organization members moving toward them. These leader dynamics include avoiding making decisions to deal with hard to resolve conflicts that may alienate, threaten, or offend organization members to maintain a sought-after friendly interpersonal world at work.

These toxic and dysfunctional leadership and organizational dynamics can be avoided by executives being thoughtful, reflective, and intentional which requires that they effectively manage their own anxieties associated with their stressful responsibilities (Chapter 14). A conscious effort to do so implies knowing oneself well enough to understand what influences one's thoughts, feelings, and actions. This includes an awareness of their all too human needs to feel accepted, respected, valued, and admired.

In sum, stress and anxiety are always present at work and they promote relying on psychosocially defensive responses that introduce interpersonal dysfunctions and fragmentation. Executives, managers, and group members who are aware of these defensive dynamics should be encouraged to discuss them when they are present. A good starting point is for leaders and consultants to make it safe enough to openly discuss dysfunctional interpersonal dynamics and fragmentation that are compromising the ability to work together. Maintaining coordination and cooperation avoids the sense that "our" ability to work together is falling apart. In sum, reflective and thoughtful responses aimed at identifying stressful organizational dynamics help to diffuse stress and minimize relying on psychosocial defenses. This process of containing and managing the stress resident in the interpersonal world at work should most wisely also be seen to be the responsibility of all organization members, not just a leader's responsibility.

A PARADOX TO CONSIDER

Organizational leaders and members shape how others know them. They may embrace perceptions of themselves that are admiring and favorable and pay less attention to less desirable perceptions. Leaders may lose themselves and their identity to a constant press of projections and transference onto them that they may resist but also embrace including attracting those that are favorable. However, when leaders and organization members try to avoid attracting usually preferred projections they are more likely to be experienced by organization members as more authentic and available to relate to by not relying on psychosocially defensive interpersonal manipulations. They are not felt to have compelling interpersonal needs to be liked or admired. When these interpersonal agendas are absent, a cultural norm emerges where working with others is safe, engaging, and fulfilling. There is, however, a darker side to creating this cultural context.

Paradoxically, a leader who is self-aware and authentic and not intentionally attracting idealizing projections may motivate aggressive organization members to see this leader as weak and vulnerable, and not effective, or taking charge, or controlling, or dominating and not respected (Chapter 14). Some organization members may believe that there is little to fear if they aggress and move against their leader. Undermining, challenging, or rejecting supervision, if not overt, may be pursued covertly behind the leader's back. These dysfunctional interpersonal dynamics of moving against the leader create a toxic and dysfunctional organizational culture that contaminates working together and the taking of opposing sides that promotes interpersonal and organizational fragmentation. Those who observe these dynamics may not agree but also may not oppose those who move against the leader to avoid becoming targeted for aggression themselves.

There is then a paradox. An effective, intentional, and reflective leader may be targeted by others who seek power and control to dominate others although this leader may well be willing to stand against those who are aggressive but at the risk of promoting more aggression. Dynamics like this sometimes require intentionally acting against them. Not dealing with persistent aggression is not a good option even if it is stressful to do so. Doing so intentionally, however, is respected by organization members who have witnessed the win-lose aggression-filled interpersonal conflict.

In sum, the leader, it may be hoped, will contain the aggression, or at least minimize it when it occurs restoring the workplace to greater interpersonal safety and operating effectiveness. However, given human nature and its effects on organizational dynamics, it must be acknowledged that there may be no easy answers to these types of toxic and dysfunctional interpersonal dynamics.

IN CONCLUSION

Effective leaders manage much more than organizational processes, people, buildings, equipment, and finances. Not often acknowledged is the importance of trying to manage defensive psychosocial interpersonal dynamics. These are usually seldom acknowledged and rarely questioned even though they contribute to a sense of interpersonal relations, coordination, and cooperation falling apart.

This chapter has pointed out that thoughtful, intentional, and reflective leaders can avoid or minimize these defensive dynamics that fragment everyone's experience of each other, their working together, and their organization. Avoiding interpersonal fragmentation that compromises coordination and cooperation requires it to be open to being safely discussed. This allows organization members to better understand their dysfunctional interpersonal dynamics. This helps them to maintain better self-integration and feel to be meaningfully joined with others in accomplishing work. Chapter 9 continues exploring organizational fragmentation by examining fragmented self-experiences and that "I" may be falling apart that results from not being able to cope with a stressful workplace.

9

Falling Apart: Personal Fragmentation

Falling apart has been discussed for organizations, groups, and the interpersonal world. How we understand ourselves and the world around us is the subject of much historical and ongoing theorizing using psychosocially informed perspectives. Any discussion of falling apart would be deficient without exploring our own self-experience. We are all faced with the challenge of knowing and understanding ourselves and managing our thoughts, feelings, and actions. We all experience at times self-awareness associated with feeling stressed and anxious and psychologically and socially defensive. This appreciation makes it important to consider how our defenses compromise work and occasionally may harm others and the organization's performance.

FALLING APART AS PEOPLE

Fragmenting self-experience opens for discussion the question of what "self" means. A healthy, consistent sense of self begins to develop during childhood and with our earliest experiences of our caregivers. These experiences ideally help us to develop an accurate, balanced, and integrated understanding of who we are and how to relate to others.

The development of an *integrated sense of self* means being able to distinguish between ourselves and others by recognizing our thoughts and feelings are separate from those of others. This self-awareness allows for successfully relating to those around us, our groups, and our organizations. These aspects of an integrated sense of self may seem obvious. This is made clearer by comparing this understanding of an integrated sense of self to fragmented self-experience.

DOI: 10.4324/9781003464464-11

People who have gaps in their self-integration experience some degree of personal fragmentation and less self-awareness. They have less ability to maintain appropriate interpersonal boundaries, especially under stress. This self-fragmenting outcome arises from a compromised development of meaningful and stable early interactions with caregivers, siblings, and others. These losses of self-integration can lead to problematic self-imposed compromises to interpersonal and working relationships. The resulting stressful sense of self can lead to compelling needs to control others to secure personal safety.

In sum, a well-integrated self-other awareness permits opposing thoughts and feelings about oneself and others to coexist without feeling anxious, fearful, or dominated. Both good and bad experiences of ourselves and others are accommodated. People with a fragmented sense of self by comparison are less able to accomplish this resulting in a splitting apart of good from bad self-experience as well as the experience of others introducing self and other fragmentation. Successfully knowing ourselves and others falls apart. We and those around us may become good or bad. This appreciation is the basis of this chapter. Self and others (us in the interpersonal world) can become split apart to keep the good (self) separate from the opposing awareness of bad aspects of self and others. This intensely personal dimension means maintaining a consistent sense of self across time in different situations is problematic and a challenge imperfectly mastered by all of us.

The inability to accommodate both positive and negative elements of self-relative to others makes it difficult for us as individuals to conceive of a single *other* (or oneself) as encompassing both good and bad. This reality-distorting split apart and fragmented way of organizing our self-experience and our experience of others results in hard-to-understand self and interpersonal dynamics. The result is at least to some degree of reliance on reality-distorting psychosocial defenses to cope with the challenges to our self-identities as we participate in interpersonal relationships, groups, and organizations.

In sum, we, along a range, compromise ourselves and our personal freedoms and autonomy to fit in. These defenses change who "I am," who "you" are, and who "we" are to be able to cope with stressful personal, group, and interpersonal dynamics that include changing oneself to become a good organization member who embraces the organizational culture and identity.

WORKPLACE RESTRUCTURING OF SELF

The workplace is a psychosocial setting that encourages its members to change themselves to better fit in to work within the organization, its work groups, and with fellow organization members. There is a coercive implicit nature to this dynamic that displaces one's sense of self with the preferred group and organizational identity to become a "good" group and organization member. This results in losses of personal autonomy and self-integration in order to stay attached to one's job and income and to be accepted as a colleague and member of the group and organization. This adaptation to social expectations includes stressful experiences as might be the case with a new Army volunteer or joining a large organization with a long history and an established culture that includes a preferred member identity to fit in. Conformity in these cases secures attachment by becoming a loyal convert who accepts the organization's culture including how power and authority are used to control the work of the organization's members. Ideally, everyone knows their job and how to coordinate working with everyone else to avoid stressful, disruptive, and potentially hard-to-manage interpersonal, group, and organizational conflict.

In sum, this restructuring of oneself becomes a self-regulatory function. Organization members are expected to willingly subordinate themselves to the power and control of, for example, a hierarchical bureaucratic organizational structure. The pressure to voluntarily conform, however, fragments the self by having to abandon or at least suppress parts of ourselves that are not valued by organizational leaders and fellow organization members. We preferably are in the same boat sharing a common workplace culture.

An example that highlights these dynamics that reshape us is what happens to a youthful recruit when confronted with military training. A developing and malleable self-identity is confronted with a stressful and demanding need to conform to become an ideal member – a soldier who submits to the chain of command. The recruit dutifully standing at attention has replaced the former sense of self by becoming a hard-to-recognize person who embraces a new *identity* and conforms to a new organizational *culture*. Much the same can be said for many types of organizations such as fire and police departments, governmental and most large organizations that have freedom stripping expectations for their members to conform.

This restructuring of new organization members is intentionally designed to be transformative creating someone who is accepting and supportive of the organization's expectations for being a good member. This accommodation on the part of individuals of accepting the organizational culture and accompanying self-identity transforms the individual into a new member. However, to be expected is that this transformation is only successful along a range. The new recruit's psychosocial defenses may also defend against what is experienced to be coercive transformational expectations. It is this tension between joining a group or organization and the new member confronting the self-compromising conformity expectations to accept the new organization's culture that is the core of this chapter.

The Constant Press of Organizational Culture

Organizational culture provides a wide range of pressures to become the ideal person and group and organizational member who conforms to expectations of how to do one's work and how to relate to others and work within groups and specialized silos that have their own subcultures. Conformity helps to allay stress about who is a member and who is not and who is with us and who is not. Organization members experience a stable culture that provides a stress-reducing way to understand life at work, including their own identity and how to think and feel.

Organization culture is hard to "see" but is nonetheless a pervasive influence on all organization members. Organizational culture is usually based on bureaucracy that provides everyone with an understanding about how to work together supported by role expectations and doing it by the book. These expectations for relating to each other usually take the form of prescribed role-to-role interactions that become the accepted way to be a member – who I am and who we are – and a good and loyal soldier.

Organization members, by accepting the culture, feel less anxious by voluntarily changing what they think and feel and how they work with others to become the ideal conforming organization member. The thoughts and feelings of organization members as a result converge on achieving comforting predictable uniformity which is especially valuable in high-stress situations such as military combat or during an organizational crisis such as downsizing. Organization members may feel that "we" are all in this together and joined in a coequality with everyone else. Interpersonal conflict and threatening autocratic uses of power and authority, it is also hoped, are minimized by the bureaucratic organizational culture that prescribes appropriate uses of power and authority creating a sense of safety and predictability for organization members. Life at work is ideally controlled, predictable, safe, secure, coordinated, and cooperative. Everyone knows what to do, how to do it, and what to expect from everyone else. Bureaucratic cultures are embraced for these reasons.

The Culture of Bureaucracy

Bureaucratic organizations (discussed below), like the military, governments, and most large companies, are social structures that regulate thinking, feeling, and behavior. This is important for the organization's members who may number in the many thousands who are scattered geographically and who must coordinate their work to produce products and services that are consistent and predictably available. This controlled productivity expectation must be met to avoid creating client and customer criticism as well as regulatory scrutiny. However, these efforts to standardize products, services, and performance are often less than fully successful when psychosocial defenses are present that, for example, defend against toxic leadership styles that are not thought to be consistent with the organization's culture and values.

These bureaucratic hierarchical organizational attributes also readily evoke stress when organization members feel over-controlled, powerless, and dependent on the organization and its leaders for direction. The psychosocially defensive responses to these stresses can lead to a defensive organizational self that conflicts with the expectations of the organization's members. Organizational structure may also implicitly include interpersonal agendas and competition for rewards. Raises and promotions may, for example, be linked to conforming and submitting to the "impersonal" organizational structure and its hierarchy of formal power and authority even when the power and authority are being wielded for personal reasons such as dominating organization members or for self-benefit.

Adapting to toxic leadership and dysfunctional organizational dynamics to secure safe employment results in some losses of personal autonomy, self-efficacy, and self-integrity. Conforming to rigid and detailed work requirements can lead to reliance on individual and shared psychosocial defenses such as actively or passively resisting performance expectations and moving against the control of the organization's leaders. Our experience of the rational and impersonal bureaucratic organizational design that ideally runs like a machine can be humbling and alienating when dysfunctions exist. We may feel that we have become little more than oppressed coequal cogs in a machine and good soldiers on the battlefield.

In sum, working within organizations is not a benign presence in our lives. Their immersive and engulfing context based on a hierarchical bureaucratic form of organizational design that ideally regulates our work lives can make us feel oppressed, overcontrolled, and dominated by autocratic authoritarian leadership enabled by the hierarchical structure. Maintaining our employment, however, depends on our willingness to change ourselves to "fit in." This transformative outcome includes relying on psychosocial defenses, such as denial, rationalization, the three directions of movement, and splitting and projection to cope with the oppressive conformity expectations. This becomes the basis for our own self-fragmentation. Our interactions with our organizations can, however, also lead to our trying to change and restructure them and their cultures to better meet our personal needs to feel less regimented and oppressed to achieve personal fulfillment.

WORKPLACE RESTRUCTURING BY OURSELVES

Our organizations continually adjust to competitors, technology, economics, and social change. They also adjust to the expectations of the people who create them every day that they come to work. Unquestioning submission is not always the case even in the military. Our organizations are filled with resistance to change and top-down unilateral and not in frequently oppressive autocratic control. These resistances are to be expected and fulfill human needs to maintain some sense of personal integrity relative to the demands for conformity and submission to authority ostensibly aimed at fulfilling the organization's mission. For example, some duties in a position description may be complied with and others modified or not adhered to including adding new self-assumed duties and ways of performing work. Individual dynamics like this passively if not actively restructure the organizational culture and bureaucracy. This informal organizational restructuring can make it more functional and livable for organization members or conversely more dysfunctional and stressful.

Organization members bring to work their personalities influencing organizational dynamics and management decision-making. This creates complexities within the interpersonal world and within groups. The cumulative effects of these individualized distortions encourage us to understand that organizational life and decision-making may not always be so rational and performance-oriented. Organization members and their lifetime experience, personal attitudes, and expectations can defeat the best-engineered organizational design and controls. This tension between this restructuring of the organization and the organization's restructuring of its members is always a conflict-filled organizational and psychosocial organizational dynamic.

In sum, being aware of the bidirectional nature of workplace transformational dynamics is important. Organizations change how their members experience themselves, each other, and their work. And conversely, organization members continually strive to make sense of their workplace and change it to better fulfill their unique personal needs and desires to maintain self-esteem, self-integrity, and self-integration. These two directions of change may improve the bureaucratic hierarchical control processes or introduce dysfunctions. This organizational context, where organizational and human needs coexist in a dynamic tension, generates the unpredictable outcomes found in organizations.

One way to better understand these individual proclivities is to use the psychosocial defensive framework described in Chapter 2 as a basis to recognize workplace dynamics that, at an extreme, can become dysfunctional and distort our sense of ourselves and others and our ability to respond to the stressors of daily organizational life. These defenses are once again adapted for this purpose as in the previous chapters. To begin it is important to first explore the intentional organization member who responds to stress with fewer psychosocial defenses.

The Intentional Organization Member

The intentional organization member is someone who does not tend to be overly anxious or defensive when confronted with stressful situations. A secure sense of self allows for thoughtful and reflective responses. This organization member feels capable in managing assigned role responsibilities while also being respectful of bureaucratic work norms but not overly dependent on them to control workplace experience to feel safe.

These individual dynamics allow for authentic responses to workplace challenges that are productive under a wide range of conditions. Initiative, flexibility, and innovation are this member's identity, and assuming personal responsibility is the norm. These organization members are accepting of others and support an open, inclusive, collaborative, respectful, and trusting work setting where conflict is discussable including being able to safely question fellow intentional leader decisions and actions.

Intentionality is, however, regrettably often lacking in organizations, especially during stressful times. Psychosocially defensive group dynamics contribute to losses of intentionality on the part of their members when everyone may feel that they are together in the same sinking boat. The defensive group descriptions in Chapters 2 and 7 are recast here to speak directly to individual defensive responses in organizations that may be familiar to readers. Understanding defensive individual and group dynamics is a major step forward in terms of managing our own self-experience when they are encountered.

Moving Against Others – Aggression

These individuals are committed to a win-lose strategy that can include being competitive, holding arrogant contempt for others, and being aggressive and intimidating, particularly toward those who resist and offend them. The vindication of personal injuries and exploiting others at work is common even if doing so compromises interpersonal relationships. These organization members are resourceful and persistent which paradoxically often makes them appear to be good leaders, especially when it is felt strong leadership is needed to take charge and manage a threatening situation. However, feeling arrogantly better than others combined with being vindictive when challenged also encourages these individuals to not be liked and often feared. These organization members, who may not be particularly concerned about being liked and approved of, feel free to aggressively compete against others since there is little to lose. Their drive to "get ahead" translates into winning out over everyone else sometimes at any cost to themselves, others, and the organization. At an extreme, especially in management roles, there is the potential that aggressive, arrogant, and vindictive behavior may have few limits. Their willingness to engage in interpersonal aggression also provides them with some immunity from being held accountable since anyone endeavoring to challenge them can expect a punishing response.

Another noteworthy aspect of moving against others is that those, in management roles, may rely on perfectionism and micromanagement. At times, no aspect of the work of organization members may seem to be too small or insignificant to be overlooked. This detailed level of oversight is autocratic, authoritarian, and oppressive especially when nonconstructive criticism is used. Denigrating and blaming others openly or behind their backs readily promote feelings on the part of organization members of being victimized for not fulfilling the leader's self-imposed perfectionistic expectations for work performance.

Those who move against others are also often self-centered and seek positions of power and authority to be admired or failing that feared. They are competitive and overachieving striving to be better than everyone else. This personal dynamic is reinforced by their tendency to over-value what they accomplish. In management roles, there is a tendency to attract attention to themselves by generating attention-getting ideas that end up having problematic outcomes that are blamed on everyone else. The challenges of managing the unintended consequences of creating change may also lead them to lose interest in their idea and move on to the next big idea. This avoidance and moving away from personal responsibility can lead to delegating to others the work of dealing with the implementation details setting them up to be blamed when the ideas fail to work out. These blaming rituals also enable these individuals to hold contempt for those who assumed the responsibility for the implementation. Few may measure up to this leader's perfectionist expectations or compare favorably to this individual's over-valued sense of self and accomplishments.

Moving Away from Others – Retreat

This defensive direction of movement is in part the result of feeling that moving against offending and oppressive others is too stressful to consider or not likely to succeed. Conflict avoidance including ignoring what others think, feel, and do is commonplace in organizations. Giving up on resisting aggressive and offending others who may hold oppressive performance and interpersonal expectations is embraced in favor of being left alone to work. Efforts by others to be interactive may be experienced as distressingly invasive and coercive. Being expected to follow rules and conform to policies and procedures is also disliked. This tendency to retire, withdraw, withhold, and be left alone, it is hoped, attracts less attention to one's presence and work. At an extreme, retreat can result in being less motivated to perform excellent work sometimes referred to as "retiring in place." The setting of personal goals that are experienced as coercive self-imposed pressures are also be avoided.

The defensive response of moving away is not usually consistent with organizational norms and expectations for organization members to submit to supervision and assume personal responsibility for performing work. Retreating from engagement, however, can also paradoxically lead to distressing conflict with others and in particular superiors. By noticeably avoiding contributing at work, moving away from others can result in others moving against this individual by trying to enforce oppressive performance expectations that compromise the success of this interpersonal defensive strategy.

In sum, retreat from interacting with others provides a sense of freedom (discussed below). However, successfully retreating to a low-stress context is problematic when accomplishing an acceptable volume of quality work may be lacking. Marginal performance and participation predictably result in attracting the attention of others and supervisors who hold oppressive performance expectations that retreat it is hoped will avoid.

Moving Toward Others – Dependency

Being dependent suggests the presence of a low sense of self-worth and feelings of competency and confidence combined with difficulties in coping with stress. When stressful experiences are present, this organization member may defensively look to others to meet security and safety needs. This dependent way of relating to others is also many times implicitly promoted by hierarchical organizations. Dependency-oriented relationships are usually encouraged by those who hold power and authority to secure control over organization members who are expected to submit to them.

Self-minimization and low self-evaluation are aggravated by holding self-defeating perfectionistic standards that reinforce the feeling that others must help and take charge. This disowning of the ability to accept responsibility and achieve excellent work is consistent with self-criticism and even self-sabotage. Depending on the support of a group may also include dependency on others who seek to dominate organization members who are willing to submit to them to secure hoped-for caretaking dependence. Submission, however, is self-compromising and reinforces feelings of low self-efficacy. Accepting and maintaining an oppressive and abusive interpersonal relationship of dependency at work is unfortunately common.

Despite this self-limiting quest for dependency that seeks safety and freedom from coercive workplace responsibilities, successful work is accomplished so long as others provide direction, approval, and reassurance. This type of interpersonal collusion is commonplace in organizations that have hierarchical bureaucratic structures that overcontrol their members reinforcing underlying psychosocial dependency needs that place a premium on feeling secure, safe, and accepting that others are in change.

In sum, those who seek roles of dependency may experience themselves as self-sacrificing loyal followers relative to others where submission secures approval and caretaking. The role of dependency is sometimes rationalized by asserting that they are being oppressed and victimized by powerful others which may in fact be true if the others are autocratic, authoritarian, and oppressive. This pairing at work and in life outside of work is all too common. Moving against oppressive interpersonal dynamics like this, which is appropriate to maintain self-integrity, is, however, avoided as being too threatening and stressful, and seeking safety and security from others is preferred.

Hope and Freedom

Feeling hopeful and seeking freedom from oppressive expectations is part of who we are as human beings. However, when these personal attributes become defensive, individual, group, and organizational dysfunctions can develop. This individual's focus on a hopeful future combined with feeling oppressed by others who may hold expectations to assume personal responsibility can lead to waiting for someone to take charge of stressful situations. This hopefulness, if joined in by other organization members, creates a cultural dynamic of feeling together in being attentive and participative in discussing problems, but there is also a lack of willingness to assume responsibility for acting to resolve threats and operating problems. Paradoxically locating someone to lead may be experienced as threatening in that the leader may expect organization members to assume personal responsibility for acting which compromises individual and group pursuits of freedom from these oppressive expectations. Paradoxically, it may, in fact, be better that a leader is not located and innovative ideas to deal with problems not thought since in either case they may be followed by oppressive expectations to assume personal responsibility to act.

In sum, this psychosocially defensive orientation and its hope to remain free from coercive and oppressive others and their expectations to assume personal responsibility to act, can generate stressful unresolved organizational problems and conflict. The pursuit of freedom from acting can paradoxically contribute to a cultural collapse toward autocratic and authoritarian leadership during stressful times fulfilling the fears of being oppressed. Unlike dependency, this defensive response avoids the submissive obligations that come with seeking out a role of dependency by being willing to resist a strong leader who holds coercive and oppressive expectations.

Togetherness and Sameness

Feeling joined with others in a common cause as equals is an all too human wish. Feeling that we are all in this together is comforting. This psychosocial defense may include a shared resistance to toxic leadership and stressful organizational experiences such as downsizing and restructuring. Events like this encourage organization members as individuals to merge for safety in a homogenized sameness and coequality based on the sharing of a common threatening experience such feeling that everyone may have a target on their back. How will a downsizing affect You, Me, and Us?

Being comfortingly together in sharing the same experience reinforces feelings of a homogenized coequality and reduces the anxiety of each organization member. Few group and organization members are willing to self-differentiate to, for example, volunteer to lead resistance to leadership toxicity or a response to a threatening operating problem. There is a tacit understanding that anyone who does try to lead may disturb the feeling of sameness, merger, and coequality. It may also be the case that anyone who decides to try to lead may be targeted as a threat by those in senior leadership roles and disciplined or terminated. Personal survival is important. However, a lack of leadership and willingness by organization members to follow a leader, assume personal responsibility, and to work on stressful problem-solving predictably leads to operating dysfunctions and organizational ineffectiveness that increases the stress everyone is individually feeling.

In sum, during stressful times organization members may become invested in psychosocial defensiveness that contributes to personal fragmentation and anxieties associated with feelings of falling apart. Organization members are striving to not set themselves apart from the crowd and the herd mentality. This, however, compromises individual and group learning from experience and the ability to work together creating organizational fragmentation. Everyone is together foremost as individuals defending against their personal fragmentation that arises from their unique experience of the stressful organizational dynamics. Defensively sticking together to seek freedom from distressing workplace experiences, however, promotes stressful organizational dysfunction that reinforces individual defensive responses. Merging with others can also result in relying on other defensive dynamics where, for example, losing one's identity and self-integrity to the group dynamic (the mob) may lead to moving away from the togetherness and sameness of merger and toward another familiar coping response, that of bureaucracy.

Bureaucratic Control

When work life is predictable and under control it feels safe. The striving for control through reliance on bureaucratic organizational design is a familiar defensive response. Individuals embrace it because it relieves stress in favor of a routine and accepted culture of control that ideally regulates even those in authority as to what they can do and how they do it. Adhering to the rules and regulations creates comforting predictability for organization members. Organization members who embrace this psychosocial defense accept the hierarchical structure and its routinized forms of hierarchically based leadership that are circumscribed and impersonal to minimize their stress by hopefully limiting unpredictable personalized uses of power and authority.

This structural psychosocial defense becomes "who I am and how we do things here." However, for each member as an individual, there are losses of personal autonomy and self-identity. This amounts to a personal trade-off to avoid stressful losses of control and predictability in the organization. The focus on stability and dependability is, for each organization member, an accepted psychosocially defensive compromise that can, however, also generate stressful operating problems as a result of the accompanying bureaucratic rigidities and the proverbial performance-robbing red tape.

In sum, bureaucratic overcontrol leads to an inability to make decisions and rapidly adapt to internal and external change and threats. When stressful outcomes like this develop, the defensive response may be an unthoughtful further reliance on doubling down on bureaucratic methods to regain control. Balancing predictability with organizational rigidities is an ongoing challenge for managing bureaucratic organizations, especially when unresolved threats and conflict lead to toxic autocratic leadership.

Autocratic Authoritarian Control

This approach to achieving control relies on individual propensities to seek out an autocratic usually charismatic leader, sometimes by governing boards, who it is hoped will get control of distressing of out-of-control operations and alleviate feelings of personal vulnerability and self, group, and organizational fragmentation that have compromised working together. When a context like this arises, organization members feel reassured by the presence of a strong, powerful, authoritative leader who assertively if not aggressively steps up to take control drawing idealizing projects that encourage feeling empowered to act. This dynamic may lead to an organization leader becoming autocratic, authoritarian, and unaccountable for creating collateral damage to organization members and the organization. This leader may succeed in mastering the situation but also set the organization up to fail by imposing poorly considered decisions that promote scapegoating, conflict, and individual, group and organizational fragmentation that again compromises organizational performance.

Some organization members may also seize upon a troubling period to try to realize their personal tendencies toward autocracy and authoritarianism to cope with their stressful self-experience. In these cases, the stressful situation, while creating a context for this to happen, also evokes anxiety that throughout life has been defended against by seeking to take charge and control and becoming authoritative and dominating – moving against group and fellow organization members. Individuals with these personal tendencies are, however, also often seen by others as stepping forward to take charge fulfilling their personal needs to feel protected and having their dependency needs met. This defensive psychosocial outcome creates a self-fulfilling dynamic where the leader feels empowered by many who are willing to follow and submit to an authority figure who takes charge and metaphorically takes no prisoners to create hope for stress-reducing change.

IN CONCLUSION

The psychosocially defensive responses, when used to inspect the self-experience of individual organization members during stressful times, inform understanding what is going on at a personal level. Organizational members, depending on the quality of their sense of self, may respond to stressful events by relying on deeply personal and familiar defensive tendencies that, for example, may include taking charge of situations that are felt to be out of control or conversely seeking to have their security needs met by embracing a take charge, autocratic and authoritative leader. These life-long psychosocially defensive strategies are how we know and understand ourselves – who we are and what our responses are to stressful workplace experiences. These defensive individual responses are also often relied upon by others and may become shared among organization members who feel that they are together in their leaky boat. This shared tendency creates an interpersonal, group, and organizational psychosocially defensive cultural response to stressful times that becomes the basis for organizational dysfunctions such as moving against, toward, and away from organization members and those in management positions.

Based upon these defensive individual, leader, and organizational dynamics, several organizational outcomes may arise. Some of these are as follows:

- Organizations can be expected to be top-heavy with those who consistently rely on autocratic and authoritarian defensive tendencies to take charge during stressful times combined with a willingness to do whatever is needed to neutralize threats – winning at any cost.
- Organization members may resist organizational change because it is stressful and can evoke shared psychosocial defenses.
- Organizations that have members who have "selected in" tend to rely on organizationally compatible psychosocially defensive tendencies that become part of the culture. The organization may, for example, be observed to have a lot of interpersonal competition and movements against others aimed at personal gain and self-aggrandizement. There may also be an abundance of people who rely on moving toward those in leadership roles seeking dependency and some may move away withdrawing from active participation to

avoid feeling dominated, manipulated, and micromanaged by those in positions of power and authority. And those who have adequate self-integration may experience the organizational landscape and its culture as hostile, competitive, rule-bound, marginally productive, and unrewarding.

• There is always the option of "selecting out" of the organization where organization members leave for positions in other organizations. Selecting in and out tends to gradually create a cadre of organization members who are left who are compatible with and supportive of the toxic leadership and dysfunctional organizational culture. They are all joined together.

In sum, the individualized psychosocial framework of this chapter depicts a situation that often "fits" with the personal experience of working within a large complex organization. It provides a conceptual framework for understanding human behavior at work. Better appreciating individual, interpersonal, group, and organizational dynamics is a fundamentally important knowledge base for improving our lives at work and the performance of our organizations.

Part 3 continues this work of better understanding toxic leadership and psychosocially defensive dysfunctional organizational dynamics. The chapters provide insights into how to not only avoid but also repair dysfunctional organizations.

Part 3

Organizational Healing

Parts 1 and 2 have provided insights into the darker side of organizational life. Destructive oppression and narcissism on the part of toxic leaders result in dysfunctional organizations. The development of individual, interpersonal, group, and organizational fragmentation pits organization members against each other reducing voluntary coordination and cooperation as well as the quality of work life. Organizational dynamics like these present organizational leaders and members challenging opportunities to avoid them. But when they do develop, there are ways to help organizations recover from toxic leaders and dysfunctional organizational dynamics.

Part 3 provides a framework for understanding how bureaucratic hierarchical organizational roles contribute to leader toxicity and organizational fragmentation. Organizational role structure enables toxic leaders who tend to be selected for powerful hierarchical roles. These often-narcissistic leaders dominate organizations and their members to meet pressing personal needs to feel admired, strong, powerful, and in control. The framework of psychosocial defenses provides a way to diagnose dysfunctional organizational dynamics and how intentional leaders, organization members, and organizational consultants can facilitate organizational change and healing.

DOI: 10.4324/9781003464464-12

Healing may seem like a strange word to use relative to toxic leadership and dysfunctional organizational dynamics. However, abusive, disruptive, autocratic, toxic leaders and the accompanying oppressive dysfunctional organizational cultures that they generate are distressing workplace experiences for organization members. They may rely on psychosocially defensive coping strategies to deal with the threatening, stressful, anxiety-ridden personal, interpersonal, group, and organizational dynamics that are fragmenting.

Responding to these dysfunctional organizational dynamics, when they are too threatening to be addressed by organization members, may require engaging an external consultant to study the underlying elements of the cultural dysfunctions. Consultants who encourage organization members to acknowledge the stressful dysfunctions must provide an open, inclusive, and transparent setting to begin to locate responses that are healing for the organization and its members.

Better yet is avoiding these toxic, harmful, and dysfunctional outcomes by adopting a leadership style that is both healing and restores organizational performance turning it into a good place to work. Intentional leadership can do this, but this requires locating what it really takes to be an intentional leader discussed in Chapter 14.

Part 3 concludes by looking backward over the journey taken in the book and looking ahead as to how what has been covered can be utilized by boards, leaders, and organization members to make their organization high-performing and a good place to work.

10

The Psychosocial Dimensions of Roles in Organizations

The interpersonal world at work is more complex than meets the eye. Two people at work, let us say a manager and an organization member who works in the manager's specialized silo, each have designated roles based on position descriptions. These roles are part of a hierarchy of roles with the chief executive officer (CEO) at the top that ideally have position descriptions that explain role performance expectations and preferred role-to-role interactions. These roles, however, may not always or often be clearly described and role performances may become modified by those in the roles to meet personal needs and to respond to changing organizational necessities. Over time these "drifts" in the roles can become accepted as the way "I" work, and how "we" accomplish working together. In sum, regardless of how clear the role descriptions are, they are occupied by human beings who bring themselves, their life histories, their skills, and knowledge to work. Organization members have personal preferences and behavioral tendencies that include functional and less than functional elements that are played out in their roles. These preferences include, as in the previous chapters, reliance on psychosocial defenses that can become dysfunctional.

So, what is really going on in organizations? This chapter explores workplace roles inhabited by people who invariably experience the stresses and strains linked to their jobs and their membership in groups and their organizations. The accompanying anxieties are coped with by relying on psychosocial defenses unique to each individual but also shared by and with others. These out of immediate awareness and hard to discuss defenses help us to control our experience of our daily work lives to make them less stressful. These defensive responses, however, create organizational

DOI: 10.4324/9781003464464-13

dysfunctions that can be confusing to individuals and pit organization members against each other compromising organizational performance.

In sum, the pursuit of control over our lives at work leads to managing stress by relying on defensive work and role-related individual and interpersonal dynamics that may become dysfunctional and compromise individual, group, and organizational performance. Better understanding these psychosocially defensive role enactments is the focus of this chapter.

WORKING WITHIN LARGE COMPLEX HIERARCHICAL ORGANIZATIONS

All kinds of organizations, especially large complex organizations, have many challenges to master that are associated with coordinating work among their members, and the hierarchical layers and siloed divisions. This challenge has historically been addressed by relying on bureaucracy to create institutionalized control. This approach to management has worked well over the millennia; however, bureaucracy also introduces dysfunctional organizational dynamics that are frustrating to deal with. Bureaucracies are not always well run by those in management roles, and this introduces frustrating, stressful, and sometimes threatening experiences for organization members to cope with. This appreciation suggests this hierarchical organization design may not be so logical and thoughtful in practice. Role-based performance limiting and distressing dysfunctional individual, group, and leadership dynamics can lead to compromising our organizations and their ability to effectively respond on a timely basis when they are confronted with demands to be innovative and productive to achieve success in the twenty-first century. Traditional management perspectives such as span of control and centralized versus decentralized organization designs must also include a greater awareness of the effects of toxic leaders and dysfunctional rigid organizational cultures. Better appreciating human behavior in our organizations must include considering that roles may have psychosocially defensive elements that reduce our experience of stress and anxiety. In particular, it is important to consider overt and covert role performances opening the door to considering their psychosocially defensive uses.

Overt Assigned Roles

Overt assigned roles are defined by job descriptions. The descriptions ideally provide for predictable thoughtful and logically designed patterns of individual and group behavior that regulate role-to-role individual and group interactions to optimize performance. An individual who acts *out of role* can be expected to attract attention. For example, a Vice President (VP) of a major operating silo may spontaneously decide to walk through a department in a different silo visiting with workers having never done this before. This visit may well be greeted with suspicion, skepticism, and defensiveness. No one wants this executive to show up like this unexpectedly. In this example, the VP has acted out of role by visiting organization members not a part of the VP's role responsibilities disrupting their sense of safety and security by the unpredictable behavior.

It is also important to appreciate that it is logically impossible to create job descriptions that apply equally well everywhere all the time. Those in organizational roles should ideally intentionally adapt themselves and their role as needed to respond to unpredictable organizational events and change to avoid disruptive uses as psychosocial defenses. This process of adaption during uncertain stressful times leads organization members to informally (covertly) modify their roles.

Covert Assumed Roles

Covert roles are a part of daily work life. They serve important adaptive purposes but also psychosocially defensive purposes by reducing uncertainty especially if overt roles have failed to regulate interpersonal and role-to-role interactions. Covert assumed roles (acting out of role) however can attract positive or negative attention and may be accepted by others or not. Covert role performances are also seldom formally acknowledged because this would be potentially threatening and confusing and introduce conflict among organization members.

For example, a new organization member is hired who formally worked for a supervisor who micromanaged the person's work stripping away feelings of being competent. The new supervisor's leadership style, in contrast, is open, inclusive, trusting, and respectful, and work is delegated with the expectation that organization members will independently pursue their work. This amounts to new role expectations for the new organization member. However, the response, in this case of delegation, may be for the individual to frequently discuss decision-making with the supervisor seeking approval before acting. Work products may also be presented for review consistent with the past role of subordination to a micromanaging supervisor. This past micromanaged role, in this case, is being informally and covertly imposed on the new supervisor to avoid feeling at risk of being criticized. In response, the supervisor may become aware of the resistance to the individual assuming personal responsibility and of being subjected to manipulation and closely supervising the new member's decisions and work. In this example, the supervisor may also not exactly be sure how to approach this problem without threatening the new organization member over not acting with more autonomy. These are some of the challenges of covert role-to-role interactions.

This example illustrates the subtle coercive nature of covert role performances. The overt role fails to meet the person's need for security to avoid feelings of uncertainty about being authorized to act and whether approval will be forthcoming. This has led to trying to impose a covert dependent role on the supervisor to avoid assuming personal responsibility. The new organization member finds it difficult to discuss expectations about how role-to-role, work, and interpersonal relationships should be structured and makes the expectations known indirectly. The supervisor gradually becomes aware of the imposition of these covert role expectations that are inconsistent with the preferred overt role description that includes expectations that responsibility will be assumed for the delegated work. This conflict is not open to being comfortably discussed, which makes ongoing coaching seem to be in order to allow the new organization member to gradually accept the new role expectations.

And to be noted is that the success of indirect approaches to assuming a covert role depends on other organization members making sense of the subtle forms of communication. The dependency on the supervisor to approve decisions and work is a form of messaging that may lead to only partial success and sometimes failure to assume a preferred covert role. If failure or partial success is the outcome, greater efforts may be made to assume the covert role. These efforts may, however, contribute to creating role-to-role uncertainty and stress relative to others who may cope with these efforts to impose covert roles on them by relying on psychosocial defenses and moving against or away from their new organization member.

USING ROLES TO CONTROL STRESSFUL WORK EXPERIENCE

Understanding our lives at work requires inspecting the underlying nature of bureaucratic organizations that have elements that facilitate psychosocially defensive responses to stressful work experiences. Organizational structure, when used as a defensive response to stressful losses of control and predictability, compromises the intended logic of coordinated role and position descriptions to achieve efficiency and effectiveness. For example, changes in leadership or organizational restructuring and downsizing are stressful disruptions to the predictability provided by familiar assumed or assigned roles.

Assigned overt roles and their job descriptions that are logically arrayed in the hierarchical chart of the organization ideally provide personal security and stress-reducing vertical coordination among the layers and horizontal coordination among the specialized silos. Rigid reliance on organizational roles and structure can, however, become dysfunctional as can the assumption of covert roles that are hard to know, ever-changing, and may be psychosocially defensive. In sum, the logical hierarchical and horizontal organizational structure of prescribed positions and roles and the assumed covert roles can both be used for psychosocially defense purposes. This makes effectively leading and managing an organization's members a challenge best met by unpacking this complexity.

The Positional Dimension of Bureaucracy

Bureaucracies are a hierarchical form of organizational design with positions reporting upward to one person at the top, a director, president, CEO, or owner, and this can promote defensive individual, interpersonal, and group psychosocial dynamics that may take many forms. These dynamics are associated with the simultaneous presence for those managers in the middle of the hierarchy of reporting upward to superiors and managing downward relative to subordinates or relative colleagues. This hierarchical context introduces the potential for conflict around who has power and authority in a given instance and how it is to be used by those in the roles that have it. Related questions are who is in charge, who will assume responsibility (or not) for a given situation, and whether the actions taken are or are not consistent with the duties that come with position's description and role in the hierarchy. The answers to these questions are important in that being expected to accept the authority of others depends on whether their formal overt role and job description authorizes them to make requests and give orders or whether the authority is being informally and covertly assumed. In the latter case, it may be felt that "I" am being subjected to inappropriate expectations held by an individual who has self-assumed authority. This can readily lead to defensively resisting and questioning the assumed authority creating dysfunctional interpersonal dynamics.

Resistant psychosocially defensive dynamics like these lead to conflict and stress in working relationships. Who is authorized to say and do what and our own readiness to assume personal responsibility for our actions and decisions create uncertainty, stress, and hard-to-resolve conflict. Also, to be considered in bureaucratic hierarchies and especially governmental bureaucracies is that no one may seem to be in charge and responsible for making decisions or holding group members accountable. This is often the case when decisions are made that lead to less than satisfactory outcomes that are too often attributed to *them* or a designated scapegoat who is metaphorically thrown under the bus. It is also common for organization members to reduce position-based stress by manipulating others and information to achieve the right mix of both being a superior to lower-level positions and a subordinate to higher level positions. Minimizing this uncertainty can become an important covert goal.

In sum, bureaucratic hierarchies of positions, whether they are assumed or assigned (overt or covert), are an accepted part of organizational life that triggers anxieties about the exercise of power and authority and the risks of assuming personal responsibility.

Successfully managing these threats is made easier by understanding psychosocially defensive bureaucratic organizational dynamics.

PSYCHOSOCIALLY DEFENSIVE ROLE DYNAMICS

Organizational life can be stressful, especially for individuals who have propensities to feel threatened or personally offended by, for example, being closely supervised or questioned about a decision. Feeling stressed out for some organization members may result in relying on psychosocial defenses that compromise working with others. Defensive responses to stress may involve relying on familiar defensive role behaviors that resemble one or more of the following defensive tendencies. Roles are focused on in this discussion as a way to better understand human behavior in large complex hierarchical organizations. We all have roles at work and outside of work as well.

Moving Against Others – Aggression

Moving against others sometimes aggressively is enabled by the power and authority that resides in the vertical hierarchy of roles with each ascending layer having more power and authority. Everyone is familiar with this type of structure-based power and authority beginning in families. The implications for everyone are also familiar. Those who have powerful positions may control and dominate and if necessary aggress anyone who is resistant. My way or the highway is the applicable phrase. Those in leadership roles may move against members of their silo when perfection is lacking but also move against the leaders and members of other silos. This defensive and toxic process of moving against others creates hard-to-resolve conflict and losses of coordination introducing organizational fragmentation. Moving against others can also be expected to generate countermeasures (resistances).

Roles-to-role conflict is common in organizations where fulfilling the responsibilities of a role creates structural conflict with those in other roles who have different but overlapping responsibilities and goals. A Chief Financial Officer may, for example, arrogantly impose budget discipline to the point of oppressing organization members in silos that require budgeting flexibility to fulfill their role responsibilities.

Defensive and dysfunctional role dynamics like this also include personal propensities such as a narcissist in a powerful role readily feeling insulted – being thin-skinned. Striking back at offending others with aggressive, punishing, and vindictive actions is attention-getting. Psychosocially defensive outcomes like this are often the root cause of hard-to-resolve interpersonal conflict enabled by the hierarchy of roles of power and authority. Movements against others, especially those who have lower-ranking roles and less power and authority, can be depended on to create disruptions and casualties – winners and losers. These distressing outcomes may be ignored by looking away or accepted because doing something about them, it may be felt, is too threatening to contemplate due to the power and authority attached to the aggressive person's role and willingness to aggress and bully others. These toxic and dysfunctional role dynamics are regrettably common workplace experiences but not the only role-based dysfunctions.

Moving Away from Others – Retreat

Moving away from performing their role responsibilities and those of others during stressful times is common in organizations. Some organization members who have stressful jobs may retreat to only assuming responsibility for some of the responsibilities listed for their position. This defensive process makes life at work less risky, demanding, and stressful but also risks being held accountable for the covertly modified role performance that does not fulfill all of the role's responsibilities. Finding a flexible balance for this psychosocially defensive retreat is important if only to stay employed. One way to manage this is to depend on others to assume responsibility for some elements of the position's responsibilities. This can seem like meaningful delegation, but it is delegation with an ulterior motive – self-protection. This "delegation" may also be incentivized by the possibility of a promotion or raise for those who assume the responsibilities that shelter this individual from stress and anxiety.

Moving away also often happens when an individual in a role avoids superiors, subordinates, and colleagues in their roles. A superior who is disliked in role may be avoided as much as possible to limit role-to-role interactions. For example, a manager may avoid performance reviews and coaching subordinates, not be available to meet with superiors, and avoid responding to emails or phone calls. These retreats from assuming personal responsibility and relating to others can leave organization members wondering who is in charge.

In sum, retreating from role responsibilities and role-to-role interactions to defensively manage stress creates uncertainty for everyone else. These defensive dynamics can leave organization members wondering who is in charge. Organizational fragmentation may also be an implicit outcome of these defensive leadership and organizational dynamics that split organizations and groups apart as a result of retreating from working together.

Dependency

Feeling like you should be able to depend on others when needed is important. However, some individuals may seek dependency as their psychosocially defensive response to stressful situations. What are you going to do about this? Dependency as a defensive strategy reinforces feelings that you are less than able, capable, and effective in your role and that an oppressive organizational hierarchy may reinforce this self-experience. Dependence may especially be the case when relating to senior-level positions but also relative to anyone who is willing to assume personal responsibility. When someone does take charge, there is a willingness on the part of those seeking dependence to follow. This may include submitting to what might become oppressive autocratic and authoritarian leadership.

The dependency defensive strategy is accentuated by thinking the person who assumes the role of leadership has superior vision and skills as compared to everyone else accentuated by projection of self-competencies onto the leader. This encourages the leader to feel self-confident, powerful, authoritative, and in charge. It is also the case that if someone does not step forward to assume a role of leadership, those who rely on dependency are frequently willing to wait even when faced with obvious threats. Waiting, however, can eventually be hard to tolerate, motivating someone who feels overly anxious to accept a leadership role. Depending on the situation it may also be the case anyone who accepts the role of taking charge may find meeting the dependency needs of fellow organization members challenging. Marginal success and the holding of threatening expectations for dependent others to assume some personal responsibility for acting may evoke disappointment, rejection, and being replaced.

Hope and Freedom

Organization members may hold the hope a leader, a new idea, or a new strategy will resolve a stressful situation. Once again there is a sense of dependency, but it also includes a hope that the situation will be resolved preferably by taking as little stressful risk-taking action on their part as possible. Many may feel that dealing with it is above their pay grade and not part of the role's responsibilities – moving away. As a result, organization members stay focused on the hope for a better future and that a leader will be identified who resolves the stressful organizational problems without expecting them to assume too much responsibility for acting. However, if a leader expects organization members to assume too much responsibility for acting, this is experienced as oppressive, coercive, and limiting their personal autonomy and freedom. These leader expectations may then be passively or actively resisted.

What is being expected by their leader may also not be thought to be an empowerment invested in the person's overt role. Role-to-role conflict is common where personal freedoms are infringed upon across role and organizational boundaries. It may then be the case that the underlying hope is that it may be better that a leader is not located out of fear that the person will hold oppressive expectations for everyone to assume some risky personal responsibility for acting. Remaining free from performance expectations by others in their leadership roles is the goal. This defensive strategy may also be supported by hoping the distressing situation will get better on its own over time. Doing nothing may seem to be a good option.

Togetherness and Sameness

Being together in groups at work is an organizational cultural norm. Organization members identify with their group or team and its members and leader, and they also know who is not a member. These organization members have accepted their role in their group or silo of specialization. These roles may differ from each other but ideally they are logically structured and coordinated with everyone knowing what their job is and just as importantly what everyone else's job is. This level of transparency creates stress reducing coordination and cooperation. However, when stressful circumstances are encountered, role responsibilities can become challenging to fulfill and there may arise a psychosocially defensive response that seeks security from feeling merged with their colleagues to deal with an operating problem or organizational threat. This result is a familiar group-based defensive response to, for example, defend against toxic leadership, misaligned organizational resources, and threatening announcements such as downsizing and organizational restructuring. We are all in this together. Many, when confronted with organizational dynamics like this, seek the safety of being a group member. Everyone might be said to be alone-together in this psychosocially defensive response to a threatening workplace experience.

Being together and knowing we are all sharing the same experience is comforting. We are all in the same experiential boat. This sense of sameness reinforces interpersonal and role-to-role acceptance of coequality where few are willing to volunteer to self-differential to assume meaningful leadership even if their roles authorize providing direction. They move away from assuming their personal responsibility. There may also be a tacit understanding that accepting a covert role of leadership not authorized by the group is problematic. These group dynamics have the effect of compromising the ability to work together for lack of clear direction. This crowd-like experience where leadership is lacking and role-to-role coordination is compromised leads to personal, group, and organization fragmentation. We may be together, but we are also alone together in our shared experience metaphorically going down in the same boat together. Waiting, hoping, and doing nothing is implicitly accepted as the way to go.

In sum, organization members may avoid stress by retreating from stressful events and problem-solving by narrowly focusing on their work and being noncompetitive and nonthreatening relative to each other. Efforts to engage, motivate, supervise, and lead when organization members defensively withdrawal into role, togetherness, and sameness are rejected. If we are all together in this experience, none of us may be responsible for acting or leading. Being held accountable for fulfilling the responsibilities of their work roles is experienced as a coercive loss of personal autonomy and freedom and to be avoided. In sum, group and organization members have retreated to only doing the work of their often covertly redefined roles trying to avoid the stressful aspects of having to assume personal responsibility for acting.

Defensive Bureaucratic Control

Bureaucratic organization design that is the basis for most large organizations includes structured hierarchical roles with descending levels of power, control, and responsibility. These role-to-role interactions attract attention to which roles are authorized to do what relative to other roles as well as to the people who occupy them. Bureaucratic roles include individual and shared psychosocial dynamics that encourage the individuals in the roles to accept the roles and voluntarily submit to the hierarchical structure that ideally circumscribes the uses of role-based power and authority. Even though individuals fill the roles, the cultural expectation is that the role performances are impersonal, depersonalized, and designed to be well-controlled and coordinated. This "rational" structuring, it is hoped, will regulate role-to-role interactions minimizing conflict and stress. Losses of personal autonomy and self-identity are accepted to avoid feeling anxious about losses of organizational control and predictability, although the cost of stability and dependability often includes the proverbial performance-robbing "red tape" that can lead to stressful role-to-role interactions.

In sum, doing it by the book on the part of organization members by adhering to their respective roles and position descriptions is expected. This psychosocial defensive reliance on a carefully designed organizational structure has become a standard operating methodology. However, this defensive approach to managing stress also forms the basis for dysfunctional leadership and organizational dynamics that are usually addressed by "doubling down" on more bureaucratic control that can lead to toxic autocratic and authoritarian leadership.

Autocratic Authoritarian Control

Hierarchal organizations have individuals in roles of power and authority who may wish to autocratically impose their authority on those in roles below them in the hierarchy but also those in lateral roles and those above them in the hierarchy. Taking charge, being in control, dictating decisions, and micromanaging how work is performed as a psychosocial defense against stressful operating problems can readily become an oppressive experience for organization members that is resisted. These conflictual leader and group dynamics can result in a growing sense of unresolved conflict, loss of coordination and cooperation, and organizational fragmentation. Organization members may hope that their leaders can overcome the threatening problems and restore coordination but without holding expectations for organization members to assume personal responsibility for acting. This dependence on roles of leadership, however, encourages those in the roles of leadership to feel overly authoritative and empowered to dominate and control, perhaps also becoming less accountable for their decisions and actions. These losses of accountability may include distressing moral and ethical violations of accepted organizational and societal cultural norms and values that often make the headlines. These outcomes may then encourage organization members to retreat from and resist the autocratic authority figure(s) leading to punishing responses and continuing conflict and marginal organizational performance.

Marginal organizational outcomes created by toxic role performances by leaders result in unresolved interpersonal and role-to-role conflict and the continued presence of threatening and fragmenting organizational dynamics. The need for organization members to regain control and limit the toxic leadership may lead to the leader's gradual rejection – movements against and away. The hope may be that a new leader can be located to alleviate the distressing and threatening aspects of the organization's oppressive operating dysfunctions healing the organization.

In sum, roles in bureaucratic hierarchies can introduce exceptional levels of organizational dysfunction when those who occupy powerful roles rely on autocratic and authoritarian leadership styles to dominate organizational members. The resulting organizational culture becomes oppressive when roles of authority are weaponized by the individuals who occupy them. The result may be a movement against these leaders or retreat from them. The defensive directions of movement may add to a growing sense of organizational fragmentation. Life at work and our ability to work together may be felt to be falling apart when everyone is hiding from or resisting toxic leaders.

The Intentional Workplace

Organizational roles arrayed in a hierarchy that have accepted expectations for role performance by those in the roles leads to fewer defensive individual and group dynamics allowing for voluntary coordination and cooperation. When organization members are valued and respected, this facilitates the development of the intentional workplace. An organizational culture that is reflective and intentional makes it easier to deal with organizational threats and operating problems. Retreats to dysfunctional psychosocially defensive responses are avoided. Organization members who understand their roles and those of others and identify their self-interest with their group's and organization's purposes and goals create well-functioning organizational cultures. There exists a mutuality of understanding, cooperation, and coordination and a non-defensive willingness to evaluate personal and leader assumptions and decisions openly and inclusively. Outcomes of decisions and actions are evaluated to promote learning from experience to better achieve individual, group, and organizational goals. A balance is maintained between individual role autonomy and being overly dependent on leaders. Tendencies to overidentify with each other and merging into togetherness that compromises role-to-role performance are avoided.

In sum, losses of reflectivity, critical thinking, and individuality are minimized if not avoided. Maintaining these functional role-to-role dynamics is, however, a challenge especially when work experience becomes stressful as may be the case with the hiring of a toxic leader who compromises feeling valued, respected, and safe. This proviso suggests developing and maintaining an intentional workplace is challenging during stressful times.

Defensive Roles – In Sum

Defensive role enactments are relied upon individually but also can become a shared organizational dynamic. They may also be combined or relied on sequentially such as first retreating and then aggressing back. Defensive role enactments detract from organizational performance. They, however, help organization members to cope with distressing thoughts and feelings arising from toxic leadership and dysfunctional organizational dynamics but also introduce hard-to-resolve conflict and fragmentation that compromise organizational performance. The defensive framework in Chapter 2, when it is used to examine hard-to-understand workplace role enactments, provides actionable insights for managing psychosocially defensive role uses, opening the door to more effectively managing and working within our organizations.

HOW TO USE DEFENSIVE ROLE PERSPECTIVES IN MANAGEMENT ROLES

Everyone in organizations assumes assigned roles. The most prominent roles are those at the top of the hierarchy that have substantial power and authority invested in their roles that may then be used in many ways. The above-mentioned framework makes clear that understanding management role performances must consider the diversity of human nature and different organizational histories and cultures. This is challenging, but the insights provided in this chapter encourage understanding how, in practice, management role performances affect organization members in their roles.

For example, an executive, when confronted with a stressful organizational event, may decide the response should be a *good offense* to attack the problem. Work becomes focused on taking aggressive action to overcome the problem or threat and this may include defeating an opposing manager or siloed group such as might occur between manufacturing relative to marketing's unrealistic expectations for developing innovative products. This focus on acting may result in those who suggest alternate approaches being ignored, rejected, or attacked. The leader in this example may aggressively press organization members to achieve higher levels of performance, and this can lead to resistance that may then be suppressed by the leader's bullying and intimidation. These movements against operating threats and problems and their root causes are accentuated by tendencies for organization members to increase their dependency on their leader to act. This defensive dependency and submissive-oriented strategy by organization members encourage the leader to feel empowered to do whatever it takes to respond to attack the problem. A focus on being led to take aggressive action can be expected to unite organization members in feeling together in responding to a common enemy or problem motivating them to achieve at a higher level.

However, the leader's aggression may also be directed at group or organization members. They may be blamed for the threatening operating problems because they failed to measure up and fulfill their assigned roles. These stressful leadership dynamics may then readily encourage defensive retreats into roles, offices, or cubicles to avoid being blamed and aggressed. However, moving away from the leader may attract the leader's attention leading to more stressful role-to-role conflict where there will be only one winner. And to be noted is that those who retreat from this organizational battlefield may also set themselves up to be blamed by their toxic leader if success is not achieved.

In sum, toxic leaders introduce into groups and organizations a number of dysfunctional dynamics. Aggressive leaders who rely on the power and authority of the role may also covertly expand uses of their power and authority beyond that originally assigned to their positions evoking resistance. They may also avoid threatening criticism and role-to-role influences by those in higher-level roles who are felt to be invasive, threatening, and coercive. Toxic leaders who encounter few resistances may also readily come to feel that there are few limits on what actions may be considered acceptable. This sense of freedom to act enables the pursuit of perfecting control over the operating problem by relying on autocratic uses of power and authority backed up by a willingness to attack anyone who resists. This leadership tendency may also include oppressive and threatening "hands-on" micromanaging control over work further introducing organizational conflict and dysfunctions. For example, organizational leaders below the CEO may be ordered to do something that is thought to be ill-conceived and is defensively resisted by not acting on or "slow walking" the instructions. This resistance may, however, attract the CEO's attention leading to an aggressive pursuit of personal accountability creating conflict within the management hierarchy that is hard to resolve. Observers of these organizational dynamics may wonder what just happened.

Who Is in Charge?

Thus far, the management role examples have highlighted their problematic nature within organizational hierarchies. If the organizational circumstance contains uncertainty that requires leadership, the question may be who is in charge. For example, for those who are trapped in a metaphoric stalled organizational elevator, the question arises as to who will do what. Who is authorized by their role inside of the elevator to take charge? There is an immediate assessment by everyone in the elevator about organizational roles and who occupies them. Someone may step forward who has a leadership role and if not someone in the group who is confident of being able to lead may step forward. The question, however, is whether those present will follow either leader? Will some in the group move against or away from their potential leaders if there is no clear hierarchy of organizational roles?

This uncertainty about who is going to do what and who is in charge is aggravated by the stressful context. In an organizational context like this when a manager is present, the manager's level of authorization to make decisions may not be agreed to by organization members and they may not be willing to follow the leader's directions. The acceptance of this leader as being effective and worthy of being followed may be further compromised by the knowledge that the leader has not avoided the problem or effectively responded to it on a timely basis. As a result, new covert role relationships may be worked out to respond to the problem. This type of restructuring of roles is often based on the perceived competence of those holding the roles and this is seldom openly acknowledged or discussed, especially during stressful times. As a result, these leader and group dynamics are often dealt with by using covert interpersonal pressures and group influence. The question becomes who other than the apparent leader might successfully meet the dependency needs of organization members to safeguard them, their group, and the organization from threatening problems. Who will press the emergency button in the elevator?

The Subtleties of Interpreting Workplace Role Behavior

Everyone in management roles has preferred ways as to how organization members should work. When these preferences are not met, managers may rely on subtle ways to communicate this other than openly and perhaps judgmentally speaking to a performance expectation gap. Managers may covertly signal dissatisfaction with body language, facial expressions, eye movements, and indirect uses of language to avoid the stress of directly confronting organization members up and down the hierarchy. For example, a supervisor may visibly act uncomfortably when organization members are indifferent to accomplishing the work being requested. However, relying on subtle forms of communication may leave group members feeling uncertain about what exactly is being communicated. The ambiguity may leave group members wondering what just happened and uncertain as to who will do what and when to respond to the performance gap or problem at hand. If the covert messaging is accurately received, the manager may then appear to be less distressed hoping everyone will find a way to respond to the expectation gap.

In the elevator example, someone may assume a role of a leadership and step forward to take charge of the situation. Should another person also offer leadership this individual's efforts may be ignored or minimally acknowledged becoming a subtle form of communication of rejection. In organizations when there is uncertainty over "management turf" those in one area who feel authorized by their roles may try to assume responsibility and control over decision-making and move against anyone else trying to take charge. This can result in disruptive if not destructive role-to-role conflict (Who is in charge?) and interpersonal competition that can make taking coordinated action to accomplish work a secondary goal.

This conflict may have the outcome of individuals seeking to have their personal safety and security needs covertly met with the result that everyone may seem to be working together separately creating organizational fragmentation.

These competitive if not combative interpersonal and role-to-role organizational dynamics add more dysfunctions to an already stressful situation. Even if much of this conflict is played out in subtle less direct ways, many organization members may feel the pressure to do something productive to keep organizational performance from getting worse. There may also emerge on the part of some members, who strongly feel action needs to be taken when leadership is not being provided, the necessity of taking charge themselves to deal with the threat. This assumption of a covert role of leadership like this may be accepted by organization members in the hope that it will restore predictable workplace experience. Will someone just please press the elevator's emergency button?

In sum, disruptions like these are stressful and trigger reliance on psychosocial defenses that evoke undercurrents of interpersonal influence and manipulation to influence organizational dynamics. The framework of psychosocial defenses offers a way to understand these types of stressful organizational dynamics and respond to them.

IN SUM, THE FRAMEWORK OF DEFENSIVE STRATEGIES

Organization members who remain reflective and thoughtful during stressful times should be able to take corrective action using the psychosocial defensive framework. These defensive tendencies and the intentional strategy are ways of thinking about workplace experience that can contribute to containing stressful and toxic leadership and dysfunctional organizational dynamics enabled by bureaucratic organizational designs with their hierarchy of roles that may be used defensively.

Organizational roles, as discussed, can serve personal defensive and adaptive needs. Assigned overt roles when paired with detailed job descriptions make clear what the organizational and senior leaders' workplace expectations are. However, during stressful times, when psychosocial defenses emerge, less well-understood, conflicting, and unpredictable covert roles develop to meet personal needs for safety and security.

And, during periods of major change such as restructuring or downsizing, overt and covert roles can become compromised creating stressful losses of familiar and predictable ways of working together. These losses can be avoided by non-defensively recognizing for discussing toxic leadership and dysfunctional organizational dynamics, with a focus on restoring an intentional and less psychosocially defensive organizational culture that restores predictable role performances.

IN CONCLUSION

Better understanding the psychosocial dimensions of roles in our hierarchical organizations informs more intentionally managing individual, group, and organizational dynamics to promote feelings of safety and security. And to be expected during stressful times is that toxic leadership and dysfunctional organizational dynamics encourage organization members to rely on the role-based psychosocial defensive framework outlined in this chapter to help them cope with their stressful work lives.

Chapter 11 continues this insight building for more effectively managing toxic leaders and dysfunctional organizational dynamics by exploring the contribution that narcissism makes to creating toxic leaders and interpersonal and group dynamics.

11

Diagnosing Organizational Narcissism

The use of psychosocial theory to study human behavior in organizations offers a way to understand complex organizational dynamics including providing a framework to understand leader and organizational narcissism informed by the three defensive directions of movement described in Chapter 2. A four-part framework will explore how organization members and consultants can make interventions to deal with toxic narcissistic leaders and organization members to minimize the organizational dysfunctions that flow from their behavior.

CONTEXT SETTING

An important aspect of human nature is our experience of ourselves. The experience of "self" begins at infancy and becomes who we are which may be someone who is a self-aware and self-confident individual or a less integrated and self-confident person who relies on psychosocially defensive responses to cope with stressful relationships and organizational situations. In the first case, successful self-development is contributed to by good enough parenting. In the second case, personal development is compromised by life experience that leads to the development of life-long dysfunctional self-awareness that includes the forms of narcissism to be discussed.

Examples of these personal and interpersonal narcissistically based dysfunctions are abundant. For example, everyone seeks to fulfill personal needs for attachment and approval. However, if these human needs are compelling and remain unfulfilled they may be responded to defensively by moving toward, away from, and against others. Moving toward others

   DOI: 10.4324/9781003464464-14

includes submitting to others to maintain attachment. This is true in dysfunctional families where attachments are problematic and abusive, and it is true in organizations leading to sycophancy. Avoidance of others and abandonment of achieving meaningful attachment, moving away from others, may also arise. Feelings of not being worthy of receiving enduring, meaningful, and secure attachments can lead to abandoning the hope of achieving these attachments and approval. These feelings of unworthiness can also lead to moving against others aggressively because it is felt there is little to be lost. This interpersonal as well as intergroup aggression can lead to hard-to-resolve conflict that compromises voluntary cooperation and coordination of work promoting organizational fragmentation. These three examples based on less-than-satisfactory self-experience and self-centered responses to the interpersonal world at work form the basis of this chapter.

Everything that happens to or around these narcissistic organization members (or group dynamics) is evaluated in terms of managing this vulnerable self-experience. These three psychosocial defensive directions of movement are used to inform the narcissistic types to be discussed that adversely affect others, groups, and organizations. Making sense of hard-to-understand, unrewarding, and threatening lived experiences in our jobs and organizations when narcissistic leaders are at work can be challenging.

AN OVERVIEW OF NARCISSISM

Narcissism is usually discussed from several perspectives ranging from being studied as part of normal development and as a psychosocial defense. The following overview of narcissism draws upon these perspectives that share much in common.

The Elements of Narcissism

Narcissism is a disturbance usually associated with problematic parenting and early life relationships that create feelings of not being accepted. There is a lack of secure meaningful attachments. This dysfunctional parenting may include being dominating, overprotective, intimidating, overindulgent, erratic, and being partial to others (favorites). There is usually a constellation of these influences at play. These aversive parenting experiences lead to anxiety-ridden insecurities and reliance on psychosocial defenses that further compromise self-experience and relating to others making it challenging to understand narcissistic dysfunctions.

In contrast, positive and good enough parenting leads to feeling safe, secure, and accepted. There develop a balanced and authentic sense of self-interest in relating to others who are accepted as having their own interests. Working together is, therefore, not contaminated by interpersonal agendas of being approved of, liked, and admired.

With this context in mind, a more detailed definition of narcissism is provided to begin developing our understanding of toxic narcissistic leaders and organization members and the dysfunctional organizational dynamics that they create.

Defining Narcissism

The attributes listed emphasize the diversity and complexity of understanding narcissism as a psychosocial defense.

- There is a focus on self-promotion as well as sensitivity to being criticized or rejected.
- These individuals lack authentic emotions and are not loyal to others but expect others to be admiring and loyal despite the presence of distressingly abusive behavior.
- Approval may be sought from envied and idealized others, and those whose approval is not sought after are denigrated.
- Anger may arise that is hard for others to respond to and sooth especially when the anger is experienced as being out of control sometimes referred to as narcissistic rage.
- Grandiosity and self-importance compensate for not having been accepted and this fuels feeling powerful, brilliant, special, and unique.
- Feelings of being personally entitled result in interpersonal exploitation, manipulation, and deception of others for self-serving purposes and without feeling guilty.
- Shame, however, may be felt but only for being weak which has been compensated for by being aggressive, dominating, and arrogant.

Combinations and degrees of presence of these attributes are to be expected, and this highlights the complexities of understanding narcissistic leaders and organization members who may act in many different ways creating a wide variety of toxic dysfunctional workplace outcomes. This toxicity may include moving against, toward, and away from organization members and, depending on the context, these directions of movement may be experienced as threatening and distressing by organization members. And to be noted, one of these defensive directions of movement may be more consistently relied upon although the other two always remain available if the first direction of movement does not reduce the unrewarding experience of relating to organization members.

Moving against others by rebelling and fighting back against those who are felt to be withholding approval, not available for secure attachment, and critical and threatening is common in organizations. These personal insults and threats may be defended against by those in positions of power and authority by arrogantly aggressing organization members. However, narcissists who identifying with an expansive and glorified sense of self paradoxically magnify their vulnerability of not being proportionately admired by organization members. The result can be hyper-vigilance that spots the slightest hints of criticism or disloyalty. These readily perceived threats require using the power and authority of hierarchical roles to bring the offending others into line. This interpersonal fragility, fragile ego, and narcissistic "house of cards," must be continually defended. Failures to protect the expansive "me first" self-experience may evoke detested feelings of weakness, unworthiness, and helplessness. Being personally reflective and insightful is not part of this dynamic.

In sum, psychosocially defensive narcissism that arises from inadequate parenting and unfulfilling early life experiences contributes to the development of a personality dominated by defensive self-absorbed character traits. This appreciation is highlighted throughout this chapter.

THE PRESENCE OF WORKPLACE NARCISSISM

Toxic and dysfunctional narcissism takes many forms in our organizations. The following discussion "frames up" understanding narcissism at work and how to respond to its presence. To begin, normal narcissism is considered to contrast it with toxic narcissism.

Normal Narcissism

Normal narcissism refers to feelings and attitudes that balance our feelings of separateness, pride, belongingness, gratitude, and concern for others. This level of personal development allows for comfortably being ourselves while relating to others neither dominating, submitting, or avoiding them. This balanced interpersonal world includes reasonable (not overdetermined) expectations that others will be suitably supportive and that there is a comfort level for speaking out when interpersonal issues do develop.

Healthy narcissism includes empathy for others and personal control over our thoughts, feelings, and actions allowing for the successful navigation of the interpersonal world and life in groups and organizations. This contrasts to people who have overdetermined needs for approval and admiration but also do not feel that they are not entitled to receive them resulting in distressing feelings of being ignored, disregarded, and harmed requiring a response.

Healthy narcissism includes the following:

- A realistic understanding of our abilities and limitations.
- An ability to comfortably accept criticism and rejection as well as accepting approval and praise.
- Developing creative ideas and fantasies that motivate achievement.
- A balanced sense of entitlement relative to others including an intentional use of hierarchical power and authority that avoids being manipulative, aggressive, threatening, or punishing.
- Empathy, compassion, and mutuality allow for meaningfully embracing commitments to others.
- A willingness to accept decision-making risks and personal responsibility for achieving personal, group, and organizational goals.
- A heightened potential for providing thoughtful and assertive leadership.

These attributes of healthy narcissism are present in each of us some of the time depending on the context. They are also often observed to be present for those intentionally fulfilling leadership roles.

In sum, many people who are talented, intellectually gifted, and able to generate inspiring ideas are committed to fulfilling leadership roles. They have a willingness to be creative combined with the ability to assume the personal risks associated with assuming responsibility to accomplish work. They are also self-aware and others aware and do not overestimate the value of their contributions that would implicitly devalue the contributions of others. This balanced, insightful, and reflective form of leadership contributes to resolving organizational operating problems that call for creative solutions and problem-solving. However, also common in our organizations are the dysfunctional outcomes of excessive narcissism that compromise work experience and organizational performance.

EXCESSIVE NARCISSISM AT WORK

There are three types of dysfunctional narcissism that will be discussed – arrogant, dependent, and avoidant. These three directions of defensive movement contribute to understanding excessive self-centered narcissism and the interpersonal, group, and organizational dysfunctions it creates. The three directions highlight, while arrogant narcissism is common, feelings of being entitled to be taken care of or left alone may also be frequently observed.

Arrogant Narcissism

Arrogant narcissism is a toxic presence in our organizations that may be a familiar experience. Arrogant narcissism includes:

- Grandiosity, arrogance, entitlement, and an overbearing perfectionistic attitude along with being "thinned skinned" and easily offended resulting in an uninhibited willingness to aggressively vindicate the offenses.
- Feelings of anger, shame, and envy are readily felt and energize excessive responses to perceived personal injuries but may also result in mood swings such as being depressed, irritable, and elated.
- Feeling entitled to receive approval, admiration, and loyalty that maintains an expansive sense of self.
- Impaired empathy and an underlying lack of commitment to organization members who are viewed instrumentally and transactionally for what they can provide the narcissist.

In sum, arrogant narcissism is associated with superiority, self-importance, and disdain for others who fail to measure up to the imposition of perfectionistic expectations. Admiration and attention are sought after by being boastful and generating grandiose ideas accompanied by aggressive pursuits of power and control to fulfill them. There is also present sensitivity to not being admired, approved of, and loyally followed that results in angry and unpredictable behavior and moving against and attacking those who are not thought to be loyal and admiring. In these instances, leaders who have powerful hierarchical positions often rely on bullying and threatening non-compliant organization members (moving against them) and they may gradually eliminate anyone who is not loyal and supportive. These aggressive leadership dynamics eventually create groups that have members who are admiring, supporting, and loyal to their leader.

Dependent Narcissism

The dependent narcissist is also a frequent defensive presence in organizations. Dependent narcissism includes:

- Being focused on receiving caretaking from others including receiving recognition and approval paired with feelings of being harmed and abandoned (victimization) if the caretaking is not good enough.
- Pursuing interpersonal control by imposing covert roles of dependency on others and by focusing on predictability and orderliness to limit stressful chaotic experiences.
- A willingness to submit to others as a "good person" and team player to receive positive attention and assurances that stressful workplace experiences will be managed by others.
- Feelings of being marginally competent, helpless, powerless, and unable to cope with workplace stresses that arise during stressful times.

In sum, the dependent narcissist is friendly and supportive of others and expects the same in return. Because these expectations are excessive, they can become oppressive and hard to manage by colleagues without feeling guilty. They may also feel that they are being manipulated. This interpersonal agenda is made clear when a dependent narcissist is a fellow group or organization member who invariably looks to others to take charge to avoid assuming personal responsibility for acting.

Avoidant Narcissism

This self-serving tendency is the opposite of the arrogant tendency. Feelings of arrogance and superiority are avoided by moving away from leadership roles and others who hold expectations for the assumption of personal responsibility for acting to respond to a stressful situation. Avoidant narcissism includes:

- Avoiding developing personal abilities and talents and appearing to be capable of acting – self-minimization.
- Feeling ashamed about having ambitious ideas out of fear of failing to fulfill them if imagined.
- A hypervigilance exists regarding being criticized and controlled leading to focusing on avoiding these aversive experiences and stressful performance expectations.
- Modesty, humbleness, and an unassuming attitude that reinforces feelings of not being entitled to be respected or admired.
- Inhibited interpersonal interactions that may include low affect and empathy – not a people person.

In sum, the avoidant narcissist can easily feel ashamed because of excessive self-criticism. They are their own worst enemy. Feeling competent and striving to achieve are avoided. This self-minimization is reinforced by feelings of deficiency and failure generated by holding an ideal of self-perfection that cannot be achieved. So why try? There is a preference for being left alone to work with little oversight, and supervision is experienced as oppressive and implicitly imposing offensive performance expectations.

A NOTE ON NARCISSISTIC ANGER

Narcissistic anger has an attention-getting lack of empathy and forgiveness. Grudges are held sometimes accompanied by revenge-taking by almost any means which can severely compromise interpersonal relationships as is often the case in autocratic and authoritarian organizational cultures. Typical behaviors include being manipulative and withholding praise, empathy, and comforting support and resources for others. Paradoxically feeling angry and acting aggressively, while obviously present and happening, may be denied (gaslighting) and even projected onto others.

In sum, retaliating against others is a defensive response that redirects outward (projects) feelings of anger relative to, for example, feelings of shame for not meeting self-expectations to be admired. Others are then known to be angry, deficient, and narcissists. This defensive dynamic regains control over self-experience, others, and the organization and wards off detested feelings of vulnerability, dependency, and defectiveness. Toxic leadership and dysfunctional group and organizational narcissistic cultures are the outcomes.

Narcissistic anger and aggressively moving against others to win at any cost to rectify narcissistic injuries can become a win-lose organizational culture that some organization members may selectively identify with allowing them to also act out their anger. However, the resulting culture of aggression and conflict may encourage organization members to move away from these distressing and toxic organizational dynamics and leave this interpersonal battlefield to feel free from coercive expectations to join in the aggression. And some may prefer to depend on other organization members whom they support to continue the fight on their behalf. These avoidant and dependent organization members, when confronted with toxic aggression-filled organizational dynamics, prefer to become witnesses to their own and the organization's fate. Toxic leadership and dysfunctional organizational dynamics usually ebb and flow in organizations remaining an ever-present threat when enemies threaten arrogant narcissistic leaders and supportive colleagues.

NARCISSISTIC ORGANIZATIONAL THEMES

Understanding organizational dynamics must include appreciating the narcissistic themes that shape our lives at work and become a part of organizational culture. This awareness provides insight into how to better manage, avoid, and repair the effects of toxic leadership and dysfunctional organizational dynamics. Better management begins with understanding how these dysfunctions spread within organizations.

Organizational Contagion

The use of the word contagion suggests that the development of shared interpersonal and group dynamics spreads invisibly in organizations like a communicable disease. Similarly, organizational narcissism is a self-perpetuating shared experience. For example, a narcissistic chief executive officer (CEO) who continually seeks admiration and loyalty from senior organization members encourages them to sacrifice their personal autonomy and self-worth to ensure their CEO feels admired and loyally supported. These personal compromises deplete their positive self-experiences creating narcissistic deficits. This may then encourage them to seek compensating support and loyalty from those around them (including at home) who may also then become depleted. This process creates a cycle of narcissistic deficits and compensation passed downward within the hierarchical organizational structure as well as across its silos.

In sum, psychosocially defensive interdependent relationships like this gradually spread the CEO's excessive narcissistic needs throughout an organization. Also, to be appreciated is that the CEO, by acting this way, implicitly "authorizes" others to act this way.

Dysfunctional organizational dynamics like this inform our understanding of how dysfunctional organizational cultures develop. The following checklists offer a framework for understanding narcissistic organizational dysfunctions.

BASIC NARCISSISTIC ORGANIZATIONAL ELEMENTS

- Organization leaders are experienced as being bigger than life.
- The organization and its leaders are promoted in the media to receive local and national attention and recognition.
- The organization, its accomplishments, and its future are described in visionary terms, and competitors and regulators are ignored and denigrated.
- Achieving grandiose ideas periodically creates marginal outcomes and failures that are ignored, covered up by scapegoating others or preempted by more big ideas.
- Organization members become split apart into those who are loyal supporters of the leader and those who are neutral or not supporters.

- Organization members idealize their leaders.
- Organizational resources such as promotions, compensation, and office space are used to reward supporters.
- Leaders are overly responsive to criticism of themselves, their followers, and their organization.
- Bad news may be ignored, and those surfacing organizational problems may be marginalized, scapegoated, or terminated for not being team players and not going along to get along.
- Customers and clients may not have their needs met and laws and ethics may be disregarded as needed by leaders and organization members to achieve their expansive goals.

In sum, these narcissistically based organizational elements may sound familiar having been ripped from the headlines. They apply equally well to organizations of all types and sizes as well as to nations that claim to be exceptional. Over time many organization members will identify with this organizational culture that encourages them to feel expansive about themselves and everyone else including their leaders and their organization. Their self-identity becomes linked to the narcissistic culture creating a shared experience of being together in accomplishing a grand vision. It may also be the case that those who do not identify with it have left to find other positions. Selecting out is a process that creates a more homogeneous organizational membership reinforcing feeling together in sharing the same grand experience.

These elements of dysfunctional organizational narcissism form the basis of the following checklists that highlight the defensive nature of the three forms of narcissism paired with the three directions of defensive movement for more insight building.

THE ARROGANT ORGANIZATIONAL DYSFUNCTION – MOVING AGAINST

- Organization leaders are proud of their organization and see few limitations on what can be accomplished.
- Organization leaders feel entitled to exploit others, customers, and the public good for their own and their organization's benefit.

- When achieving goals is frustrated organizational leaders respond by expending as much time, energy, and money as needed to defeat anyone, group, or an organization that is blocking achieving success.
- Non-supporters who do not identify with the arrogant culture are terminated, marginalized, transferred, or demoted and management by intimidation is common.
- Accurate reality testing is suppressed in favor of a preferred favorable flattering management narrative.
- Information is manipulated to glorify leaders and minimize threats to them, and it may also be hoped that operating problems will simply go away freeing everyone up from having to take risky corrective actions.
- Avoiding recognizing management decisions that have created organizational problems is important in terms of minimizing the blaming and scapegoating of organization members for problems created by their leaders.
- The organizational culture contains disorienting unpredictable elements such as successes being excessively celebrated followed by feelings of failure and despair over not achieving lesser goals.
- Organization members, as a defensive response to confusing, threatening, and sometimes oppressive organizational dynamics, may move away from their toxic self-absorbed leaders to avoid their dysfunctional leadership.
- Group dynamics may include polarized good versus bad views of each other and many in the organization's layers and silos leading to distressing and destructive internal competition and hard-to-resolve us versus them conflict.

In sum, this conflicted threatening authoritarian organizational culture contains arrogant and aggressive leaders who take unilateral autocratic action. This aggressive management culture also authorizes aggression on the part of organization members. The result is the splitting of the organization into groups with different values and subcultures and psychosocially defensive strategies. This fragmentation, fueled by unresolved conflict and operating problems, contributes to the feeling that the ability to work together and the organization is falling apart. Despite the apparent organizational dysfunctions that these self-absorbed, self-centered, arrogant, and autocratic leaders create, the response to threatening situations always seems to be the same, doubling down on the aggressive arrogant movement against anyone who gets in the way.

THE DEPENDENT ORGANIZATIONAL DYSFUNCTION – MOVING TOWARD

- Effective leadership may be absent because leaders avoid accepting role responsibilities in order to avoid risking not being liked and admired making it seem as though no one is in charge, especially during stressful times, although there may also be a hope that effective and consistent leadership will emerge.
- Feelings of helplessness and indifference about achieving group and organizational success lead to a lack of motivation on the part of organization members to accept potentially threatening personal responsibility to succeed.
- The status quo and mediocrity are accepted and lead to few being willing to assume responsibility for solving operating problems to avoid narcissistic injuries which is a dysfunctional organizational dynamic aggravated by some of the best people leaving – selecting out.
- There is a history of failures to effectively respond to crises and threats and take advantage of opportunities to succeed that contribute to a sense of vulnerable self-experience from the directionless, hopelessness and that failure is an option.
- Organization members who embrace self-centeredness believe success will eventually be achieved but without expending much effort to accomplish it.
- There may be a focus on being a team player and together in feeling vulnerable that discourages individuals and groups from trying to independently achieve success to avoid being targeted for aggression for being self-serving and not being coequal team members.
- There is an unwillingness to address performance issues based on an organizational history of double standards such as poor performers being promoted and rewarded for loyalty over competence.
- Pursuits of self-centeredness, perfection, and being in control may become the enemy of progress in that leaders avoid taking what they believe will be imperfect actions (analysis paralysis) that may threaten being admired and loyally followed.

- Dependency upon some who volunteer leadership may lead to them being destructively envied discouraging other organization members from volunteering leadership.

In sum, there is a stressful organizational malaise associated with unresolved operating problems and internal conflicts combined with a lack of effective and timely decision-making on the part of leaders who are focused on being liked and admired. Organization members feel that they share in the experience of these dysfunctional leadership and organizational dynamics and that they cannot do much about them. The status quo under these conditions provides comfort that reinforces the tendency to wait for new leaders to emerge who are not narcissistic. However, the hope remains that these new leaders will not hold expectations that these dependency-oriented organization members should assume stressful responsibility for acting to achieve organizational success.

THE AVOIDANT ORGANIZATIONAL DYSFUNCTION – MOVING AWAY

- Leaders and organization members are marginally invested in making the organization work better preferring to avoid accurate reality testing by embracing nonthreatening poorly informed and arrogantly speculative decision-making and actions.
- Organization members identify with a self-centered self-reliance and a culture of individuality even though at times it is clearly nonadaptive and splits organization members apart creating threatening dysfunctional organizational dynamics and fragmentation.
- There are present feelings of being victimized by leaders who are arrogant and coerce organization members into accepting responsibility for acting against internal and external threats.
- Individual achievement is emphasized to receive approval, and working together as a team is avoided because it compromises individual autonomy and self-serving pursuits.
- Recognizing threatening external influences is avoided because doing so may increase personal awareness of vulnerabilities that require autonomy stripping teamwork to create adaptive change.

- Doing nothing in response to operating problems and unresolved organizational conflicts is an option, and planning, goal setting, and achieving measurable operating objectives are felt to introduce coercive expectations that are to be avoided to maintain personal freedom.
- A nonthreatening status quo is preferred resulting in little initiative-taking and leadership to create needed changes.
- Organizational fragmentation that thwarts voluntary coordination is accepted to avoid threats to an expansive sense of self and losses of personal and group autonomy.
- Many organization members believe that someone (a new leader or consultant) will save the organization but without compromising their personal freedoms to do what they want.

In sum, this organizational cultural context includes members identifying with an autonomous individuality and working separately "together" which is becoming more common as technology facilitates working remotely either in the office or at home. These organizational dynamics are attention-getting and attract those who seek out a culture that allows them to maintain their narcissism by contributing autonomously. The pervasive sense of organizational fragmentation that develops is an inhibitor to anyone in a leadership role trying to draw organization members together to respond to opportunities and operating problems.

In sum, the thematic dysfunctional organizational dynamics discussed suggest that organizations will over time have some of these narcissistically based dysfunctional organizational cultures and subcultures. Also, important to consider is that these organizational dysfunctions are dynamic and although one type may rise to prominence more frequently the others remain available as defensive psychosocial possibilities. This makes keeping an open mind important in terms of understanding how to manage and change dysfunctional leadership and organizational dynamics.

ORGANIZATIONAL INTERVENTION CHALLENGES

Understanding the narcissistic organizational context sufficiently to place it into this framework is the first step in creating organizational change. Gathering the necessary information requires organizational leaders or consultants to be willing to pay attention to what they see and hear or do not to develop an overarching perspective of the unique nature of an organization's culture and its interpersonal and group dynamics. For new leaders and consultants interviewing and the use of focus groups should be considered for learning about what it is like to work here. This learning process combined with studying available quantitative organizational data that, while perhaps not timely, representative, and distortion-free, does provide insights into organizational performance using commonly available information about operations. What is being learned should preferably be open to discussion and confirmation with organization members. This diagnostic work should include:

- Developing an organization history that includes key events, growth rates, leadership style changes, and the experience of work across time that reveals how the organization's leadership, size, operations, and culture have changed.
- An orientation to the organization's work during a walk-thru informs the subsequent listening analysis.
- Information gathering should include acquiring the mission and values statements, planning, internal and external performance assessments, and audits and receiving a historical overview of organizational successes and failures, descriptions of current problems, and perceived strengths and weaknesses.
- Developing an understanding of member experiences of the organizational culture and dynamics provides a framework for appreciating the organization's past, present, and probable future.
- Capturing subjective impressions developed during this diagnostic process facilitates making sense of what has been learned that can be shared back to organizational leaders and members to validate everyone's understanding of the organization.

Members of narcissistically oriented organizations, however, may be invested in avoiding recognizing problems, especially those created by powerful self-absorbed autocratic leaders. These defensive dynamics when confronted promote anxiety and more reliance on accepted psychosocially defensive individual, group, and organizational dynamics (doubling down). In these instances, the prevalence of denial and poor reality testing can make organization members feel that failure is an option creating hopelessness and depressive withdrawal that encourages excessive dependence on idealized organizational leaders. This type of cultural context makes change from within the organization or change facilitated by external consultants a challenge in that cultures of narcissism can be depended upon to be aggressively defended to avoid the threats of powerful narcissistic leaders.

IN CONCLUSION

The narcissistic organizational disorders and their accompanying organizational dysfunctions that have been described provide a way to understand organization dynamics that can open the door to creating a safer and more fulfilling workplace that is inclusive, cooperative, and reflective. The work of developing and preserving organizational performance and a good enough work experience is a worthy challenge.

Chapter 12 continues the unpacking of toxic leadership and dysfunctional organization dynamics to meet the challenges of individual, group, and organizational change.

12

Understanding Dysfunctional Organizational Dynamics and Leadership

Human nature is the commonality that all organizations, groups, and leaders share. It can generate caring and enlightened interpersonal, group, organizational, and societal dynamics or as in Part 1 autocratic authoritarian oppression that harms people, groups, and organizations. These dark outcomes are attention-getting. This chapter applies the analytical framework in Chapter 2 to understand the dark side of human nature that contributes to autocratic authoritarian, oppressive, toxic leadership, and dysfunctional groups, organizational, and social dynamics.

The framework of organizational culture and organizational identity, the defensive directions of movement, and defensive group and organizational dynamics will be used again to unpack toxic and dysfunctional organizational experience. Three short case vignettes begin this chapter and will be analyzed to promote critical thinking about how to apply the defensive framework to understanding toxic leadership and dysfunctional organizational dynamics. The framework will be briefly explained again as a memory refresher before exploring what each contributes to understanding the leader and organizational dynamics in the cases.

INTRODUCTION TO THE CASE EXAMPLES

The cases are brief but provide the key elements necessary to understand common group and organizational dynamics that arise when toxic leaders create dysfunctional organizational dynamics. These examples may

DOI: 10.4324/9781003464464-15

be familiar to readers who work within hierarchical layers of power and authority in large organizations and within their specialized silos.

Case 1 – Is There a Leadership Problem?

A large complex organization has had frequent leadership changes over the past decade. These changes have created losses in leadership continuity and unresolved operating dysfunctions most of which have been created by these leaders. Several leaders provided little to no direction and several others introduced authoritarian and autocratic leadership styles demanding changes that served their self-interests. These ever-changing leadership dynamics created uncertainty about the organization's direction and well-being.

The turnover of leaders, some of whom have left shortly after starting to work for new higher-level positions in other organizations, has been accompanied by a growing number of unresolved operating problems and conflicts and this has raised the question for a local newspaper, "Is there a leadership problem?" Organization members have, however, stayed focused on their respective areas of responsibility, feeling that they together could master the operating challenges after being abandoned by their leaders. This "can do" organizational culture has encouraged everyone to take action individually and in their respective work groups to cope with the ever-evolving problematic aspects of maintaining organizational performance. However, unresolved operating problems have contributed to losses of longer-term organizational planning and there have been some compromises to cooperating and coordinating among the layers and silos creating organizational fragmentation. Working together seemed to be at times falling apart.

Case 2 – Regime Change

A vice president (VP) of operations has had exceptional control over all aspects of a thousand-employee and hundred-million-dollar organization. This level of control has led to losses of personal accountability as represented by some glaring examples of unethical self-serving behavior. No aspect of operations has been too small to ignore. Many organization members fear this executive who bullies, threatens, and intimidates anyone who resists being micromanaged. Survivors of this toxic leadership style who have not voluntarily left feeling exhausted, drained, and unsure of themselves. After many years, this VP is replaced and to everyone's dismay the new VP is a micromanager who relies on even more oppressive intimidation to crush resistance. Organization members have continued to feel dominated, oppressed, overcontrolled, and at risk of losing their jobs. They have, as a result, focused on avoiding being targeted. There are, however, prominent exceptions to these leadership dynamics. Those who "sucked up" to the new leader and became favorites received rewards for their loyalty. They also became a threat to the organization's members who feared that they might be reported to the VP for what they were thinking, saying, and doing that was resistant and nonconforming. These threatening dynamics contributed to splitting the organization members and the organization apart creating hard-to-manage organizational fragmentation.

Case 3 – Life in the Trenches

This local service organization collects and distributes biological products but has historically suffered from turnover in their leaders who have been recruited from within the organization. These new leaders who are healthcare professionals have been eager to improve operations, but they have lacked leadership and managerial skills. This has created a chaotic sense of top management. Given the leadership turnover, the marginal leadership skills, and the resulting chaos, it has been the organization members who have compensated by dealing with the resulting dysfunctional organizational dynamics. They and their specialized silo leaders have been committed to the organization's mission, and they have done what is necessary to keep the organization running even though this initiative taking has threatened the new leaders of the organization who feel that they should be in complete control. They have sometimes punished these threats to their status, power, and control.

The Cases – In Sum

These three cases of toxic leadership and organizational dynamics illustrate the often-distressing lived experience of organizational members who want to keep their jobs by trying to maintain organizational performance. These and many dynamics like them can be understood by using the framework of organizational culture, organizational identity, the defensive directions of movement, and the defensive group dynamics. These perspectives are overviewed before using them to analyze the three cases.

ORGANIZATIONAL CULTURE AND ORGANIZATIONAL IDENTITY

These two perspectives provide a framework for understanding the less visible side of organizational dynamics at both a global level of analysis, that of culture, and at an individualized level, how organizational members come to understand themselves and their lives and identity at work.

Organizational Culture

The idea that organizations have cultures is a way of understanding organizational life. Leaders play a key role in creating and managing organizational cultures that provide a framework that informs organization members how to respond to stressful changes in the workplace and external threats such as the actions of competitors and government regulators. What is found to work is logically retained, and this makes organizational performance and workplace experience more manageable. What has been learned from experience becomes a taken-for-granted way of thinking, feeling, and acting and an accepted, safe, and secure way of maintaining stable role-to-role and organizational performance. Organizations, even under the worst operating conditions, usually remain sufficiently cohesive, functional, and productive to survive. If the culture does become dysfunctional, leaders, as expected and hoped, help to guide organization members to learn new more adaptive cultural assumptions that hopefully avoid excessively stressful organizational dynamics that lead to relying on psychosocial defenses.

Changing organizational cultural elements, however, can be a slow process even when rammed through top-down by management. Autocratic change, however, increases the risk of evoking resistance to change because these unilateral actions are frequently threatening and alienate organization members. Human nature also suggests leaders may, in addition to acting with clear intentions, act to support their own self-interests by, for example, seeking to appear to be in charge by acting aggressively to impress board members and stockholders during stressful times.

It is also the case that many organizations in the twenty-first century are rapidly developed and scaled up. They cannot be expected to develop stable, familiar, and shared histories and cultures that provide accepted, predictable, routine operating methods and ways of thinking, feeling, and working together. Planned and unplanned leadership turnover in new organizations also contributes to losses of cultural continuity and a sense of organizational chaos. Who is in charge or just as often who is to be blamed?

Yet another consideration is that large organizations have leaders of specialized divisions and silos who create unique subcultures that may or may not be compatible with the larger organizational culture. These sub-cultures are common and have their own goals, language, and operating procedures. Organizations may then not be the sum of their parts. They often suffer from losses of internal integration that introduces fragmenta-tion and a sense that effectively working together has fallen apart. Losses of continuity in leadership, values, and tactics can have profound impacts because they contribute to solving the problem of the day, week, or month, as well as planning and implementing change.

Case Discussions from an Organizational Cultural Perspective

Organizations and their cultures can become dysfunctional perhaps lead-ing to a new leader or consultant being hired to reengineer the culture. Many organizations suffer from unresolved conflict, operating problems, and dysfunctions where they may not fail but they also fail to succeed. The three case examples raise different issues about organizational cultures and subcultures.

Case 1 illustrates chaotic leadership and cultural changes when there are a series of new leaders hired. A history like this leads to a culture where organization members must deal with the chaos that the leadership changes create. Leadership in the divisions and departments keeps it run-ning (functional subcultures), compensating for the dysfunctional discon-tinuities of the leadership changes. When these organizational dynamics develop, organizational fragmentation is also present. Organization members may feel the organization is falling apart when the specialized silos, divisions, and departments and some individuals pursue their own self-defined goals. These dysfunctional leaders and organizational dynamics compromise coordination, cooperation, and overall performance.

Case 2 is the opposite of the first case. A leader of many years is replaced by another new leader who has the same familiar punishing high-control autocratic leadership style. As a culture, there is an ongoing sense of autocratic and authoritarian oppression and fear of being suddenly singled out for discipline. Management by intimidation leads organization members to focus on keeping their jobs by "staying out of the line of fire" and keeping a low profile. The hope for good leadership and positive cultural change in the case is diminished if not lost. In sum, the micromanagement combined with punishing interventions has created a threatening cultural context of trying to personally survive while the organization seems to be slowly failing to succeed.

Case 3 illustrates losses of leadership continuity that are aggravated by selecting leaders who have marginal skills and experience. This has resulted in an organizational culture that is dysfunctional and effectively managing the organization is problematic. There is a shared workplace distress for failing to meet personal, group, and organizational performance expectations. The dysfunctional management hierarchy has created a culture of confusion and chaos for organization members who have focused on coping with the accompanying operating dysfunctions. They are committed to carrying on the mission by volunteering leadership even when top management has criticized them for doing so. There is nonetheless a culture of shared pride in the organization and its life-giving mission. Organization members, however, also feel that they are together in the same leaky boat that they have managed to keep afloat.

In Sum Organizational Culture

Cultural perspectives encourage critical thinking about what is really going on in organizations including the visible and less so. However, not addressed by culture are the underlying psychosocial drivers of leadership and followership in organizations and *why* leaders and followers may act in ways that do not appear to be adaptive. Poor cultural leadership can result in losses of sustainable stabilizing and functional cultural elements that make failure at times seem like it may be an option. Organizational identity helps to explain "why" this happens by exploring the human side of organizational life.

Organizational Identity

Organizational identity addresses elements of organizational life that are usually taken for granted. People join and stay in organizations for both logical, rational, and conscious reasons and also for personal and out-of-awareness reasons. Organizational identity helps to explain these reasons by focusing attention on less than fully aware and discussable individual and group dynamics.

Definitions

Chapter 2 overviewed the key elements of organizational identity. Psychosocially defensive responses to stressful organization dysfunctions can create a binary split-apart world where there is usually a good self or group and a bad other group, organization, or nation. Self-experience may also be split apart where, for example, feelings of fear or malignant intent on our part are denied and attributed to an individual or group. The workplace can become an us versus them, win-lose, and a zero-sum experience resulting in being able to work together falling apart. The finance department and its desire to manage costs can create oppressive and limiting experiences for the specialized silos that need financial resources to respond to customer expectations and new marketing opportunities. These conflicted individual, group, and organizational dynamics are often hard to discuss and can become not only who we are but also how we work together or do not – our culture. Accurate reality testing as a result is degraded. We simply think, feel, and act in ways relative to others consistent with our split-apart world. For example, if others are thought to be bad we act as though they are. Paradoxically, if others challenge this perception of themselves, they validate the negative split. They are bad for resisting our view of them.

Organizational identity also involves feelings from the past being felt in the present. A "bad" supervisor may be felt to be like an abusive parent (or past supervisor), evoking feelings that may not be consistent with the nature of the supervisor's actions in the present. This creates what some might call a "hot button" response that is disproportionate. The individual may, for example, respond to a supervisor by becoming resistant, unduly submissive, or withdrawn for little to no apparent reason. Accurate reality testing is compromised for everyone.

Organizational identity emphasizes these usually out-of-immediate awareness individual, interpersonal, and group dynamics that contain psychosocially defensive responses to stress. Poor quality workplace attachments that do not support feeling connected and mutually understood can readily compromise organizational performance by creating fragmentation.

In sum, the reasons for the patterns of interaction within work groups and among organization members are not always self-evident. There are out-of-awareness elements of organizational experience that create a familiar structuring of organizational life to manage stressful workplace experiences. Ideally, organization members and leaders are aware that their thoughts, feelings, and actions are affected by what is going on around them and that distressing experiences can result in reliance on psychosocial defenses that split organization members and groups apart. Being aware of these aspects of organizational life underscores the importance of managing individual, group, and organizational experiences to create a welcoming and safe workplace that promotes reflectivity, intentionality, and non-defensive responses to stressful operating problems (Chapter 14).

Case Discussion

Case 1 is a context where senior leadership frequently changes along with the direction of the organization's work. The new leaders understand that they may not hold their position very long, and this encourages them to make their self-centered mark quickly and sometimes arrogantly on the organization by canceling projects and replacing them with new ones. Resistance to their new agenda is "bad" and not tolerated for long. They all have imposed their will on the organization and its members creating an autocratic and authoritarian good versus bad win/lose cultural dynamic.

Self-serving leadership dynamics like this are common in organizations often accompanied by the presence of excessive narcissism, arrogance, and overdetermined vindictive triumph over anyone who resists the leader's authority. Authoritarian leaders usually want to be seen as strong and powerful and generating visionary ideas in order to feel admired and followed or failing that feared. The result is some organization members leave while others may drop out in place for safety metaphorically hiding out in their organizational foxholes, not openly resisting but also not pursuing the new directions with much enthusiasm passively resisting.

Case 2 is an organizational scene filled with high control by the leaders enforced by reliance on the raw uses of power that contain some punishing and sadistic features. Organization members must accept this oppression and give up some of their personal integrity and autonomy in order to keep their jobs by submitting to these powerful autocratic authority figures. However, in cases like this, some organization members may accept the risks of not submitting and resist the oppression. A few may focus on finding new jobs. Autocratic and narcissistic leaders, however, when they encounter resistance, can be expected to aggressively use the power of their positions to threaten and punish those who oppose being dominated. These toxic leadership dynamics encourage the leader to be thought of as bad by organization members who then feel that they are good as well as being abused and dominated. However, some organization members may feel reassured by the presence of a controlling, dominating, and powerful idealized leader who takes charge and protects them. In their dependency, they willingly submit. These leaders often find organization members are marginally capable and competent and must be micromanaged. Resistance to being micromanaged is usually felt to be a personal insult and narcissistic injury that must be aggressively responded to, if necessary by terminating the bad organization member(s).

Case 3 is a context that promotes defensive psychosocial dynamics within the leadership group and the organization members. The members feel limited by the ineffectiveness of their management's ability to lead and manage the organization. This "us versus them" outcome has split the organization apart creating a culture where management is felt to be marginally competent (bad), and the good employees feel loyal and joined together to keep their organization running. Management's response has been to feel organization members are resisting their authority by taking charge of their work and implementing change without consulting with them. Organization members and their silo leaders are, therefore, considered to be rebellious (bad) and if necessary controlled autocratically. The result is a lose-lose outcome. If things are not going well, management asserts it is the fault of the bad unruly organization members and not themselves – the good leaders. In contrast, the good identities of the organization members keep the organization running despite bad management.

In Sum Organizational Identity

Organizational identity emphasizes our lived experience at work and the often-ignored defensive psychosocial complexities that influence leaders and organizational dynamics. Understanding autocratic, authoritarian, oppressive leaders and the toxic dysfunctional organizational dynamics that threaten organization members and organizational performance is essential for change. For example, changing an organizational culture that has had an arrogant, aggressive, combative leader that led to the hiring of a motivated cadre of opposing equally arrogant and combative silo leaders is challenging even when a new psychosocially aware leader is hired. In cases like this, it is wise for the new leader to start with an organizational assessment to better understand the organization's history and its split-apart "us versus them" aggression. In particular, by not engaging in splitting and aggression with the organization's members, the ambient cultural level of organizational aggression may become open to discussion and change. However, changing an organizational culture like this with its good versus bad splitting and its aggressive silo leaders who, as individuals, identify with and have "selected into" these familiar dysfunctional organizational dynamics that they like may not be readily achievable.

This example suggests an in-depth understanding of psychosocially defensive group and organizational dynamics is important for improving organizational functioning by changing workplace culture and member identities – who we are, who You are, and who I am at work. The framework in Chapter 2 is once again adapted to create insight into these hard to understand and manage psychosocial complexities that human nature introduces into our organizations.

THE PSYCHOSOCIALLY DEFENSIVE WORKPLACE

The two approaches for understanding defensive leadership and organizational dynamics in Chapter 2, the three directions of movement and the defensive group dynamics, offer complimentary insights. They shift our focus from the psychosocial elements of cultural and identity dynamics toward understanding the defensive psychosocial dynamics of groups in our organizations. They are discussed separately as a two-part analysis.

The Defensive Directions of Movement – Part 1

Groups and organizations that are focused on achieving goals and objectives are compromised by three familiar psychosocially defensive group dynamics that are responses to stressful times. They are briefly reviewed before using them to discuss the case examples.

Aggressive groups that move against others rely on their leaders to lead the group or organization against an "enemy" or threat. It may be felt only the leader can save us and our organization. Thoughtfulness and reflectivity are reduced as the focus becomes on taking action against a problem or threat. This intense self and group experience surfaces strong emotions that energize attacking the threats within the organization as well as from other organizations or nations.

Dependency groups seek security by moving toward a leader who will protect the group or organization. There is a shared sense that the organization's members are unable to take care of themselves or deal with operating threats and they need help. When an organization member, or leader, is identified to take charge, the person assuming this role feels needed and self-confident enough to lead. If no leader is identified, the group waits expectantly for a leader to emerge. Eventually, someone (or a group) who cannot tolerate the inaction any longer steps up to lead. However, anyone assuming this leadership role is faced with the possibility that the dependency needs of this group's members cannot be entirely met. Marginal success can arouse disappointment and their leader being replaced by someone who it is hoped will meet everyone's dependency needs.

Retreating from stressful workplace experience, movement away, becomes a group focus when there is hope that things will simply get better with time or that a leader, a new idea, or a new strategy will be located that will "magically" deal with the stressful situation. Organization members are attentive and focused on the hope for a better future but paradoxically avoid assuming stressful personal responsibility to respond to threatening operating problems. This defensive strategy leads to hiding out in one's metaphoric organizational foxhole to avoid the stress. However, identifying a leader who holds expectations for organization members to take action may be resisted in favor of the leader assuming all of the associated stressful risks for taking action.

In sum, group dynamics that include these three defensive psychosocial directions of movement compromise accomplishing the organizational mission, especially during stressful times. Leaders are often depended upon to provide reassuring direction by taking charge. By doing so, however, organization members become dependent on them. The leader may also encourage dependency by withholding information and resources that encourage organization members to not feel capable of dealing with internal and external threats. But, if the leader is ineffective or one is not located, the group may believe if they wait long enough a leader or idea will be located to save them. Doing nothing is many times an option in organizations if the stress of doing nothing can be tolerated. These psychosocial defenses provide insights into the three case examples.

Case Discussions

Case 1 and it's leadership turnover present organization members with both a leadership vacuum and autocratic top-down changes in direction when a new leader is hired. Despite the leadership chaos, the organization's members continue to perform their work and feel free to act on their own and in groups to hold the fort. This setting suggests that there is hope that someday effective and stable leadership will be located. However, since the new leaders do not stay in their role very long, this also fulfills the defensive expectation that organization members will not be expected by those in power to assume personal responsibility for acting other than feel free to choose what they will do to respond to the operating problems. Doing nothing institutionally may also seem to be an option and that the status quo is good enough. However, when no one is dealing with organization-wide unresolved operating problems and conflict, this makes holding the fort unnecessarily difficult. These dynamics suggest there are dependency assumptions that are not being met. In sum, organization members seem to hope a leader will emerge who will save them without making coercive demands on them to assume stressful risk-taking personal responsibility for acting.

Case 2 portrays an organization dominated by autocratic leaders who control everything and aggressively suppress opposition. People who resist are forced out or into hiding and some are terminated. These organizational dynamics contain elements of aggression and movements against others in the form of micromanagement that is stressful for organization members. Their leaders are willing to attack anyone opposed to the micromanagement and following orders. Organization members who remain practice avoidance moving away or accept submitting to their leader moving toward. The harsh treatment of an occasional employee who steps forward to question these leadership and organizational dynamics sends a clear message that anyone who does this might suddenly go missing. Organization members understand this palpable reality and that they are always at risk for resisting. Going along to get along is the safest way to go for many organization members.

Case 3 is a story about dependency on silo leaders to keep the organization running. The absence of effective senior management has led to the silo leaders stepping up to the plate to keep the organization functioning. Organization members are respectful and dependent on those among them who are willing to lead. The willingness of their colleagues to take up the slack, however, comes with risks. Those in senior management roles occasionally feel threatened by their leadership and move against these leaders who are willing to assume personal responsibility to keep the organization running. Their response when challenged by those in senior leadership positions is to move away from them to avoid being aggressed. These risk-taking silo leaders are also seldom acknowledged for their good work, and life at work for them is usually unrewarding if not punishing. This is a toxic leadership organizational culture.

In Sum

These analyses suggest that a stable, rationally managed organization that optimizes its performance can be problematic. This conclusion that defensive and dysfunctional organizational psychosocial dynamics are often present in our organizations is supported by spectacular failures such as the General Motors bankruptcy in 2009 and the global failure banking/financial industry during the Great Recession in 2008. Many organizations that fail or fail to thrive disappear – being sold, merged, ending in bankruptcy, closed, or bailed out by the government.

In sum, the psychosocially defensive directions of movement discussed are a way to understand complex and ever-changing organizational dynamics. The directions of movement provide a framework for thinking and reflectivity that encourages understanding dysfunctional organizational dynamics and toxic leadership and why changing these dynamics is important but also challenging. Each defensive response and direction of movement (against, toward, and away) offers its own unique challenge to overcome as does the framework of defensive group dynamics.

The Defensive Group Dynamics – Part 2

Defensive group and organizational dynamics are also common workplace experiences. The following psychosocially informed framework contributes to understanding under-recognized and misunderstood defensive dysfunctional organizational dynamics that are a coping response to stressful organizational leadership and operating problems. This defensive struggle is waged between maintaining personal autonomy and integrity and submitting to leader, group, and organizational dynamics that result in accepting losses of personal autonomy and integrity. And to be noted is that the more stressful the work experience becomes, the more likely dysfunctional individual and group psychosocial defenses will arise. These defensive coping strategies are briefly overviewed and then used to inform understanding the case examples.

Togetherness and Sameness

This pursuit of group member safety and security arises as a response to, for example, poor or absent leadership, misaligned organizational resources, and internal events such as downsizing and restructuring. These events are stressful and split organization members apart. Who will be next? This loss of voluntary coordination and cooperation introduces organizational fragmentation that may lead organization members to feel that their ability to work together is falling apart threatening organizational survival.

Organization members who feel threatened may find themselves merged in a defensively oriented group dynamic focused on working together in the hope they will not be next. The desire within this group is to maintain a non-threatening group culture and member identity that emphasizes coequality, togetherness, and everyone being treated the same way since they are all faced with the same threats. However, the paradox remains that this sense of being joined together can leave organization members feeling anxious about losing their identities. The expectations of the merger into togetherness may be felt by individual organization members as also including oppressive features. This experience may encourage some group members to move away from this defensive group dynamic to find their own solitary ways to defend against threats and stress. This tension between the safety of being a merged group member and feeling anxious about losses of identity can lead to lapses in developing thoughtful, intentional, and integrated plans for problem-solving. Compromises to voluntary coordination and cooperation may also develop among the group or organization's members when acting is expected. As a result, they may have the experience of being alone together as might be the case for a table of friends all working on their phones.

Bureaucratic Control

This experience, in contrast to group and organization members compensating by merging in a coequal togetherness as a team, encourages individual and group acceptance to a controlling, hierarchical bureaucratic structure. This defense contains anxiety by relying on an impersonal, controlling, and rigid structure and leadership that regulates work and minimizes unpredictability and stress by following bureaucratic policies and procedures. Losses of personal autonomy and self-identity are accepted in favor of avoiding threats arising from losses of control. This comforting focus on control and compliance with routines, it is hoped, will provide stability, dependability, coordination, and cooperation to avoid work groups and the organization falling apart. Organization members are together in accepting this defensive approach to managing stressful times at work.

Autocratic and Authoritarian Control

This group relies on a charismatic autocratic authoritarian, often oppressive leader, who provides unilateral direction aimed at limiting the out-of-control self-experience of workplace stress. This leader is admired for taking charge and possessing exceptional leadership qualities in part because organization members, by comparison, feel that they are less than capable (via projecting their competencies onto their leader) of dealing with operating problems. This leader is free to act powerful and is admired for doing so but may also be feared by anyone who is not a loyal follower. These defensive group and organizational dynamics can result in the leader becoming unaccountable for violating moral, ethical, and social values. However, if this leader fails to meet the dependency needs of organization members to feel safe and secure, the leader may be rejected in the hope a new leader will gain better control, resolve operating problems, and limit their distressing workplace experience. It may also be the case, as is sometimes said, only this leader can save them.

The Work Group

This group is not that common in large complex hierarchical organizations. The group works effectively to accomplish organizational goals learning from experience. Members are open to their work and methods being questioned including the leader's decisions and actions. Intentionality, reflectivity, and awareness are valued by the group's members who understand and respect each other which creates a trusting bond that is collaborative and cooperative and promotes critical thinking while avoiding retreats to psychosocial defenses.

Case Discussions

Case 1 has a focus on togetherness with everyone committed to keeping the organization running. The changes in leadership have created leadership vacuums and limited consistent overall direction that has compromised the benefits of a hierarchical bureaucratic organizational structure. This chaos encouraged employees to retreat from their leaders and focus on taking individual and group initiatives to keep the organization running. There is also a loss of pride in being a member of an organization with such poor leadership. The freedom to take independent action, however, can also split an organization apart with some groups not working together collaboratively and cooperatively. Dysfunctional organizational dynamics can then develop where, for example, it is culturally accepted that pursuing your own and group goals and self-interests seems appropriate even when marginally coordinated with other organization members and groups. As a result, it is easy to feel working together on the organization's mission is problematic and that the organization has become fragmented.

Case 2 resembles the autocratic authoritarian organization. The leaders have acted unilaterally to control organization members, and resistance to being dominated is not tolerated making life at work threatening. Stories about people being abused and forced to quit encourage organization members to feel powerless and vulnerable. Their leaders have been unrestrained by board members, ethics, or morality. Personal safety is sought by remaining silent and avoiding attracting the attention of their leaders – moving away. An image of an authoritarian totalitarian police state where everyone is being watched for deviances is not far removed from this experience.

Case 3 has many of the elements of bureaucratic work experience. The employees are compensating for their management's ineffectiveness by sticking closely to established processes and methods. The organization members are self-led to get work accomplished and resist management changes that they believe will compromise their work. Effective executive leadership is not a prerequisite in terms of keeping a bureaucratic organization running sometimes referred to as the "deep state" in a governmental organization. Steadfast reliance on policies and procedures and prescribed cooperation and coordination creates predictable as well as sustainable organizational performance.

In sum, the defensive group framework offers insights into the "why" of familiar organizational dynamics. The case discussions illustrate a way to understand organizational life grounded in psychosocially informed perspectives. Psychosocially defensive leadership, group and organizational dynamics are a frequent presence in organizations that, if recognized, should preferably nonthreateningly be made open to discussion. Recognizing their presence is step one toward improving everyone's work experience and healing dysfunctional groups and organizations.

IN CONCLUSION

The psychosocially defensive group and organizational perspectives discussed provide a framework for understanding organizational dynamics. Organizational culture has merits but may not be applicable to new organizations with a limited history. Culture emphasizes being aware of workplace elements that are created by and manipulated by leaders to provide guidance to organization members. Organizational identity emphasizes usually out-of-awareness individual, interpersonal, group, and organizational psychosocial dynamics. Together these two perspectives increase our awareness of our lives at work.

The directions of movement and psychosocially defensive framework also provide important complimentary perspectives for understanding and managing organizational dynamics. They provide leaders, organization members, consultants, and researchers with insights into managing and changing organizations to limit the presence of psychosocially defensive individual and group dynamics. This complexity also suggests that there is no "cookbook" approach to knowing and changing dysfunctional leadership and organizational dynamics in large complex usually hierarchical organizations. This is a humbling appreciation but also a challenge that merits being met.

In sum, this chapter has focused on how leaders, organization members, and consultants can better understand and work toward overcoming dysfunctional leadership and group and organizational dynamics. Creating a sustainable productive and enjoyable workplace is a worthy goal for organizational leaders and members who may be helped along by psychosocially oriented external consultants, the subject of Chapter 13.

13

Consulting to Dysfunctional Organizations

Contemporary organizations large or small, public of private, family owned or corporate share the complexities that human nature introduces into how they run and "What it is like to work here." Our organizations are invariably split apart into vertical hierarchical layers of power and authority and horizontally across specialized siloed functions like finance, human relations, marketing, and production. This organizational fragmentation creates a milieu that is hard to understand and sometimes changes by the hour as the problems of the day or month are dealt with and plans made and implemented to take advantage of new opportunities. These organizational attributes and operating dynamics are confounded by a range of leadership styles some of which are effective and some of which are toxic and contribute to hard-to-manage stress on the part of organization members who rely on psychosocial defenses to cope. This is the context organizational consultants are confronted with. They must be able to understand the psychosocial nature of dysfunctional organizations and toxic leadership to facilitate change that improves organizational life and operating performance.

Culture and identity, how we work together and who we are, are two ways to understand this dynamic complexity. A dysfunctional leader may, for example, have the toxic behavior accepted and rationalized away. This flight from contemplating corrective action is especially likely when a punishing response from the leader is expected. An unchallenged dysfunctional leadership dynamic like this becomes a part of the organization's culture that members identity with locking in the leadership toxicity and the resulting organizational dysfunctions. Organization members understand that "you must go along to get along to keep your job."

DOI: 10.4324/9781003464464-16

CONSULTING TO ORGANIZATIONAL CULTURE AND IDENTITY

Organizational culture and identity include a variety of organizational attributes that new organization members learn. This organizational socialization may approach indoctrination as in the military and police or fire services. This process may include job training and informal learning from colleagues about the organization's rituals, history, and myths as well as the defensive psychosocial dynamics shared by organization members that help them to cope with their stressful work experience. This process of becoming an ideal organization member may be punctuated by unexpected and hard-to-understand organizational events like a chief executive officer (CEO) suddenly becoming enraged in a meeting, yelling accusations at some of those present, and then leaving the room slamming the door on the way out. Events like this are sometimes followed by aggressive actions against an offending organization member in the meeting. The actions may take the form of reduced chances of being promoted, being publicly humiliated, or being terminated by, for example, being included in a downsizing, restructuring, and reengineering that targets some offending organization members in addition to the metaphoric "organizational fat." Aggressive destructive toxic leadership dynamics like these are threatening, stressful, and unreasonable and send a clear message to potential future offenders of their leader.

In contrast, organizations that nurture intentionality do so by being open, inclusive, transparent, and collaborative which promotes mutual respect and trust. These organizational values form a secure basis for organizational effectiveness and a workplace that is less stressful reducing the need to rely on psychosocial defenses. However, many leaders, along a range of dysfunction, deskill and alienate their members. Employees may feel misled, threatened, helpless, and fearful, especially when they and their organization are faced with hard-to-resolve internal and external conflicts, operating problems, and organizational change imposed autocratically top-down. Coping with stressful organizational dynamics like these leads to relying on reality distorting psychosocial defenses that, when accepted as a part of the culture, become depended upon to cope with dysfunctional organizational dynamics and toxic leadership. These defenses, however, also result in losses of self-integration, group cohesiveness, and organizational adaptiveness making it seem as though our ability to work together is falling apart. This experience is accentuated by familiar but problematic bureaucratic organizational rigidities that defend organization members from stressful unpredictability.

For example, members of a large organization controlled by a CEO and a closely knit group of senior-level executives understand that they are to make all the decisions and are self-authorized to "drill down" in the organization to micromanage work and projects. Explanations of management decisions are minimally provided and supported by financial analyses that no one has enough knowledge of to understand to be able to question them, which would also be hazardous in terms of staying employed. Organization members are expected to accept the decisions and analyses and tolerate the intrusive micromanagement. The culture that is observed by a consultant to have developed around these organizational dynamics may be one of the organization members being indifferent and withdrawn and sticking with doing "my" job. Instances where management decisions generate unintended negative consequences are being dependably blamed on those associated with working on their implementation. There may also be a history of organization members being suddenly terminated, reorganized, or downsized out of their jobs. Organizational experiences like this, the consultant should understand, reinforce organization members identifying with being passively dependent, feeling vulnerable, and retreating from active participation.

In sum, organizational culture and identity that include interactive, shared psychosocial defenses that defend against stress contribute to organizational operating dysfunctions. Understanding these oppressive organizational dynamics and their accompanying operating problems must include developing insight on the part of consultants into the psychosocial defenses that are a part of every member's identity and the organization's culture – who I am at work and how we work together. One way for consultants to develop insight into these complex organizational dynamics is to develop an organizational analysis.

DEVELOPING AN ORGANIZATIONAL ANALYSIS

Developing an analysis begins by confidentially interviewing executives, managers, and a cross-section of supervisors and employees who represent all sites and shifts. The analysis should also include reviewing mission statements, strategic plans, overviewing budgets, and a "walk through" of spaces and operations. These two levels of analysis, qualitative and quantitative, are further informed by paying attention to the consultant's subjective reactions to what is being observed and listened to as experience of the organization and its members accumulates during the diagnostic work.

Diagnosing Organizational Culture and Identity

Understanding organizational life requires paying attention to what is observed and heard and what is not observed and heard that reveal some of the less obvious elements of organizational culture and member identity. These diagnostic elements include employee reactions to questions, how information is volunteered during walk throughs, opinions volunteered about top management, and descriptions of what it is like to work here revealed by open-ended questions during interviews that generate attention-getting responses in the presence of a "listening" consultant. The interviews, when understood as a whole, tell a story that describes what it is like to be an organization leader and member. These organizational themes are often communicated metaphorically in the telling stories that are intended to evoke thoughts and feelings on the part of the consultant. The consultant must "listen" to these self-experiences that are being evoked by less than obvious covert forms of interpersonal communication aimed at controlling what the consultant thinks, feels, knows, and understands. This reflective self-awareness is critical in terms of imagining the overall organization and its members and what is like to work here.

In sum, the consultant's listening diagnostic work enables understanding organizational life in sufficient depth to appreciate both the functional and dysfunctional aspects of the organization's leadership and dynamics that enhance or compromise organizational performance and the quality of work life. For example, an awareness of acts of management intimidation, scapegoating, unresolved interpersonal and intergroup conflict, and organizational problems informs locating meaningful and implementable change. What has been learned and proposed change recommendations must be thoughtfully shared back with the organization's leaders and members to encourage their non defensive listening to promote their intentional responses in support of locating meaningful organizational change.

CREATING AN ORGANIZATIONAL INTERVENTION

Two kinds of organizational data must be interpreted. One data set is the *concrete* factors that affect organizational performance that include such things as regulation, funding, space, equipment, technology, and externally marketplace dynamics and competitors to list but some examples. The second data set is the psychosocial factors that influence the use of concrete organizational elements by leaders and employees to make the organization effective and to respond to operating problems and external threats.

For example, organizational leaders and members might be encouraged to rethink their resistance to solving a problem that they imagine will require risk-taking, more work on their part, and a commitment of scarce organizational and financial resources. Rationalizing the problem away as not solvable may arise if it is thought that there are not enough resources and time available which can make doing nothing an option. Consultant facilitation of a discussion of this resistance that explores underlying thinking and feeling and a less-than-accurate problem definition is a step forward to contemplating planning and implementing change. Also, to be appreciated is that anticipating change can be threatening to organization members encouraging them to rely on psychosocial defenses such as denial and rationalization to make change unnecessary.

Doing nothing and moving away to maintain freedom from having to act, consultants frequently find, seems like a good option for organization members even though the organizational dysfunctions are obviously stressful. In the example, the dysfunctions are less stressful than contemplating the risk-taking and demanding work of planning and implementing change. Overcoming group and organizational resistances like this is challenging. However, facilitating the development of a safe enough context where the resistances and threats can be openly discussed does move organizations toward creating change.

Creating A Safe Enough Workplace

Recognizing that change is needed and that planning and implementing change is stressful for organization members suggests that avoiding psychosocial defensive responses to change is essential. Containing these stresses and the accompanying anxieties minimizes resistance to change, blaming rituals, and scapegoating requires consultants to create a safe enough facilitated context to accomplish working on organizational change. Organization members must feel that they can safely share their thoughts and feelings about the uncertainties and vulnerabilities resident in acknowledging problems and threats exist, and planning and implementing change is necessary. This process usually also includes the stressful admission that errors in management decision-making have contributed to some poor organizational outcomes. Acknowledging these leader decisions and actions may have been defensively avoided, denied, rationalized, and tolerated. This defensiveness makes getting the diagnostic findings about dysfunctional organizational dynamics, performance problems and the cultural themes of the psychosocial defenses acknowledged requires creating a safe context. Getting the organization's leaders and members to recognize the origins of their operating problems and accept some of the likely solutions is a challenge for consultants only eclipsed by getting organizational leaders and members to take action.

In sum, the creative potential of a facilitated safe enough organizational setting that encourages the organization's leaders and members to openly confront their organization's operating problems must be appreciated. Organizational leaders and members who feel safe are more easily facilitated to generate innovative solutions to improve organizational performance and their lives at work. Creating an open, inclusive, transparent, and collaborative process for locating and implementing change can be expected to encourage a positive embrace of change by organization members or at least change that is minimally defended against.

However, consultants may be confronted with a worst-case scenario that is hard to turnaround and may not be salvageable. Outcomes like this are regrettably a part of the practice of organizational consulting including recently hired turnaround executives. The following example is about an ultimately unresolvable set of organizational leadership and organizational dysfunctions.

A CASE EXAMPLE: FOR SALE

The organizational assessment and intervention process, in this consultation, revealed many challenging dysfunctional leaders and organizational dynamics deeply embedded in their culture and identities – how we work here and who we are. Organizational dynamics like this regrettably lead to organizations being sold, merged, or simply ended as in this case.

Background and Presenting Problem

A successful former marketing executive who was the new president of a midsized division of a large corporation hired a consultant to help salvage a failed effort to convert an out-of-date management information system to a new one. This problem was created by the CEO of the parent corporation who contracted with a large national consulting company to provide a new computerized operating system with a price and date certain for completion of the work. This was announced in a corporate quarterly report and proved to be a fateful pronouncement.

The consulting company developing the new software used several non-compatible software packages that had to have programmed bridges developed between them to permit communication, an approach that would require continuous costly maintenance when one of the packages is upgraded. The consulting company began to run behind schedule and over budget. When the previously announced time to implement the software package was reached, the CEO ordered the conversion to be made even though the consulting company had not finished its work creating the bridges. The consulting company's contract was terminated, and the company was sued. This compromised opportunities to receive the company's assistance going forward. The CEO, to avoid additional operating costs, decided not to run the old software in parallel for backup. There was no going back.

Major system operating problems immediately developed among the software components that failed to pass data between them. This is the operating context that the consultant was confronted with to keep the company operating and its organization members employed it was hoped.

The Organizational Diagnosis

Understanding the organizational dynamics that are the origins of a presenting problem like this provides consultants insights into how to help organizations to recover. Interviews were conducted throughout this division. They revealed that organization members were struggling to maintain production, sales, inventories, and services. It was also understood within the division that the CEO and executives in the distant home office had made decisions that set them up to fail. They were not so angry as they were overworked and fatalistically reconciled to slowly failing. However, they also took pride in suffering through the many operating problems together.

The managers of this division were faced with operating problems that so far have been impossible to resolve. The new software interfaces between the non-compatible software packages were not sufficiently developed to permit seamless communication, coordination, and management. These dysfunctions were aggravated by increasing sales volumes. Ironically the more successful they were, the bigger became the operating problems.

The consultant was allowed to recruit an organization member to evaluate the databases being used, and this work yielded that the customer database included inaccurate, duplicate, and untimely information that further compounded the problems associated with keeping the division operating. Another example was a large warehouse that had to abandon the new automated inventory management system that did not work. The manager had to resort to using a manual system that consumed time and effort that detracted from order fulfillment.

The parts of the new system that were usable were not user-friendly in addition to not interfacing with the rest of the software. Those using the system were required to move through multiple screens to take orders, which slowed down their work and introduced human error. Orders once taken required considerable time to be committed to manually manipulating the order data so that it could be accepted into the next software package.

Yet another set of problems was eventually discovered. Information in some of the software packages could not be uploaded to the corporate headquarters systems without once again being manually manipulated. This reduced real-time management information and transparency about what was going on at their division's site raising suspicions in the home office about their performance.

In sum, the members of this division were burdened by operating dysfunctions to the extent that a fourth of their time and effort was being devoted to overcoming system limitations introducing error, increasing operating costs, and eventually dooming the division to fail.

The Home Office

A visit to the home office by the consultant was revealing. An interview with a key administrator revealed that the current president of the division was the most recent of several recent changes in leaders. This discontinuity of leadership had crippled efforts to avoid but also deal with the operating problems created by the CEO and senior home office staff members' decision to go live on a nonfunctional software platform. It turned out this division was not alone. Several other divisions had similar software problems. It was also revealed that the CEO was surrounded by loyal senior staff who were committed to covering up the operating problems created by the fragmented operating systems for their job security. From a diagnostic perspective, it did not seem as though meaningful improvements could be made without acknowledging that the CEO and the senior staff were part of the problem, something they were defensively steadfast in not having acknowledged. The decision to go live with an inoperable system had created a catastrophe that everyone knew about, but no one was willing to speak about it out of fear of retribution.

A Note on Organizational Culture

The culture of the division is discernable from this case description. The employees worked hard and valued what they were doing but felt they were going to fail because they were using a computerized system that did not work. There was, however, camaraderie and a sense of togetherness in coping with their many operating problems. Organization members darkly joked about all the problems that had been created by the CEO and senior staff. They also shared a fatalistic awareness that failure was becoming an option that had to be accepted.

Within a context like this a consultant, by simply listening, provides some comfort for organization members by their knowing that the consultant understands their many operating problems. The challenge in a case like this for consultants is locating what can be done if anything. The covering up of the problems and blaming others was the "go to" defensive strategy in the home office. The implementation decision and the fact that it was dangerous for division members to discuss operating problems with the home office was an accepted part of the organizational culture. Good versus bad identities emerged that included feeling being victimized by the CEO and home office by division members and the division being suspicioned as incompetent and blamed for poor operating results by those in the home office.

One way to understand an organizational dynamic like this between the home office and a division is to examine the contribution that concepts like organizational fragmentation and internal splits can make to unpacking why organizations seem to be falling apart.

Internal Splits

Internal splits in organizations are usually self-evident. In this example, the home office is poorly informed about if not in denial of the root causes of the operating problems at the division level. This makes the leaders in the home office unreceptive and defensive about dealing with the problems that they have created. They in fact blame the division's employees for the operating problems. The division's staff sees the home office's staff as ignoring and even threatening them about the unresolved system operating problems that they created by going live before the interfaces were finished. Pointing out the root causes of the problems to the home office is also known to be hazardous even for the consultant. This dysfunctional organizational dynamic made the victims of the poor decisions responsible for protecting the CEO and home office senior leaders from having to acknowledge and deal with the information system operating problems that they created.

Psychosocially defensive organizational dynamics such as blaming, denying, and not assuming responsibility are common. They make clear that organizational fragmentation is present, and that organization members and the siloed divisions (division operations versus the information systems division) are moving against each other as part of a good versus bad split. Being able to effectively work together is falling apart. Organizational fragmentation in this example confronts organization members of the specialized divisions with collaborative discontinuities that have undermined performance. The losses of cooperation and coordination were also contributed to by the psychosocially defensive culture of protecting home office senior leaders and the CEO from acknowledging that they created the operating problems. Responding to an operating context like this for any consultant is a worthy challenge, especially when funding is made available to hire only one consultant.

Recommendations for Change

Given this organizational context of a dysfunctional organizational culture, what might be recommended to regain profitable operations? The early efforts by the consultant to locate ways to smooth out the operating difficulties did help to limit the extent of damage, although it took more staff time to walk data between the incompatible software packages and manage product inventories. Recommendations to deal with the root causes of the system failure made the new division president anxious because correcting the problems would promote conflict with the home office. There would be only one winner. The home office staff already thought that the division's members were out to get them by blaming the CEO for the decision to go live. An onsite discussion of one element of the new system that was particularly dysfunctional did lead to feedback to the home office. Predictably several senior staff asserted it was an attack on them and the CEO. The defensive response by the CEO was to terminate the consulting engagement and several division staff – metaphorically killing the messengers.

The many time-consuming workarounds that permitted the division to operate did not "turn around" the disastrous implementation of a marginally functional information system with no backup. There were few meaningful recommendations for remediation that did not threaten the CEO and the cadre of home office senior staff loyalists. The division was doomed to fail.

The End Result

Everyone understood that salvaging the situation was not possible so long as the home office defended its leaders and decisions. Improving sales only served to aggravate the operating problems by increasing the workload for those manipulating the system to get it to work. The Plan B solution implemented by the president of the division to salvage part of the company's investment in the division was to "dress up" the numbers as best as possible (putting lipstick on the pig as this is sometimes referred to) and selling it to another organization that had its own systems and wanted to acquire the customer base. The acquiring organization gradually moved operations to another state and the division's members had to accept being laid off. Failure turned out to be the only option.

INTERPRETING THE CASE EXAMPLE AND OTHERS LIKE IT

Understanding this case example seems simple, but it is more complex than meets the eye. The enduring split between the home office and the local organization created a dynamic where catastrophic decision-making by the CEO could not be addressed in any meaningful way. This was consistent with the recent history of unresolved operating problems that led to the resignation or firing of several past presidents of the division who recognized that they could not succeed without major changes. They had been forced out of their roles for advocating that the operating problems generated by the home office leadership group be recognized and addressed.

The proposed interventions recommended by the consultant were also rejected by the home office staff who were defensive and pursued a strategy of eliminating the irritating consultant. The president of the division, who could be the head of any division within any organization sufficiently large to have specialized operating units, came to understand, like the past presidents, that these defensive organization dynamics ruled out meaningful change. Accepting the inevitability of being doomed to fail led to the strategy of selling the division to avoid a complete monetary loss.

The defensive psychosocial dynamics in this case example were intense. Fear and animosity are present in the division and the home office where the CEO and senior staff feared being exposed for poor decision-making to keep their jobs. Everyone was at risk of losing their job including the CEO. This highlights the defensive splitting that was present that contributed to the fragmented working relationship where the bad "other" was a threat and to be blamed. The division was seen by many in the home office as being run by people who were incompetent and irritating (bad) by their pointing out the operating problems created by their decision-making. This mutually antagonistic view (movement against) of the opposing groups was unresolvable and led to the elimination of, in this case, the division. There is also to be noted a depressive quality that pervades this organizational culture where division members had to accept their eventual fate of failure. In the home office, there was a sense of feeling that they were under attack by the division members and the consultant. Some home office staff below senior levels, however, understood the many operating problems and what had caused them but, in order to keep their jobs, had to depressingly say and do nothing. Within the division, the psychosocially defensive response was one of moving away from the home office and toward each other to survive and depressingly becoming silent to avoid threatening and punishing home office interactions to keep their jobs. The hoped-for solutions by the consultant did not fulfill their dependency needs and their movement toward the consultant. Failure was not avoidable.

<hr>

IN CONCLUSION

Large and small organizations possess the challenges of managing the operating complexities of human nature and the accompanying dysfunctional psychosocially defensive individual, group, and organizational dynamics. Organizational hierarchies and their many layers and specialized divisions are hard to manage, and this is made more difficult by less-than-effective and even toxic leadership. It is also natural for organization members who experience stress to rely on defensive psychosocial responses that can take many forms that contribute to organizational fragmentation.

Organizational culture and identity are concepts that provide consultants with useful ways to understand these dynamic complexities that are stressful. Organizational consultants must appreciate that the psychosocially defensive responses help organization members to cope with the inevitably presence of workplace stress. Being able to making sense of toxic leaders and defensive organizational dynamics is a gateway to imagining meaningful organizational interventions that improve operating performance and the work lives of their members. And to be appreciated from the case example is that some organizations may become zombies to be sold off.

Chapter 14 turns our attention to how leaders can be more effective in managing their organizations and their members by promoting organizational cultures that are open, inclusive, transparent, collaborative, trusting, and respectful.

14

Intentional Leadership

This chapter is about locating an approach to leadership that can make a difference for our organizations. More specifically it is about *intentional* leadership that is characterized by a set of values and an organizational culture and identity that embraces openness, inclusiveness, transparency, collaboration, mutual trust, and respect. These cultural values are the foundation for creating an organizational space and time where new ideas and solutions to problems can emerge and be effectively implemented. Intentional leadership provides direction without becoming top-down unilateral autocratic command and control. Intentional leadership is, however, more challenging than it sounds.

AN INTRODUCTION TO LEADING INTENTIONALLY

Leadership is a topic that has been around for thousands of years. Reviewing the vast literature on leadership and management styles, methods, and skills is not the goal of this chapter. Countless leadership studies have been published in academic books and journals, business practitioner magazines, and on the internet. Neither does this chapter easily fit within the scope of what has been traditionally considered to be leadership. Intentional leadership diverges from leadership that emphasizes unilateral, autocratic sometimes authoritarian command and control organizational management. Intentional leaders instead focus on listening and reflectivity to help contain, absorb, and respond to the stress and anxiety organization members experience that may lead to reliance on

DOI: 10.4324/9781003464464-17

psychosocially defensive dynamics. The goal of intentional leaders is to maintain a non-defensive focus for creating an organizational culture and identities that minimize relying on psychosocially defensive organizational dynamics.

Controlling everyone and everything in our organizations is a challenge that is never successfully achieved as discussed in Part 1. Perceived gaps in control can result in oppressing organization members to perfect top-down management control. Defensive resistance to these toxic leaders (moving back against them), however, is not a good option and can threaten continued employment. Moving away from these leaders offers some safety. So does embracing a loyal and unquestioning role of moving toward the leader in dependency and submission. Also, to be considered at the other end of the autocratic leadership spectrum are leaders who are less overtly controlling of organization members and their organizations. These leaders are passive, self-serving, and risk-averse. They slow down decision-making, problem-solving, and innovation by moving away from their decision-making responsibilities.

In sum, organizational entropy and losses of coordination arise by relying on these defensive directions of movement that compromise the ability to work together and create organizational fragmentation. These defensive organizational dynamics can make understanding leadership and how best to lead an elusive and aspirational goal. If there was one "right way" to lead, it might be assumed it would have been discovered over the millennia. In general, well-conceived leadership studies that focus on types and methods seldom evaluate the influences of leaders and individual, interpersonal, group, and organizational psychosocial defensive dynamics. This chapter peers inside the "black box" of workplace experience and leadership and the challenges leaders encounter when managing themselves, others, groups, and organizations. To be explored are losses of self-awareness on the part of leaders that compromise fulfilling their responsibilities and achieving the organization's mission, vision, strategic plan, and making their organization a good place to work. This chapter explores the *intentional* leader's approach to managing that includes self-awareness, reflectivity, listening, and relying on the six cultural values: openness, inclusiveness, transparency, collaboration, mutual trust, and respect that contribute to maintaining personal, group, and organizational intentionality.

DISTINCTIVE LEADERSHIP STYLES

Hierarchical bureaucratic organizational structures are designed around layers of power and authority and specialized departments such as accounting, finance, operations, marketing, sales, transportation, and human resources. These vertical layers and horizontal departments or silos are staffed by members of professions who have specialized skills, language, and knowledge that can contribute to organizational fragmentation. This makes leading in a context like this challenging. The result often is a variety of self-generated ways leaders exercise hierarchical organizational position-based power and authority.

Hierarchical organizations concentrate power in roles at the top of what is a pyramid as illustrated by organization charts both for the organization as a whole and within the specialized silos. Leaders frequently rely on the power of their position to be in charge and make decisions without much regard for what others think and feel and the collateral damage that they create including sometimes abusive sadistic uses of their power. Looking and acting *strong and powerful* as is sometimes heard in politics in the first quarter of the twenty-first century fulfills their self-expectations as to what organization members should think and feel about them. These autocratic, oppressive, and frequently narcissistic and charismatic leaders feel that it is their personal destiny to oversee organization members who should loyally submit to their control.

In contrast, intentional leaders avoid relying on top-down autocratic command and control and micro-managing tendencies as well as not being abrasive, intimidating, bullying, and dominating. They prefer to be open, inclusive, collaborative, and willing to meaningfully support their organization's members' work and their personal development. They preferably provide direction and decision-making, time permitting, that is arrived at through consensus building. This is not to say intentional leaders are laissez-faire, self-absorbed, risk-averse, and unwilling to make tough decisions to avoid offending others and losing their approval. It is, however, less stressful to make demanding decisions when organization members have been meaningfully engaged and have contributed to the decisions making them easier to implement.

In sum, what is different among these leadership styles is how the leadership role is performed. Consider the following story that illustrates two contrasting leadership styles.

A STORY OF LEADERSHIP: MUSICAL CHAIRS

Tom is hired to replace a long-term senior-level executive Dick in a large complex organization. Dick's history of abusively dominating his division members and the lagging performance of his division led to a reorganization to remove him and a few of his immediate staff. These departures presented Tom with a recruiting challenge to fill the management vacuum.

Tom began his job by meeting with division and organization members to better understand their history and culture. A meeting was scheduled with Jill, a mid-level manager. When Jill showed up at the open door to his office, Dick's former office, he interrupted a call to greet Jill inviting her to have a seat at a small round conference table. As he was ending the call, he noticed Jill was still standing at the door and again invited her in. When the call ended, Jill was standing by the table. As Tom approached, Jill appeared to be anxious. He once again invited her to sit down. She stood frozen and then asked where Tom was going to sit. He grabbed a chair and sat down. She then sat down. During the meeting, she eventually shared that Dick had "his" chair and that she had unwittingly sat down in it when she was new to the organization. This led to a punishing and humiliating response by Dick, something never to be forgotten.

A week later, Tom was to meet Maggie. She had canceled several previously scheduled meetings. Maggie appeared at the door to his office, and after being greeted by Tom, she would not enter the room. A second invitation yielded the same results. She said she could not overcome her anxieties about entering Dick's former office. She asked Tom if they could meet in a nearby conference room and he agreed. She confided to Tom that she had been abused by him over the years – suffering not to be forgotten.

Several months later, while Tom was eating his lunch at the conference table with his office door closed, an explosion occurred. The walls shook and the ceiling tiles slightly raised from the concussion and the change in air pressure. A light dust from the tiles filtered down. This was followed a few seconds later by another concussion. Tom now very alert located the source as his closed door. When he opened it, there stood an intense and angry Harry, a manager of a division Dick had dominated. He had pounded on the closed door that was mindfully associated with Dick's abusive uses of his power. When Tom greeted him nondefensively his intense posture relaxed, and he was invited in.

After the unscheduled meeting with Harry ended, Tom reflected for a moment. If sitting down at a table or entering the office was so foreboding, then, for Harry, the fact that he was confronted with a closed door to his former enemy's office must have been unbearable – something to assault to express the anger that remained from his harmful combative relationship with Dick.

Discussion and Analysis

This story illustrates how autocratic oppressive intimidating leadership creates defensive organizational dysfunctions. The traumatic memories of organization members of their recently departed leader were all too fresh in their minds. Dick was gone, but the memory of his many years of abusive dominating uses of power haunted the organization influencing how everyone began to develop their working relationship with Tom.

These kinds of psychosocial dynamics exemplify how traumatic the experience of past (toxic) leadership and working relationships lives on. Tom had to appreciate how others were not responding to him and that their thoughts, feelings, and actions were being fueled by these past experiences transferred onto him. He understood he had to allow time for everyone to process the change in leadership and what had happened to them resembled post-traumatic distress. Psychosocial healing had to be allowed to gradually happen.

This work began when Jill insisted on standing until Tom sat down, and when Maggie refused to enter Tom's office. In both instances, he did not respond defensively realizing that he was not the problem and that what was happening was that the years of traumatic experiences with Dick still dominated their self-experience. Similarly, when Harry pounded on his closed door, he did not interpret this as something related to him. He understood the door seemed to symbolize something else – the hated foreboding presence of the former occupant. Tom was thoughtfully and reflectively responding to the interpersonal, group, and organizational dynamics that arose from Dick's ghostly presence. To be appreciated then is that new leaders (or employees, or consultants) do not start with a "clean slate." They inherit historical attitudes, feelings, myths, and fantasies that can readily be evoked by a new leader striving to turn around the organization's culture and performance.

In sum, organizations can be haunted by zombies sometimes symbolized by the presence of organizational objects and spaces such as a conference table with chairs, an office, or a closed door. Organizational dynamics like this strongly indicate that there must be a better way to lead and manage.

DEVELOPING A BETTER UNDERSTANDING OF INTENTIONAL LEADERSHIP: AN OVERVIEW

There are several intentional leadership attributes that are interrelated. Ideally, all are relied upon in the process of creating a safe, welcoming, and fulfilling workplace experience and culture that forms the basis for a high-performing organization.

Listening

Intentional listening is a respectful learning process aimed at gaining insight into an organization's dynamics, operating problems, and the subjective experience of organization members of their organization's culture and history of leadership. Listening on the part of new leaders and organizational consultants encourages organization members to also listen. Tom, for example, proved to be a good listener hearing spoken and unspoken messages and responding to them in thoughtful, reflective, and non-defensive ways. This began the process of changing the organizational culture and how organization members identified with their new leader, each other, and their organization.

Containment

Intentional leaders do meet some of the dependency expectations of organization members by being active listeners. They also do not neglect the equally key role of facilitating the containment of anxiety arising from stressful organizational events and uncertainty that promote retreats to psychosocial defenses to cope. Leaders who help to contain stress and anxiety that is always present in our organizations by not becoming defensive themselves, as Tom did, enable organization members to feel less uncertain and fearful, and psychosocially defensive. Organization members are then better able to focus on the problem at hand including intentionally dealing with dysfunctional defensive psychosocial dynamics that may be contributing to the problem.

In sum, organization members who experience less stress are less likely to resort to psychosocial defenses. Tom helped organization members by non-defensively accepting and absorbing their strong left-over feelings. He assumed an intentional listening and reflective interpersonal stance that began the process of healing past traumas. This healing dynamic contrasts to organizational leaders who continually point out organizational threats to mobilize fear and anger as a way to motivate organization members to higher levels of performance. Regrettably, motivational strategies like this, to be sustainable, require the leader to continually locate threatening operating problems that keep organization members continually anxious and defensive and less able to effectively work together.

Safety

Safety is important for achieving creative problem-solving. But feeling safe at work can be problematic in many organizations that are filled with institutionalized management-driven pursuits of power and control and ever-present threats of punishing aggression as was the case for Dick's behavior. The threats can take many forms such as using performance reviews to control and dominate organization members, and at a more global level, there are the threats of organizational restructuring and downsizing. In contrast, feeling safe is encouraged by intentional leaders who embrace openness, inclusiveness, transparency, collaboration, mutual trust, and mutual respect. Tom was open, inclusive, and trusting when he encountered the traumatized organization members who had to be respected for what they had been through over many years.

Playfulness – The End Result

Intentional leaders who successfully facilitate containing stress by calmly listening to organization members signal that a caretaking mutual understanding is possible and that this, by contributing to containing stress and anxieties, encourages organization members to feel safe enough to consider innovative possibilities for change. Intentional leaders who help to create a safe culture where organization members feel accepted and understood by their leader avoid fragmenting defensive retreats. In the case example, Tom acknowledges and helps organization members to manage their past traumas, dysfunctional organization history and culture, and the accompanying fears and stress. Organization members grow to feel valued and understood allowing for feelings of interpersonal safety and playful creativeness to emerge that encourage exploring the possibilities for positive organizational change. Organizational cultures like this that are inclusive, transparent, and collaborative facilitate organizational commitment to locating and implementing meaningful organizational change. In sum, organization members who feel that they are valued contributors and who feel free to question their organization's dynamics and management decision-making, unlike the experience of many organization members in the American workplace as illustrated by the case example, can create a playful organizational culture.

HOW TO DEVELOP AN INTENTIONAL WORKPLACE

Thoughtful and reflective intentional leadership of groups and organizations promotes a safe enough workplace experience that minimizes relying on psychosocial defenses. The leader appreciates that organization members bring with them to work their desires and personal hopes and aspirations regardless of whether they are openly acknowledged or not. The psychosocial dynamics in our organizations can be meaningfully embraced as compared to traditional ways of managing people that transform human beings into human resources. Intentional leadership also creates an operating context in which illegal, corrupt, unethical, and antisocial leaders and organizational behavior are safely open to inspection. The careers of organization members should not be on the line for respectfully asking difficult and probing questions.

Organization members who have their humanity, individuality, creativity, and work valued by their leaders, who actively listen, are authorized to ask tough questions and embrace critical and reflective thinking that helps to get everyone's best thinking on the table or whiteboard. Decisions and their implementation are open to discussion as compared to a leader who hands down decisions and micromanages their implementation. In sum, non-defensive and open discussion creates a cultural context of mutual trust and respect that promotes ownership of the decisions made improving implementing them by minimizing resistance to change.

Stated differently organization members are encouraged to discover and analyze operating problems and join in open inclusive discussions of what to do about them. A safe and playful workplace experience for problem recognition and solving engages everyone's creativity and innovative ideas within a culture of being open, inclusive, transparent, collaborative, trusting, and respectful.

In sum, it is possible for tough decisions to be made without the leader seizing unilateral control of the work. Making challenging decisions and implementing them can be an inclusive group and organizational experience. The stressful work of problem-solving and creating change can be a positive experience for organization members as compared to what too often are secretive and unilaterally imposed decisions by organizational leaders.

INTENTIONAL LEADERSHIP SKILLS IN MORE DEPTH

American organizations too often have narcissistic, top-down, command and control leaders who try to micromanage everyone and everything. They also can have sharp elbows when relating to organization members – My way or the highway. These leaders rely on their power and authority to make decisions and then ram them through the organization moving against the organization's members. This management style almost assures resistance to change will develop among organization members who move back against or away from the proposed changes and how they are being implemented. These defensive organization dynamics usually lead to overcoming the resistance by these leaders relying on bullying, threatening, and intimidating organization members which only serves to further alienate them. Equally attention-getting is that unquestioning loyalty and conformity by some organization members may be rewarded with favored "insider" status and receiving raises and promotions. Autocratic authoritarian leaders rely on these methods around the world where loyalty is emphasized many times over competency. Many spectacular business scandals such as Enron and Tyco underscore what can happen when powerful people act unilaterally supported by obliging and sycophantic organization members. In sum, organizations large and small fail for many reasons. Poor management is, however, invariably one of the root causes. The creative and generative energies of organization members have usually been limited or suppressed.

The four intentional leadership skills (listening, containing, and promoting safety and playfulness) while challenging to put into daily practice, can, with patience and persistence, become a seamless part of leading that can be expected to be adopted by others in leadership roles. It is suggested that it is a worthy challenge to engage organization members in an energized and creative process to better achieve organizational performance. These considerations invite a more in-depth inspection of the four elements and what it means to master this style of leadership.

Listening in Practice

We all hear but may not listen to what others are saying. Our listening can be cluttered with our own thoughts and feelings that interrupt listening. This is true of leaders who prefer to not hear about distressing operating problems, new ideas, and opinions that differ from theirs. For instance, someone may point out the risks of a decision or something harmful or illegal about a decision. The messenger of this bad news may be disregarded by the leader in preference to listening to what loyal and supportive "team players" have to say.

Listening to different points of view is challenging during stressful times that encourage relying on psychosocial defenses to cope. When stressful situations arise, it is comforting for leaders to presume defensively and arrogantly to know what to do and make all the decisions. By taking charge leaders may limit the anxiety organization members experience by their moving toward their leader and accepting roles of dependency and submission. In contrast, intentional leaders, who maintain a listening and reflective presence, and openly and transparently confirm with organization members what has been said has been accurately understood by everyone promote "organizational learning." Organization members are encouraged to evaluate their understanding of what the leader and group members are thinking as a part of a thoughtful, critical, and reflective group dialogue where everything that is being said, even by their leader, is open for discussion.

Implicit for intentional listening is that it helps to contain personal and group emotions such as fear and anger about not being listened to that can, for example, lead to resistance to change and aggression (moving against others) or avoiding acknowledging operating problems and what is being said (moving away). An intentional leader's listening presence promotes organization members' feelings of being accepted and respected, minimizing reliance on psychosocial defenses and the three directions of movement.

Creating Workplace Containment

Creating workplace containment of stress that limits anxiety creates a "calm pond" allowing organization members to stay focused on their work and minimize retreats to psychosocial defensiveness that can lead to the taking of reckless actions or not acting at all. Intentional leaders who strive to manage their self-experience and defensive tendencies contribute to containment by being calm and steady in the face of stressful organizational events. Limiting stressful self and group experiences encourages organization members to feel safe enough to be open, inclusive, creative, and able to act. They are better able to tolerate the ambiguities attached to being responsible problem solvers. Leaders who trust and respect organization members free up their contributions to resolving operating problems, implementing change, and improving organizational performance.

In sum, leaders who master containing their own anxieties and self-experience combined with self-reflectivity permit everyone to develop deeper insights into organizational dynamics. This is a leadership skill that is not often considered to be a traditional management leadership course. In practice, maintaining self-integration and not falling apart during stressful times is based on the ability to maintain self-awareness and reflectivity. For example, "If I am experiencing or feeling anxious about a stressful situation, organization members are as well." This appreciation underscores that self-reflectivity permits understanding others and group dynamics and proactively facilitates containing stressful individual and group dynamics by being able to listen nondefensively.

Creating Safety

Listening that supports containment contributes to feeling safe enough to, for example, openly and collaboratively explore operating problems, opportunities, and the possibilities of creative new ideas. If organizational

dynamics are not felt to be safe, open, inclusive, transparent, collaborative, trusting, and respectful, timely and effective responses to problems
and opportunities may not develop. Creating feelings of safety is, however,
more challenging when there is an organizational history and culture of
resistance on the part of leaders to considering new ideas and change. "We
don't do *that* here." Organization members may be fearful and defensively
risk-averse to offering new ideas. In contrast, a safe and playful group and
organizational culture facilitate generating ideas and possibilities and the
creation of a consensus that reduces resistance as to what should be done,
how, when, and by whom.

In sum, developing a sustainable, safe enough workplace is a challenge, especially in organizations that have cultures that have historically lacked it. Intentional leaders who are patient and persistent can,
however, gradually change dysfunctional organizational dynamics
toward being more open, inclusive, and welcoming of everyone's creative
contributions.

Nurturing Playfulness

Leaders who work toward containing fears, anger, and psychosocially
defensive organizational dynamics allow organization members to focus
on their creative problem-solving abilities to improve organizational
performance. A shared culture of trust, respectfulness, openness, and
inclusion fosters playfulness that releases imagination and free associations that fuel creativity and metaphorically "thinking outside box."
This contrasts to top-down, command- and control-oriented hierarchical organization responses that foreclose learning from organization
members.

New ideas do not occur in a vacuum. A safe and playful context enables
organizations to realize their fullest creative potential because their members are not preoccupied with defending against stress associated with
generating new ideas where their ideas and themselves may be attacked.
For example, the questioning of past management decisions that have contributed to current operating problems is all too often avoided out of fear
of being ignored, rejected, and even disciplined for not being a conforming team player. Many times, operating problems created by those who
have power and control go unquestioned and doom organizations to failing to succeed or eventually failing.

TWO STORIES OF INTENTIONAL LEADERSHIP

Intentional leadership may take many forms and these two examples highlight this.

The First Story

A new chief executive officer (CEO) of an organization has replaced a secretive and data-manipulating CEO who suppressed employees with restrictive rules and punishing micromanagement. The new more intentional CEO created a cross-functional group to analyze the current less than functional state-of-affairs. This work revealed how poorly the organization had been managed including losing millions of dollars that could have been avoided. Many of the findings were of a hard-to-believe nature. Rather than locating who could be blamed, the focus was on problem recognition and problem-solving, what the new CEO referred to as "No fault change." Repairing the many problems and moving forward was the goal, not looking back.

Solutions to operating problems were rapidly located and implemented. Organization members began to feel safe, respected, heard, and effective. They began to surface more operating problems including problems created by some former "sacred cows" for resolution. This newfound enthusiasm not only led to locating hard-to-resolve operating problems and conflicts, but also new ideas were generated and implemented to further improve processes and systems to capture the lost millions of dollars and take advantage of new opportunities. Organizational culture turnabouts like this speak to a notion like organizational plasticity where springing back to a more open and inclusive organizational culture revitalizes the organization is possible. Organization members recover feeling engaged and committed to making their organization and their work lives better.

The Second Story

After starting to work, a new CEO of a division within a large international organization realized that organizational life was not as expected based on the interviewing process. The division had a toxic culture much the same as the parent organization. Toxic leadership, competitiveness, and infighting had been the norm for many years. This had created a dysfunctional organizational culture that had become accepted as business as usual. Collaboration and cooperation were absent. There was a pervasive lack of trust and respect as well as excessive conflict among the organization's leaders, divisions, and members.

The new CEO, after listening to division members, reached the conclusion that a constellation of issues contributed to this toxic and dysfunctional culture. The CEO developed and posted a values list for the division: openness, inclusiveness, transparency, collaboration, respect, and trust. These values challenged the culture of hoarding and weaponizing power, control, and information to attack other organization members. The history of problematic decisions being made without including organizational stakeholders was acknowledged. These new cultural values were patiently and persistently pursued creating a constant press for cultural change that gradually improved the division's culture and performance. However, division members were ill at ease about their new values and culture because no one else in the organization practiced them. They reported feeling "disarmed" when dealing with their aggressive colleagues from other divisions who continued to be competitive and move against them. Division members, however, gradually recognized that changing the nature of the parent organization was not an option and that they had to accept this. They, however, took pride in practicing their new cultural values and saw themselves as taking the "high road."

Discussion and Analysis of the Two Stories

The two stories are about leadership succession illustrate the healing and restorative nature of the intentional leadership style. They exemplify both this leadership style's possibilities and its limitations relative to a larger parent organization.

In the first story, the new CEO replaced a top-down, command and control leader who relied on secretiveness to maintain control. The development of a cross-functional leadership team signaled a change toward a new style of leadership and a more open, inclusive, and collaborative organizational culture. Organization members were encouraged to not feel defensive about the past and its many operating problems and focus their energies on nondefensively spotting and repairing the problems and resolving unresolved conflict by embracing a policy of "no fault change."

The second story illustrates how behavior and attitudes can diverge from what is optimal. The new CEO's attitude and behavior were congruent with the posted values statement, and this encouraged organization members to gradually accept and identify with them spreading them throughout the division. And even though the members of the division were developing an organizational subculture that worked, the rest of the organization retained its dysfunctional dynamics making it challenging to adhere to the values when faced with aggressive and combative competitiveness.

The stereotype of an organizational leader, at least in the United States, is usually someone who takes charge of the organization by controlling and dominating it and its members. This approach to leadership is about dominance and submission. The intentional leadership style may by comparison be viewed by these traditional leaders as not acting authoritatively or autocratically and not going to work. Yet that would be mistaken. Challenging decisions are being made but in a *manner* that is inclusive instead of exclusive and based on respectful listening rather than decisions being made unilaterally and then imposed on organization members. Put a different way, intentional leadership includes organizational stakeholders in designing and implementing changes that may span boundaries (silos) within the organization. The uniqueness of this culture of openness and inclusion, it should be noted, amounts to, in dysfunctional organizations, a deviant subculture that threatens those who identify with the organization's culture of power and control based in a hierarchical structure and bureaucratic norms.

In sum, intentional organizational cultures encourage organizational members to feel valued and engaged leading to their acceptance of consensus-built decisions. This facilitates the implementation of their decisions by avoiding the psychosocially defensive resistances that often accompany autocratic, top-down unilateral decisions. And to be noted is that within this intentional group and organizational culture of inclusion and collaboration some members may not agree with the decisions that are made by consensus, but everyone has had the opportunity to be *heard without the fear of punishment*. The result of the new culture is that, while the official organizational structure remains and *appears* hierarchical, the top of the hierarchy *relinquishes* the traditional management model of command and control and dominance and submission by embracing a culture of openness, inclusion, transparency, and collaboration that promotes trust and respect.

CONCLUDING THOUGHTS ON INTENTIONAL LEADERSHIP

The values embraced by intentional leaders create a safe, playful, and creative workplace that allows organization members and managers to experience themselves as *part of* a process rather than *subject to* it. This approach to leadership aspires to create valued work experiences for organization members to improve organizational performance.

Chapter 15 concludes this book by looking back over what has been shared and examined its implications for changing organizations and leaders in the future.

15

Looking Back and Looking Forward

This book has taken a hard look at the human side of our organizations and organizational life. Psychosocial defenses have been discussed from multiple perspectives as an important but frequently overlooked organizational dynamic, especially in those cases where they become dysfunctional. Leaders of organizations who promote safe intentional and reflective workplace experiences to reduce stress and anxiety are admired for doing this. Organization members who are encouraged to develop themselves and each other's skills and live a fulfilling life at work are more collaborative and creative. This is to be applauded everywhere all the time. It is however the case, as this book highlights, the dark side of organizations driven by toxic leaders and defensive dysfunctional organizational dynamics creates workplace trauma sometimes punctuated by extreme cases of organizational violence such as threatening and humiliating interpersonal assaults by those in power. This organizational violence at an extreme includes traumas like downsizing, restructuring, and mergers sometimes announced in electronic messages transparently managing up stock value and the chief executive officer's (CEO's) reputation. This book, by focusing on the darker side of human behavior in our organizations, has provided insights into these performance-stripping and humanity-crushing aspects of our lives at work.

THE PSYCHOSOCIAL PERSPECTIVE'S

Understanding human behavior in organizations requires using psychosocially informed perspectives that provide insights for understanding organizations of all sizes and kinds – public or private or not for profit. The perspectives used in this book are established ways for understanding

DOI: 10.4324/9781003464464-18

toxic leaders and dysfunctional organizational dynamics. They, when used together, form a much-needed complementary multidimensional way to "unpack" organizational life that includes toxic leadership and dysfunctional organizational dynamics.

Understanding Toxic Leaders and Dysfunctional Organizational Dynamics

Organizations are with some frequency led by toxic leaders who are empowered by traditional hierarchical structures. These stressful dysfunctional organizational leadership dynamics encourage organization members to defend themselves sometimes splitting apart and fragmenting their work lives, especially during stressful times. These defenses promote polarized us versus them group dynamics and hard-to-resolve conflicts that are not usually safely open to being questioned or challenged. Personal danger may be attached to calling into question these toxic workplace experiences that degrade accurate reality testing, especially when the split-apart experience leads to *hot button* responses linked to group members reexperiencing past distressing work-related experiences.

Understanding these and similar psychosocial dynamics within an overarching *organizational cultural* perspective that contains familiar bureaucratic rigidities and problematic uses of power and authority by those in leadership roles is challenging. Leaders, to be effective, ideally must intentionally manage organizational cultures to maintain superior performance. Changes in leaders, however, can introduce sweeping cultural change such as changes in directions and reorganizations that are stressful for organization members when familiar ways of operating and relating to each other are compromised or lost. The coping response to these stressful experiences may be reliance on psychosocial defenses by organization members to manage their distressing self and group experiences.

Organizational identity is a complementary perspective for understanding psychosocial organizational dynamics. It provides for understanding how a shared sense of us – who we are as a group and organization develops. Organizational identity emphasizes individual, interpersonal, and group attachments and feelings of connectedness, togetherness, and mutual understanding (or lack of it). However, within a split apart and polarized good and bad world of fragmented selves, interpersonal relationships, and group and organizational dynamics, organization members from other groups and specialized divisions and silos may simply be thought of and felt to be uncooperative, unsupportive, and bad. This psychosocially defensive-based organizational fragmentation creates an easy-to-understand but performance-limiting binary black-and-white world. These toxic leadership and organizational dysfunctions may become so frequent and pervasive that they are accepted as the organizational and group identity and culture and who we are and how we work.

PSYCHOSOCIALLY DEFENSIVE GROUPS AT WORK

Psychosocially defensive responses to stressful group dynamics are the workplace experiences discussed in this book. It has been discussed that groups at work may become aggressive relative to each other, withdraw and retreat from dealing with problems and each other and stressful situations, or dependently seek out a leader or group that will take charge and restore predictability, resolve conflicts, and deal with threatening and stressful situations. There may also be instances when a lack of adequate leadership is the source of the problem, and it may then be hoped an effective leader will eventually take charge. While waiting for this to happen, group and organization members focus on being good team members who embrace feelings of togetherness and coequality with their fellow organization members to keep the organization running. Yet another common defensive response to stressful times is to rely on rigidly following bureaucratic policies and procedures and doing it by the book. Organization members are willing to accept, if necessary, autocratic and authoritarian leaders who are empowered by the hierarchical organization structure. However, organization members may still hope that more effective leaders will emerge but paradoxically also fear new leaders who may make demands on them to be loyal followers and willing risk-takers potentially exposing themselves to blameworthy actions (or inaction) for assuming personal responsibility for problem-solving.

In sum, organizational dynamics like these and the directions of movement are different forms of psychosocially defensive group dynamics that lead to the emergence of stable and accepted organizational cultures and member and group identities – who we are and how we work here. These dysfunctional leaders and group and organizational dynamics are briefly looked back upon as a reminder that they may all come into existence from time to time in our organizations.

THE DEFENSIVE DIRECTIONS OF MOVEMENT

The defensive directions of movement are intuitive in terms of relating to others, groups, and leaders. They can be observed to be occurring in our organizations relative to others and within our groups, organizations, and societies. They provide a useful framework for thinking about what is happening around us, especially when our organizations encounter stressful times.

Moving Against Others – Aggression

This direction is informative for understanding leaders who act aggressively toward individuals, group members, or perceived threats. This leader expects organization members to act affirmatively if not aggressively to address operating problems and threats. Organization members also implicitly accept that there may be member casualties from acting aggressively as may be the case in most forms of combat such as hostile takeovers, wars, or athletic events. Their narrow focus, limited reflectivity, and a lack of careful planning (shooting from the hip), however, can also result in creating stressful unintended consequences that may lead to "doubling down" on their aggression.

Moving against threatening others and groups is a familiar individual, group, organizational, and national response that usually includes intensely experienced feelings of fear and aggression – fight or flight. Split apart and fragmented hierarchical organizations foster these movements against the bad others both within and outside of the organization. These organizational dynamics may well create harm to organizational performance when winning at any cost becomes the only thing that matters. This is especially true for the leader who identifies with acting aggressively (identifying with feeling strong and powerful), seeing the enemy as bad and worthy of destruction, and being seen as a competent take-charge leader.

Moving Toward – Dependency

This group dynamic expects their leader to provide responses to threats and control stressful organizational dynamics by restoring predictability, security, and safety. Group members feel that they are less than able to deal with the distressing situation on their own. This may include not feeling authorized to act by their leader who embraces an organizational culture of autocratic authoritarian control. When someone does take charge everyone is thankful. This formal (or informal leader) is accepted as being in charge and knowing what to do. If a leader is not available, organization members are willing to wait up to the point that the stressful situation becomes too hard to tolerate. The ever-increasing stress of not acting may motivate a group member to try to lead the group or organization even though leading may be hard to do without being authorized to do so. If the leader is compromised for lack of authority, the outcome may be that only marginal success is achieved which raises the specter of being rejected and replaced. Organizations sometimes go through several leaders when trying to locate a leader who has sufficient competence and a willingness to act and assume responsibility to restore operating predictability and member safety and security.

Moving Away from Others – Retreat

This group culture is one of not engaging in either dealing with distressing operating problems or turning to a leader to take charge who might expect organization members to assume risky personal responsibility for acting. This group acts as though the problem or threat is not too threatening and can be tolerated and may go away on its own. Doing nothing many times in organizations seems like a good option or the default option. It is safer for the group members to go along to get along and maintain the status quo to avoid the stress of having to confront the operating problems or conflict. Retreat leads to these organization members staying in their cubicles or offices to avoid stressful operating problems and interpersonal and group conflict. They just want to be left alone to do their jobs.

These defensive directions of individual and group movement are common. They also implicitly include psychosocially defensive dynamics that further inform trying to manage toxic leaders and dysfunctional organizational dynamics.

ORGANIZATIONAL DEFENSIVE DYNAMICS

These psychosocially defensive dynamics provide more insights into the complexities of organizational life. They complement the directions of movement in organizations.

Hope and Freedom

Consistent with moving toward a leader, this group hopes a leader, a new idea, or a new strategy will resolve stressful threats and operating problems. Everyone is attentive and participative in meetings when they are discussed. However, seldom are corrective actions identified that everyone agrees should be taken. There is rather a focus on hoping an ideal leader will assume responsibility but not hold oppressive freedom stripping expectations for group members to assume personal responsibility for responding to the operating problems and threats. The expectation of organization members is that their new leader(s) will save them. If their leader does expect the group's members to act, resistance may develop to what is felt to be freedom-limiting coercion. Paradoxically, this freedom from leader expectations may conflict with the hope of locating a leader to solve the operating problems. Organizational members simply hope things will get better on their own. Doing nothing avoids losing their personal freedom to a leader's coercive expectations that they assume risk-taking personal responsibility to respond to operating problems that may include being scapegoated for poor outcomes.

Togetherness and Sameness

This psychosocially defensive organizational dynamic may arise as a response to toxic leadership that has misaligned organizational resources or created stressful organizational events such as downsizing and restructuring. Organization members feel that they are joined together in seeking security in numbers because everyone is threatened. We are all in this together and sharing equally in the same stressful workplace experience. Within this context, an organization member who steps forward to lead disturbs this shared sense of coequality and can expect to be minimally accepted. Who authorized this? There is also always the threat that volunteer leadership may result in a harsh response from senior organization leaders who find this assumption of personal authority unacceptable.

This form of nonthreatening group membership makes coping with distressing workplace experience easier, although this defensive dynamic also contributes to creating stressful leadership voids and operating ineffectiveness. No one may want to take the risk of being set apart from the group to lead the group. There may also develop performance stripping group and organizational splitting and fragmentation and an inability of organization members to agree on how to respond to operating problems and threats. This outcome may eventually lead to autocratically imposed solutions. For example, restructuring and downsizing may be unilaterally imposed by organization leaders who are felt by organization members to be bad powerful "others" who have blamed the organization's members, the bad organizational fat, for the current distressing situation. In this example, organizational members find themselves to be both the cause and solution to the problem having become disposable.

Bureaucratic Control

Reliance on hierarchical organization structures and defined roles including those of leaders create an impersonal, depersonalized, controlling, and predictable but also defensive organizational culture that it is hoped minimizes stress. This approach to working also becomes who we are, our identity. Organization members accept the structural performance limiting operating rigidities – the red tape bureaucracies are famous for. Doing it by the book on the part of everyone is the way to provide stress-reducing predictability and normality.

These structural trade-offs between achieving comforting predictability and the resulting compromises to organizational performance and losses of personal autonomy and self-identity are common. Bureaucratic public, private, and not-for-profit organizations all share the challenges of maintaining control over operations, achieving optimal performance, and not alienating their organization's members. However, persistent unresolved operating problems may result in leaders becoming autocratic, authoritarian, and over-controlling in the hope that more control will yield more predictability and better performance. These escalating uses of power and authority can become a self-defeating leadership strategy. There may never be enough power and control to continually master threats and operating problems sometimes generated by the unintended consequences of their own decisions. Toxic leadership and dysfunctional organizational dynamics like this are also aggravated by organization members becoming progressively more resistant to the ever-greater autocratic uses of power and authority by their leaders.

Autocratic Authoritarian Control

It is the hope of organization members that, by accepting this form of organizational control, distressing out-of-control workplace experiences will be diminished. Organization members want to believe their leader has the knowledge and skills to make good decisions that minimize their stressful experiences. This dependency and accompanying member authorization to take control encourages the leader to feel respected, admired, and depended on to take charge. Organization members become loyal and submissive followers, and this can result in the leader feeling free to violate moral, ethical, and social values. This leader's expansive self-experience also encourages the envisioning of overreaching goals that result in marginal implementation and organizational outcomes that are then blamed on organization members who are judged to be deficient in managing work on the goals. It may also be the case that uninhibited changes of direction can lead to unpredictability. Organization members, who experience the chaos of grand and ever-changing ideas as stressful, may become disillusioned and gradually reject their leader hoping a better leader will get control without creating chaos. Paradoxically, in cases like this, leadership failures can lead organization members to double down on selecting an even more autocratic and authoritarian leader who makes promises to smooth out operations. An outcome like this also signals the presence of an organizational culture that unthoughtfully embraces a psychosocially defensive repetition.

Healing dysfunctional psychosocially defensive organizational dynamics like these is possible if they are understood. Organization leaders and their members, including external and internal consultants, can contribute to developing a more thoughtful, reflective, and intentional organizational culture.

The Intentional Work Group

This organizational culture solves operating problems by avoiding psychosocially defensive strategies. Leadership is provided that promotes member reflectivity and intentionality that contributes to optimizing organizational performance. Stress and anxiety, which are inevitably present in our organizations, are open to safe discussion and this minimizes retreats to psychosocially defensive responses. Organization members identify their self-interest with that of others, the groups they work within, and their organization and its mission. They accept a culture of being open to learning from reflectivity and critical thinking. Unthoughtfully merging to become coequal and conforming team players is avoided in favor of mutual understanding that creates non-defense bonds between group members. This trusting and respectful context facilitates working openly, inclusively, transparently, and collaboratively. Maintaining intentionality is, however, always a challenge in our organizations no matter how they are structured and led. Changes in leaders and major threatening organizational events can disrupt intentional organizational cultures, increasing member stress and the likelihood of resorting to the psychosocial defenses to cope with shared distressing experiences.

In Sum: The Psychosocially Defensive Types – Looking Back

Psychosocially defensive dynamics are common in our organizations. Organizational culture and identity and the psychosocially defensive individual, interpersonal, group, and organizational dynamics are challenging for organizational leaders and members to manage. These defensive strategies, when taken together, provide a framework that increases our awareness of the powerful influence of the psychosocial side of organizational life that includes defensive responses to stressful workplace experiences. This appreciation also suggests that understanding the defenses is a good starting point for avoiding and healing the effects of toxic leadership and organizational dysfunctions going forward.

LOOKING FORWARD

This book has explored organizational dynamics using a psychosocially informed framework that illuminates the frequent presence of all too human defensive responses to stress at work. The defensive directions of movement when merged with the defensive strategies suggest that appreciating their impact on organizational culture and identity is a way forward for improving our lives at work and the performance of our organizations.

THE FORWARD-LOOKING THEMES OF THE BOOK

The themes are "cognitive organizers" for thinking about leadership and organizational dynamics and doing something about those that are dysfunctional. The advocacy for intentional leadership and accepting personal responsibility for preventing and healing organizational dysfunctions provides a forward-looking approach to better managing all organizations.

You Can Understand Organizational Dynamics

The discussion of dysfunctional leadership and organizational dynamics used a framework and language that should be familiar to everyone in organizations. The discussion, while not an overly simplistic self-help approach, provides an accessible framework that organizes the workplace into understandable categories of experience. This is the first step toward making meaningful change to avoid toxic leadership and dysfunctional organizational dynamics. You can understand this and do something about it.

You Can Do Something About It

A better understanding of toxic leadership and dysfunctional organizations permits doing something about them. The framework promotes critical thinking for better managing psychosocially defensive organization dynamics and avoiding their development. It also provides strategic pathways for improving yourself and your approach to providing leadership, participating in groups, and working within your organization including finding meaningful ways to contribute to our societies. Recognizing the presence of psychosocial defensiveness is a step toward intentionally creating organizational change.

You Can Create Meaningful Organizational Change

Creating meaningful organizational change starts with self-observation and self-reflection that has a positive empowering effect on leading, relating to others, and participating in groups in a less defensive way. Change begins with "us." The framework for understanding psychosocial defenses is a good starting point for leading meaningful group and organizational change that limits, avoids, and heals the harm caused by unthoughtful reliance on the psychosocial defenses. You can facilitate and lead meaningful organizational change by being thoughtful and reflective which encourages organization members to embrace the possibilities of creating a less toxic and dysfunctional organizational experience.

You Can Be a Better Leader

Our hierarchically structured organizations create roles of power and authority that are expected to provide leadership. However, leadership is not exclusively located in these formal roles and anyone in an organization can provide leadership. The framework of psychosocial defenses provides organization members a guide for intentionally leading that avoids creating stressful and anxiety-ridden organizational dynamics and relying on individual, groups, organizational, and leader psychosocial defenses. Being aware of and having a framework for understanding what is happening opens the door to providing intentional leadership that helps organization members to feel less fearful, oppressed, uncertain, and defensive. The intentional leader, who may be any organization member, who listens to everyone is acting to encourage organization members to become thoughtful and reflective critical thinkers. This helps individuals and groups to become less defensive and more open, inclusive, transparent, and collaborative in terms of locating shared solutions to organizational problems. These cultural themes promote trust and respect and form the basis of a non-defensive intentional organizational culture.

HEALING ORGANIZATIONAL CULTURES

The six words – openness, inclusiveness, transparency, collaboration, trusting, and respectful – are frequently missing or minimally present in our too often toxically led and dysfunctional organizations. The words may, however, be embraced by some groups and organizational divisions that "live" them. Embracing the possibilities of these six cultural themes is achievable when intentional leaders are patient and persistent in both embracing them and encouraging their broader adoption.

Inclusive leadership and organizational dynamics avoid splitting the organization into good and bad others and groups that create organizational fragmentation. Fragmentation compromises the ability to work together that can lead to dysfunctional interpersonal and intergroup competitiveness and hard-to-resolve conflict.

Conducting a listening-based organizational analysis to improve problem-solving and decision-making is a way forward to promote inclusiveness. Important knowledge and ideas can only be offered if organization members are recruited to contribute by listening to them. Practicing inclusiveness is, however, a challenge in organizations that have a culture and history of unilateral top-down autocratic oppressive management control. Even so, inclusiveness can be practiced in silos and work groups where insights from others are welcomed informing decision-making and taking action to resolve problems and promote working together.

Transparent workplaces invite inclusiveness. Large, complex, hierarchical organizations sometimes scattered in different geographic locations make being transparent a challenge. Local leaders and group cultures, especially within specialized silos, discourage transparency. Transparency may in fact be thought of as an unnecessary time-consuming process that invites innovative ideas and critical thinking that run counter to the leader's preconceived ideas and plans. Keeping organization members marginally informed is a defensive strategy that avoids leader frustration of having to deal with new ideas but also cuts off receiving potentially helpful contributions that might, for example, avoid unintended consequences. Organization members are frequently subjected to the fact that what is happening, especially within the higher levels of management, is not transparent. Few may know what management is thinking or doing. This predictably leads to speculation, myths, and rumors that may be threatening to organization members and promote more dysfunctional psychosocially defensive retreats. Transparency, while challenging to achieve, promotes a workplace experience of inclusiveness that opens the door to collaboration.

Collaborative groups and organizations generate better outcomes than individuals and groups that pursue their own self-interests in terms of what should be done. Effectively facilitated collaborative groups locate better descriptions of operating problems and systemic solutions to respond to operating problems that avoid the development of new problems from unintended consequences. Collaborative working relationships are inclusive and transparent and encourage voluntary coordination and cooperation that enables implementing solutions to problems that include ongoing critical thinking and feedback loops to resolve implementation issues. It is also the case that the best problem is the one that is avoided, and collaboration also contributes to this. The next best problem is the one that is resolved by trusting organization members to locate a solution that not only resolves the problem but also reduces defensive resistance to its implementation.

Trusting relationships at work are often lacking especially when toxic leadership creates stressful organizational dynamics by cutting staffing (downsizing) and then expect those who remain to cover the work of their departed friends and colleagues. Top-down unilateral decision-making that excludes organization members does not signal those in management roles trust the organization's members. It is common for organizations to have cultures that include losses of inclusion and transparency that promote suspicion and rumors that contribute to organizational fragmentation and losses of mutual respect. Developing sustainable trusting working relations depends on creating open, inclusive, transparent, and collaborative organizational cultures.

Respectful relationships at work are also not a common feature when there are toxic leaders who do not respect each other and do not promote an open, inclusive, transparent, collaborative, and trusting workplace culture that organization members can identify with. News stories about dysfunctional organizations are filled with depictions of autocratic, arrogant, and disrespectful leadership dynamics that generate harm for organization members, their organizations, and their communities. Creating a trusting and respectful organizational culture is the ultimate challenge for leaders to achieve. This culture can change the future of our organizations making them succeed by creating valued workplace experiences that organization members welcome.

MANAGING FOR THE FUTURE

A better understanding of defensive psychosocial organization cultures that compromise performance and lead to organizational fragmentation and failure is a major step forward in terms of avoiding these outcomes.

The framework of defensive perspectives reminds us that the only thing that is predictable is unpredictable organizational dynamics and change. Anyone who endeavors to plan and implement organizational change will encounter confounding complexities and resistances within our bureaucratic hierarchical organizations and their specialized divisions. Reenvisioning our organizations and how they work, however, should not be dismissed as too hard to try to do – only challenging. Successful change, however, should wisely avoid threatening CEOs and senior leaders who drive top-down organizational change that predictably encounters unanticipated difficulties and resistances when organization members have been excluded from open, inclusive, transparent, and collaborative participation.

Organizational change must include managing the psychosocially defensive nature of the workplace. Leaders and organization members must appreciate these defensive workplace dynamics that are always present, although they are also too often ignored because they seem to be too hard to understand and manage especially during stressful times. Organizational dynamics that are stressful and make their members feel anxious and defensive must be open to inspection in order to develop an intentional and reflective organizational culture that minimizes defensive responses to change. Finding creative ways to acknowledge, address, and cope with the stressful threats, operating problems, and organizational change is a worthwhile goal that facilitates creating a more intentional workplace that minimizes these experiences.

We are left with this question. Are toxic leadership and dysfunctional organizational dynamics an inevitability? The answer is Yes and No. The framework for understanding toxic leadership and dysfunctional organizational dynamics has hopefully made clear that psychosocial defenses are commonplace, natural, and can become dysfunctional if they are not acknowledged to exist and organization members are not recruited to the project of understanding their presence and how to effectively manage them. Leaders, organization members, and psychosocially aware internal and external consultants can be effective leaders of cultural change that starts with diagnostic listening that leads to thoughtful and reflective intentional facilitated change based on the cultural themes of being open, inclusive, transparent, collaborative, trusting, and respectful. They can become a cultural norm everyone identifies with. Looking back over organizational landscapes of toxic leadership and individual, interpersonal, group, and fragmenting organizational dysfunctions that compromise effective functioning makes clear that a future that includes creating organizations that avoid toxic leadership and organizational dysfunctions is an aspirational goal worthy of trying to achieve. Our organizations should be intentionally managed to create high performance and good places to work. These are doable goals for all leaders and organization members.

Index

Printed in the United States
by Baker & Taylor Publisher Services